The radicalism of ethnomethodology

MANCHESTER
1824

Manchester University Press

The radicalism of ethnomethodology

An assessment of sources and principles

MARTYN HAMMERSLEY

Manchester University Press

Published by Manchester University Press
Altrincham Street, Manchester M1 7JA, UK
www.manchesteruniversitypress.co.uk

British Library Cataloguing-in-Publication Data is available

ISBN 978 1 5261 2462 3 hardback
ISBN 978 1 5261 4590 1 paperback

First published by Manchester University Press in hardback 2018

This edition published 2019

Typeset by Toppan Best-set Premedia Limited

Contents

Preface

When I was an undergraduate student at the London School of Economics in the late 1960s, ethnomethodology was not mentioned on the courses I took, nor for that matter were social phenomenology and symbolic interactionism.[1] However, in the library I did find Cicourel's *Method and Measurement in Sociology*, Berger and Luckmann's *The Social Construction of Reality*, the (then) three volumes of Schutz's *Collected Papers*, Blumer's *Symbolic Interactionism*, and Becker's *Outsiders*, and I read them as representing a new approach to studying the social world, one that I found more interesting and worthwhile than much of what was on the official curriculum. When it came to choosing a place to study as a postgraduate, I selected the Department of Sociology at the University of Manchester largely because I knew that some staff there had an interest in interactionism. When I arrived, I found that several of them had moved on to ethnomethodology and conversation analysis. While I was familiar with Cicourel's work, I had not read Garfinkel's *Studies in Ethnomethodology* and knew nothing of conversation analysis. I spent much of my four years in Manchester reading whatever I could get access to, particularly Sacks' lectures, then still in mimeographed form, as well as Garfinkel's book. I also participated in tutorials on conversation analysis in the Department.

I found Garfinkel's arguments appealing because they raised fundamental questions about mainstream social science, and did this from a scientific rather than humanistic point of view, by contrast with many other influential critiques at the time. However, I never quite converted to ethnomethodology – initially I remained closer to Schutz, Berger and Luckmann, and Blumer, and much later came to adopt a largely Weberian methodological position (see Hammersley 2014). Nevertheless, I kept in contact with developments in ethnomethodology and conversation analysis, and from early on I produced various drafts of a paper about ethnomethodology, though never completed it. Then, in the mid-2000s, I wrote a piece comparing conversation analysis with an influential form of discourse analysis that had developed within psychology, critically assessing each of them. I gave this paper to seminars at the Open University, Brunel, Manchester, and

---

1 Paul Rock, who wrote a key book on *The Making of Symbolic Interactionism*, was teaching at LSE but, unfortunately, I did not come into contact with him.

Preface

Loughborough; it received, at best, a mixed reception, not least from ethnomethodologists and conversation analysts in the audiences. It was later published and led to an exchange in the journal with Jonathan Potter.[2] What prompted me then to go on to produce this book was an invitation to speak at a *Mind and Society* conference in Manchester in 2015. This regular conference brings together many people with an interest in ethnomethodology and in Wittgenstein's philosophy, particularly as regards its implications for social science. The invitation prompted me to re-read the book *There is No Such Thing as a Social Science*, co-authored by influential figures associated with the Conference, and I gave a paper dealing with that book (Hutchinson et al. 2008; Hammersley 2017a). Attending a subsequent conference at Manchester on *Radical Ethnomethodology*,[3] and engaging in conversations with various people there, launched me into the reflections that are presented here. As its title implies, it is the product of a critical engagement with ethnomethodology: I have tried to understand the character and appeal of this approach to studying the social world, but what I offer is nevertheless a reading and assessment from outside.

I am grateful to the organisers of the conferences just mentioned, and to participants in them for helping me to gain what understanding of ethnomethodology I have achieved. Longer term, as well as more recently, I have also benefited from occasional contacts with Bob Anderson, Alex Dennis, Lewis Hyland, John Lee, Wes Sharrock, Rod Watson, and others. I doubt that any of them will share most of my conclusions, but I hope that they will at least feel that I have made a serious attempt to understand what they said.

This book does not, however, stem solely from my personal entanglements with ethnomethodology. It also relates to a general concern I have about the nature of sociology as a discipline, and indeed about the social sciences generally. I am sceptical about the validity and value of much of what social science currently offers, and this is an attitude I share with many ethnomethodologists. So, part of the motivation behind the book was to explore common ground as well as to investigate areas of disagreement.

2 See *Discourse and Society*, 14:6, 2003.
3 See http://radicalethno.org/.

Introduction

Many years ago, Bergner (1981) argued that the very nature of modern social science means that there are many starting points leading to multiple perspectives, so that there is no prospect of a single coherent and comprehensive scientific paradigm prevailing in the field as a whole, or even separate but related ones within each of its constituent disciplines in the manner proposed, for example, by Parsons (Parsons and Shils 1951). Bergner claims that this stems from the commitment of social scientists to neo-Kantianism, with its insistence that all inquiry is perspectival and constitutive, each perspective potentially generating knowledge of some aspects of the world while always obscuring others. In fact, Bergner did not take full account even of all the sociological approaches prevailing at the time he was writing, though he does briefly mention one of the more radically distinctive ones: ethnomethodology. And it is by no means clear that there ever was, even less that there is today, general adherence to a neo-Kantian philosophical position in social science. Many ethnomethodologists, as well as representatives of some other approaches, would dissent from that position.

Of course Bergner's conclusion – that social science is irredeemably plural – may yet be true.[1] But it should be noted that representatives of the various competing approaches within social science are usually in favour of pluralism only as a matter of convenience: generally speaking, they do not celebrate it but are tolerant of diverse perspectives because this is required for the survival of their own approach. In the words of one ethnomethodologist: 'many sociologies if necessary, but preferably only one' (Sharrock 1974). There are, of course, those who champion pluralism, but, as Goldthorpe (2016: 127) has insisted, there is surely a point at

---

1 As an illustration of the diverse character of 'sociologies' today, one could compare Goldthorpe's (2016) *Sociology as a Population Science* with Fox and Alldred's (2016) *Sociology and the New Materialism*; two books that share very little in common. Goldthorpe champions a longstanding tradition – investigations of population regularities based on survey research, for example on the topic of social mobility – whereas what Fox and Alldred propose, as their title indicates, is of newer provenance. Goldthorpe offers a well-defined conception of sociology that is very narrow in comparison with what currently comes under that disciplinary banner. The kind of sociology prompted by 'the new materialism' is more wide-ranging, but is still at odds with most conventional sociological work, not least that promoted by Goldthorpe.

which pluralism becomes a liability rather than an asset. And it must be suspected that this point was reached some time ago in the case of sociology, whose labelled varieties are now beyond worthwhile count.

Towards the end of the twentieth century, Huber (1995) had sounded a warning that the subject lacked a disciplinary core. Nearly twenty years earlier, Hindess (1973: 9) had written about 'the chaotic and frequently incoherent state of modern sociology, reflected in its theoretical anarchy and the coexistence within it of radically heterogeneous and often incompatible positions'. In fact, concerns about the discipline's lack of coherence can be traced back to the beginning of the twentieth century (see, for example, Käsler 1983), or even into the nineteenth century, with Simmel's distinctively narrow definition of its focus challenging Comte's and Spencer's much broader ones, and in its turn being rejected by his contemporaries, not least by Durkheim (Frisby 1981: 56–61).

Of course, the differences among sociological approaches vary in depth and significance. In the case of ethnomethodology there is, I will suggest, a deep divide from most other versions of the discipline. This is not to say that it shares nothing at all with them, but the differences are much more striking than the similarities. My task in this book will be to examine these distinctive features, their implications for its relationship with more conventional forms of social science, and the arguments that underpin its radical stance.

Among those who deplore the proliferation of paradigms, of whom I am one, there is often a tendency to assume that it stems from spurious causes: self-promotion on the part of individual social scientists, the force of their ideological convictions, an excessive concern with 'innovation', mere following of fashion, etc. However, it seems to me that, to some degree at least, the divided state of social science arises from fundamental, unresolved problems. This is also the view of many ethnomethodologists, and I believe that much is to be learned, both positively and negatively, from their diagnoses and proposed solutions. Hence this book.

The history and character of ethnomethodology

Ethnomethodology was invented by Harold Garfinkel: both the name and the distinctive approach to the study of social life to which it refers (see Garfinkel 1968: 5–11). There is a contrast here with Comte's invention of sociology, since – while he was the first to use that term (in print in 1839) – in many respects what he proposed was not sharply different from what is to be found, for instance, in the writings of Saint-Simon and Condorcet. Moreover, histories of sociology often go back well beyond even these writers.[2] In the case of Garfinkel, however,

2 For example, in his classic account of the development of sociology, Aron (1969) begins with Montesquieu; and some commentators trace it further back to the Scottish Enlightenment, to medieval social and political thought, or even to the writings of Aristotle and Plato.

ethnomethodology is a line of thinking and a form of practice that, in many respects, is strikingly at odds with nearly all previous types of sociological inquiry.[3]

At its most basic, the term 'ethnomethodology' refers to the study of how processes of social interaction generate the intelligible world we all experience, and largely take for granted. It stemmed originally from Garfinkel's recognition that, in some contexts at least, lay people operate with similar concerns and methods to social scientists, and that it is on the basis of these that they make sense of the world and, simultaneously, make the world intelligible for one another. Thus, when he was employed in a study of jurors, Garfinkel observed that they deliberated in a practical way about methodological issues in much the same manner as social scientists: they were concerned with what counts as reliable evidence, what can legitimately be inferred from the evidence available, how competing explanations should be assessed, and so on. He also noted that, in determining what conclusions they should reach, jurors drew not just on what they had been told about relevant legal matters but also on background knowledge about society: about what normally happens in particular sorts of situation, types of people and their characteristic concerns and behaviour, and so on. And, importantly, they routinely assumed one another to have such knowledge. Another key point was that this process took place over time, so that people's practical reasoning operated both retrospectively and prospectively in making sense of 'what must have happened', 'who must have been responsible', 'what is the correct legal judgement', and so on. Furthermore, Garfinkel notes that they drew on this knowledge in essentially *ad hoc* ways suited to the requirements of the situation. As part of this he concluded that legal rules and other principles are actively used by people to make sense of particular contexts, *and that this involves simultaneously making local sense of the meaning of those rules or principles themselves* (see Garfinkel 1967a: ch. 4; Hill and Crittenden 1968: 5–11).[4]

Garfinkel formulated the name 'ethnomethodology' on analogy with 'ethnobotany', 'ethnophysiology', and 'ethnophysics': anthropological sub-disciplines concerned with documenting the distinctive cultural knowledge and practices of people in 'pre-scientific' societies about plants, bodies, and physical phenomena, respectively.[5]

---

3 Some have argued that there is strong continuity between ethnomethodology and 'classical sociology', for instance Hilbert 1992, but I find this argument is unconvincing. Nevertheless, there are some shared themes; indeed, I will point to some interesting parallels with Simmel's 'formal sociology' in Chapter 2.

4 For clear, though not easy, introductions to ethnomethodology, see, for example, Heritage 1984 and Sharrock and Anderson 1986. See Lynch and Sharrock (2003) for a multi-volume collection of papers about Garfinkel and ethnomethodology. Rawls 2002, 2006, 2008, and 2013, and vom Lehn 2014 provide information about Garfinkel's career. A good illustration of ethnomethodological work, in one of its early forms, is Wieder 1974.

5 On the nature of ethnoscience, see Sturtevant 1964. The method it employs was sometimes labelled componential analysis; see Goodenough 1956.

So, the term 'ethnomethodology' was intended to refer to the common-sense knowledge and methods relevant to social affairs deployed, and assumed, by members of a society. It is worth noting at this point, however, that there is a significant difference between those anthropological sub-disciplines and ethnomethodology, in that the former do not imply that how people make sense of plants, bodies, and physical phenomena determines the nature of those phenomena, whereas Garfinkel claims that the methods ethnomethodology studies produce the very phenomena to which these methods relate.[6] However, there was, and is, a significant tension within anthropology between a view of the sciences as a superior source of knowledge, with anthropology itself being one of the sciences, and attachment to a form of cultural relativism in which, at the very least, Western ideas, including those produced by science, are to be suspended in order to try to understand the belief systems of non-Western societies in their own terms. As we shall see, there is a parallel issue within ethnomethodology concerning its own relationship to conventional professional and lay understandings of the social world.

While Garfinkel developed ethnomethodology over the course of the late 1940s and 1950s, it was not until the 1960s that a significant body of researchers began to adopt it, at a time when dominant sociological approaches were coming under challenge from several directions, leading to a sense of fundamental crisis (Friedrichs 1970; Gouldner 1970). This was also a time when the number of sociologists was increasing significantly, against a background of broader sociocultural changes in Western societies (Bell 1976; Martin 1981; Denzin 1989). Looking back, Wieder et al. (2010: 128) report that: 'Given the struggle to understand what was later to be more widely known as EM, there was a sense of being involved in something new, something revolutionary, and something that offended established sociology – all this, perhaps, being in keeping with the spirit of the 60s' (see also Mehan and Wood 1975).

In the mid-twentieth century, a variety of approaches arose that suspended the assumption, previously widely taken for granted, that social phenomena – institutions and structures – exist and have particular characteristics independently of the perceptions and actions of people in the society concerned; indeed, that they determine those perceptions and actions. Also challenged was the idea that lay people's perspectives routinely involve misconceptions that need to be corrected by social science; on the grounds that they are either only proto-sociological in character, or are the product of ignorance and ideology. Instead, it came to be

---

6 Interestingly Wieder (1977: 2) distinguishes between ethnomethodology, concerned with the formal features of accounting practices, and ethnosociology, which focuses on the substantive content of the accounts people provide about life in their society. For critical discussions of the differences between ethnoscience and ethnomethodology, from an ethnomethodological perspective, see Wieder 1970 and Wootton 1975: ch. 2.

argued that cultural variation involves not just differing values and attitudes but also fundamental differences in perception and cognition; so that the task of sociology, for some, became exploring and documenting this diversity. Indeed, it was often proposed that people belonging to different groups live in different 'worlds', or experience different 'realities'; and the challenging task was to understand each of these in its own terms. Particularly significant developments here, besides ethnomethodology, were Berger and Luckmann's (1966) *The Social Construction of Reality*, which reformulated the sociology of knowledge partly along phenomenological lines (see also Psathas 1973); the increasing importance of symbolic interactionism and the development of labelling theory in the sociology of deviance (Becker 1963; Pollner 1974); Winch's Wittgenstein-inspired critique of social science, and exploration of the problem of understanding other cultures (Winch 1958, 1964; Lerner 2002; Hutchinson et al. 2008); and the emergence of various kinds of constructionism (Weinberg 2014).

An important influence on many sociologists at the time was Kuhn's (1970) analysis of the history of science, as punctuated by the emergence of a succession of incommensurable paradigms. As a result, natural science was no longer to be seen either as the progressive accumulation of facts or as the testing of hypotheses against incontrovertible evidence. Rather, Kuhn portrays it as operating within a host of untested assumptions on which it necessarily relies, these even determining what would count as sound evidence. His work prompted the development of a relativist version of the sociology of science, concerned with explaining 'what passes for' scientific knowledge (Barnes 1974; Bloor 1976).[7] The fact that natural science displayed 'incommensurable' paradigms was widely taken to challenge any sharp epistemological distinction between scientific and other kinds of understanding, and any insistence on the superiority of the former. At the same time, this view of science opened up what was a largely new terrain for sociology, bordering on and potentially taking over territory from both philosophy and psychology; and it was also used to legitimate the diversity of approaches emerging in the field.

The sites where ethnomethodology initially became established were various campuses of the University of California in the 1960s and 1970s. Garfinkel taught at UCLA, stimulating several generations of students there, some of whom went on to carry out ethnomethodological work themselves and to teach on other

7 For discussions of Kuhn's work, which has often been seriously misinterpreted by social scientists, see Bird 2001 and Sharrock and Read 2002. For later developments in the Sociology of Scientific Knowledge, and Science and Technology Studies, see Pickering 1992 and Sismondi 2010. These involved a considerable diversification, some taking a radical constructionist line, for example Woolgar 1988 and Ashmore 1989, others adopting a more strictly ethnomethodological orientation, notably Lynch 1985, to mention just two approaches. For interesting discussions of recent developments, see Lynch 2013 and Woolgar and Lezaun 2013.

West Coast campuses, and elsewhere.[8] Among the most important were Harvey Sacks and Emmanuel Schegloff, whose work on conversation analysis came to provide an influential model for one kind of empirical work that ethnomethodologists could do. Others – such as David Sudnow, D. Lawrence Wieder, Egon Bittner, Melvin Pollner, and Don Zimmerman – carried out ethnomethodologically-informed ethnographies. As this brief account implies, while Garfinkel published several articles, some subsequently being included in his seminal book *Studies in Ethnomethodology* (Garfinkel 1967a), much of his influence took place through teaching, and this was true later in his career as well. In this and other ways, at first ethnomethodology was to a large extent based upon a predominantly oral culture. Also important was the circulation of unpublished materials by Garfinkel, some of which came to be published towards the end of his life (Garfinkel 1948/2005, 1952/2008, 2002).[9]

Garfinkel's writings, published and unpublished, have constituted a rather equivocal stimulus – not least because of his increasingly enigmatic mode of expression – in response to which readers, both ethnomethodologists and others, have frequently offered competing readings.[10] The early death of Sacks, and the fact that most of *his* writings were in the form of lectures, unpublished in his lifetime, but again available in mimeographed form, may, over and above intrinsic merit, have facilitated the development of a thriving movement, while also leading to accusations that ethnomethodology constituted a 'sect' or a 'cult' (Coser 1975). At the same time, the highly successful development of conversation analysis as a research programme – by Sacks, Schegloff, Jefferson and others – had the effect of raising the profile of ethnomethodology considerably within social science and beyond – notably in linguistics and even in psychology.[11] Furthermore, while conversation analysis was subjected to considerable criticism, its empirical and constructive character, and the cumulative nature of its findings, matched some of the ideals to which many mainstream social scientists were committed; and arguably did so more effectively than other approaches.[12]

As I noted earlier, ethnomethodology survives today more successfully than most other radical new approaches announced in the 1960s and 1970s – such

8 For details regarding personnel, albeit not entirely accurate, see Mullins 1972: ch. 8 and Flynn 1991: ch. 1.

9 For accounts of Garfinkel's pedagogical practices see Lynch 1999: 215–17, Wieder et al. 2010: 130–2; Liberman 2013: Intro.

10 For diverse views about Garfinkel's style of writing on the part of ethnomethodologists, see Wilson 2003: 491; Rawls 2006:5; Watson 2017: 16–18. For the view of a far from neutral outsider, see De Mille 1990: 80.

11 Schegloff (1992a, 1992b, 1999; Prevignano and Thibault 2003: chs 2, 9) has provided detailed accounts of the development of conversation analysis.

12 On the failure of mainstream sociology cumulatively to develop knowledge, see Rule 1997.

as 'conflict sociology', 'humanistic sociology', 'existential sociology', and 'ethogenics'. While it has remained relatively marginal to the discipline overall, in both institutional and intellectual terms, clusters of ethnomethodologists still operate in the USA, the UK, Germany, France, Australia, and elsewhere, forming part of a loose global network. Indeed, these clusters probably represent amongst the most durable networks to be found within social science over the past 50 years.[13]

One could argue that part of the reason for the endurance of ethnomethodology, despite never having been dominant in most of the fields in which it has had a presence, is that it displays a continual strain towards purity. Generally speaking, a radical identity in any social movement must be actively sustained both by drawing sharp dividing lines that mark it off from competing approaches, and by strongly criticising and marginalising members who are judged to deviate from its ethos. Both these processes can be found within the history of ethnomethodology. For example, like Garfinkel, Erving Goffman was also teaching in the University of California during the 1950s, and some of his students later became influential ethnomethodologists, notably Sacks, Schegloff, and Sudnow. Initially, the boundary between ethnomethodology and his work, and that with symbolic interactionism more generally (represented by Blumer at Berkeley), were blurred. Garfinkel, Sacks, Goffman, and Blumer all shared a concern with closely examining processes of social interaction *in situ*, a focus on the role of communication within these processes, and a resistance to the dominance of conventional quantitative methods. However, ethnomethodologists came increasingly to insist on the radical difference between their own approach and the work of Goffman and the symbolic interactionists (Zimmerman and Wieder 1970; see Chapter 2).[14]

The strain towards purity has also involved criticising internal variants that were judged to have deviated from the central principles of ethnomethodology. For example, the distinctive positions of Cicourel and his students, of Blum and

13 These clusters are partly coordinated via the International Institute for Ethnomethodology and Conversation Analysis: see http://www.iiemca.org/_wp_live/. See Psathas 2010, and the editor's and author's introductions in Garfinkel 2002. Psathas (2008) discusses two 'schools' of ethnomethodology beyond the West Coast: those at Boston University and in Manchester (UK). Conversation analysis has grown increasingly independent, and has become even more widely institutionalised: see Sidnell and Stivers 2013: Intro.

14 On these differences see Dennis 2011. See also Gallant and Kleinman 1983; Rawls 1985. Fine (1993: 61) has noted a different outcome from that of ethnomethodology in the case of symbolic interactionism; he writes that 'Once considered adherents of a marginal oppositional perspective, confronting the dominant positivist, quantitative approach of mainstream sociology, symbolic interactionists find now that many of their core concepts have been accepted. Simultaneously their core as an intellectual community has been weakened by the diversity of interests of those who self-identify with the perspective.' For an illuminating analysis of radicalism by an ethnomethodologist that, unfortunately, does not apply it to radical movements within social science, see Bittner 1963. However, Maynard and Clayman (2018) apply his analysis to the position adopted by some of their fellow ethnomethodologists.

McHugh, and (later) of Pollner came to be viewed by many ethnomethodologists as beyond the pale. There has also been marginalising of work on 'institutional talk' (Schegloff 1991, 1992a; see also Hester and Francis 2000, 2001), and even conversation analysis itself has been criticised, in the highly influential form practised by Schegloff and his associates, as well as that more recently characteristic of Heritage and his collaborators (see Lynch 1993, 2016a, 2016b; Lynch and Bogen 1994; Livingston 1987; Lynch and Macbeth 2016). There have also been discussions in which competing versions of the approach have been distinguished within the work of Garfinkel himself: the 'protoethnomethodological' versus 'postanalytic ethnomethodology' (Lynch 1993), 'classical' versus 'radical' (Wilson 2003, 2012), and ethnomethodology 1.0 and 2.0 (Pollner 2012a).[15]

In light of the fundamental challenge it poses to conventional sociology, heightened by this strain towards radical purity, it is perhaps not surprising that the reaction of most mainstream sociologists to the emergence of ethnomethodology, where they took any notice of it at all, fell short of enthusiastic adoption. It ranged from cautious interest in what usefully might be learned from it methodologically (see some of the contributions to Hill and Crittenden 1968), through attempts to incorporate elements of it into more conventional sociological approaches, whether through a merger with symbolic interactionism (Denzin 1969) or through integration with some other form of social theory (for example Giddens 1984; see Tucker 1998), to hostile rejection, treating it as suffering from 'sterility', 'inadequacy' and 'banality' (Coleman 1968), as 'an unfruitful approach to sociology that impedes its development' (Blau 1969: 128), or as the ephemeral product of West Coast fashion (Gellner 1975).[16]

Subsequently, attitudes towards ethnomethodology within the discipline have generally amounted, at best, to grudging tolerance; though this has not prevented it having considerable influence. In particular, it has shaped some of the many forms of discourse and narrative analysis that have come to be practised across a variety of substantive areas, as well as the development of actor network theory and related approaches.[17] There have also been effects on the practice of ethnography, and on other kinds of qualitative research, within and beyond sociology; particularly in encouraging a focus on the detailed analysis of patterns

15 See also Liberman's (2013: 1) reference to 'old school ethnomethodology'. Some ethnomethodologists have adopted a more catholic stance, accepting the diversity of ethnomethodology; see for instance Maynard and Clayman 1991, Psathas 1995.

16 For other external commentaries from sociologists with diverse commitments, see Wilkins 1968; Gouldner 1970: 39–5; Goldthorpe 1973, 1974; Coser 1975, 1976; Grabiner 1975; McNall and Johnson 1975; Maroules and Smelser 2006. For replies by ethnomethodologists to some of the attacks, see Benson (1974), Mehan and Wood (1976); Zimmerman (1976).

17 See Latour 2005. For relevant discussion of the relationship of ANT and some other approaches in Science and Technology Studies to ethnomethodology, see Lynch 1993; Sharrock and Button 2011.

of social interaction, with a view to identifying processes of social construction and/or the operation of social forms of one kind or another (see, for example, Holstein and Gubrium 2008; Silverman 1993a; Atkinson 2015; see Chapter 5 in this volume). It has also been influential in interdisciplinary fields like Communication Studies, the investigation of Human-Computer Interaction, and Science and Technology Studies.[18] However, in this book I will examine ethnomethodology primarily against the background of its relationship to the discipline of sociology.

Sociological background

In order to understand the significance of Garfinkel's ideas we need to consider the state of US sociology in the 1940s and 1950s, a period punctuated by the Second World War.[19] Sociology was in the process of expansion and institutional diversification over this period (see Odum 1951), with other centres, notably Harvard and Columbia, taking over the Chicago Department's previously dominant position (see Bulmer 1984). Garfinkel initially studied business accounting at the University of Newark,[20] where he became friends with several individuals who were later to become influential in their fields – Melvin Tumin, Herbert McClosky, and Seymour Sarason – as well as coming to know already established figures in sociology like Paul Lazarsfeld and Philip Selznick, who were then at Columbia University. He began his graduate studies at the University of North Carolina, where a distinctive brand of empirical sociology was being taught, broadly in the spirit of the Chicago tradition but with a strong emphasis on contributing to the solution of social problems.[21]

Garfinkel later moved to Harvard, where Parsons, with others, had established the Department of Social Relations: an interdisciplinary unit that drew together sociology, anthropology and psychology (Schmidt 1978). Parsons led a strong push for systematic sociological theory, and also for the clarification and development of its relations with other disciplines. This was promoted not just in his individually produced books at the time –The Structure of Social Action and The Social System – but also in interdisciplinary collaborative work concerned with developing various aspects of his theoretical framework (Parsons and Shils 1951; Parsons et al. 1953).

18 The interdisciplinary connections of conversation analysis are particularly wide: see Sidnell and Stivers 2013.

19 On the effects of this on sociology, see Parsons and Barber 1948.

20 Pollner (2012b) has explored the possible influence of this on the subsequent emergence of ethnomethodology, notably through the concept of 'accountability', as well as the 'selling' of ethnomethodology as a business.

21 While at North Carolina he wrote a short story about racial discrimination which was published – Garfinkel 1940 – and reprinted in a couple of collections. See Doubt 1989 and Hama 2009.

Other important developments were the growth of research on small groups (the study of jurors in which Garfinkel participated was part of this) and on decision-making in organisations, both of which were stimulated by practical as well as theoretical concerns. Garfinkel was involved in one of the major post-war projects relating to these areas, involving psychologists and economists as well as sociologists, run by Wilbert Moore at Princeton, an older-generation student of Parsons (see Rawls 2008).

The ethos of the environment in which Garfinkel was trained was one of optimism about the development of sociology and about its significant social role. Moreover, the conception of science involved had moved on considerably from the earlier Chicago focus on case studies of groups involved in social problems, on community studies more generally, and on the statistical documentation of social trends. There was a much more explicit concern with developing and testing sociological theories, and with investigating forms of social organisation at micro and macro levels through both theoretical and empirical work, the latter often quantitative in character.

Garfinkel's relationship to prevailing forms of social science seems to have been increasingly ambivalent.[22] Much of his early work was concerned with problems in carrying them out, for instance in coding (for sociological purposes) records produced by bureau officials and others. On the basis of these investigations, Garfinkel raised fundamental questions about what was being achieved and how the study of social order, social organisation, and practical decision-making was being pursued (Garfinkel 1948/2005, 1952/2008). His doubts were centred on his concern with 'the problem of meaning', this having developed especially through a reading of the phenomenological writings of Schutz and Gurwitsch. In order to explore this he deployed informal experiments, perhaps modelled on some of those in small group research at the time (on which see Strodtbeck and Hare 1954), to reveal the practices in which people engage so as to make sense of situations. This was achieved by intentionally disrupting these practices (Garfinkel 1963: 187 and *passim*; 1967a: chs 1–3).[23]

---

22 After noting the 'immense sums of foundation money' that had gone into social science, he comments that 'it is common knowledge that in the overwhelming number of researches that are methodologically acceptable, and, paradoxically, precisely to the extent that rigorous methods are used, dramatical discrepancies are visible between the theoretical properties of the intended sociological findings of inquirers and the mathematical assumptions that must be satisfied if statistical measures are to be used for the literal description of the intended events' (Garfinkel 1967a: 101–2).

23 There is an interesting parallel, for example, between Garfinkel's experiment on pre-medical students designed to engender consternation and confusion and Asch's (1951, 1955) experiments on conformity (Clayman and Maynard 1995: 5). However, Psathas (2012) also points out that Garfinkel's breaching experiments were a practical implementation of Husserl's notion of 'free variation'. These 'experiments' attracted considerable attention. Here was a sociologist *instigating* social disorganisation, rather than studying it with a view to finding a

Perhaps reflecting Garfinkel's ambivalence towards prevailing forms of social science, the exact relationship between ethnomethodology and its source discipline, as well as with other related disciplines, is rather uncertain (Dennis 2003; see Chapter 3 of this volume). While he has often claimed no more than that ethnomethodology opens up a new realm of phenomena for investigation, one that had previously been largely overlooked, his arguments have generally been taken to carry profound implications for social science and its relationship to the people and activities it studies. On the one side, it is often held to undercut social scientists' stereotypical treatment of lay people's understandings of the social world as generally false and/or irrational, and as in need of replacement by sound social scientific evidence. On the other side, Garfinkel's work implies that, contrary to the claims of many social scientists to rely solely on 'logic' and 'evidence', in pursuing their work they actually deploy more or less the same kinds of reasoning and data as the people they study, and rely upon common-sense knowledge, this raising questions about their claim to a scientific approach. Furthermore, their explanations typically treat commitment to particular values and norms as causal factors explaining people's behaviour. Yet, if the meaning of rules and principles cannot be specified independently of their use, as Garfinkel's own work suggested, then (he argued) these could not serve as causal factors. And this connects to the more general problem of the relationship between the concepts that lay people employ and those that social scientists produce in order to explain their actions (see Winch 1958; Louch 1966; Hutchinson et al. 2008).

What all this makes clear is that, at a minimum, ethnomethodology involves suspending the assumption that what conventional social science produces is superior to practical common-sense knowledge and skills. This suspension is partly a product of the way that ethnomethodology shifts the focus of inquiry on to the role of such knowledge and skills in social life. In this way, it distances itself from what Garfinkel later began to refer to as 'constructive analysis', 'formal analysis', or 'the world wide social science movement'. He came to argue that ethnomethodology is simply 'incommensurable' and 'asymmetrically alternate' to this (Garfinkel and Wieder 1992). However, as already noted, many ethnomethodologists have explicitly challenged the claims to validity and value that conventional social scientists make for their work. For instance, Mehan and Wood (1975: 63) declare that ethnomethodology has 'found social science out'. To quote another

---

remedy for it. In the 1960s and 1970s this was misguidedly taken by some as a form of political radicalism, as indicating the possibility of fundamental social change. There was, nevertheless, a significant resonance between Garfinkel's experiments and the fact that, as Schegloff 1992b: xiii reports, in the name of political radicalism 'violations of politeness had become … a systematic political tactic on university campuses'. See also Gouldner (1970: 394) on the parallel between Garfinkel's experiments and the 'happenings' of the 1960s' counterculture.

particularly strident example, it has been suggested that what social science produces is no different from 'journalism or [ideas put forward by] political parties and pressure groups, technology enthusiasts or conspiracy theorists or, indeed, the person standing next to you at the bar' (Button et al. 2015: 137). These latter authors propose that 'ethnomethodology would do away with social science' (p. 135). Meanwhile, others have insisted that 'there is no such thing as a social *science*' (Hutchinson et al. 2008, emphasis added; Hammersley 2017a).

A radical project

There is little doubt, then, that ethnomethodology presents a fundamental challenge to conventional social research, and that the sorts of investigation it proposes are very different from the mainstream, despite the latter's diversity. There are several aspects to its distinctiveness.

In the 1960s, ethnomethodology formed part of a broader movement concerned with the sociology of everyday life, in which the work of Goffman also played a central role (Truzzi 1968; Psathas 1980).[24] Where other interactionist work at the time focused on the study of deviance, on forms of occupational work, or on distinctive types of local community, Goffman was interested in relatively universal processes of face-to-face interaction. In effect, this new movement sought to promote a change in 'news values': it announced a focus on issues that, in conventional sociological terms, were trivial. While Simmel had earlier opened up the study of everyday life, in this respect he had had few followers within the discipline.

Furthermore, the new field was often treated by its exponents as having theoretical priority: it was insisted that studying the nature of mundane processes of social interaction provides an essential foundation for social science; that this area had been neglected as a result of sociologists' concern with producing abstract theoretical accounts of social structures, or with addressing high-profile social problems. Also at fault, it was argued, was sociologists' reliance upon highly structured methods of data collection that cut them off from what normally happens in natural settings.

As this suggests, there was also often a methodological critique of mainstream social science. In one of the most influential early presentations of ethnomethodology, Zimmerman and Pollner (1970: 80–1) open their discussion as follows:

> In contrast to the perennial argument that sociology belabors the obvious, we propose that sociology has yet to treat the obvious as a phenomenon. We argue

---

24 Subsequently, the study of everyday life has recurrently been revived, in a variety of forms: Sztompka 2008; Pink 2012; Kalekin-Fishman 2013; see also *Human Studies*, 3:1, 1980; *Sociology* 49:5, 2015.

that the world of everyday life, while furnishing sociology with its favoured topics of inquiry, is seldom a topic in its own right. Instead, the familiar, common-sense world, shared by the sociologist and his subjects alike, is employed as an unexplicated resource for contemporary sociological investigations. (pp. 80–1)

In line with Garfinkel's early writings (see Garfinkel 1962), Zimmerman and Pollner insist on the need for a 'principled respect for the distinction between the world of common-sense as a resource and the world of common-sense as a topic', implying thereby that conventional sociology is unprincipled in this regard (p. 84).

While Zimmerman and Pollner do not spell out exactly why sociology's reliance upon unexplicated resources is a problem, it was not difficult at the time to understand the challenging implications of their argument. These are signalled when they write that: 'sociology apparently is in the position of providing a professional folklore about the society that, however sophisticated, remains folklore' (p93). The predominant methodological views within sociology in the 1950s and 1960s were what could be broadly described as positivist, and a key element was the idea that scientific knowledge is founded on empirical givens accessed by scientists employing objective methods. As already noted, this necessarily implied a contrast with the informal and 'subjective' perception and cognition of non-scientists, of 'ordinary folk'. To show, as Zimmerman and Pollner go on to do (pp. 86–92; see also Cicourel 1964), that, in practice, sociologists rely upon common-sense knowledge and members' methods for making sense of the world, amounts to a damaging critique of this position: it documents the failure of sociology to live up to the precepts that were its scientific credentials. This was, in effect, an internal critique of conventional sociology, but it was also the case that ethnomethodologists themselves insisted that, in studying the social world, researchers must not simply *trade on* the background knowledge of it they have as participants, *that this knowledge must be the focus of inquiry if that inquiry is to be rigorous.*

In this emphasis on rigour, ethnomethodology differed from many of the other new approaches to sociology that emerged in the 1960s and 1970s, including those that made up the study of everyday life. Indeed, ethnomethodologists put forward an alternative conception of rigorous inquiry, and of what the task of sociology should be. This was initially modelled on phenomenology, to a considerable extent, but appeal was also sometimes made to a specific natural science model, what Sacks (1984: 26) referred to as 'primitive sciences', such as nineteenth and early twentieth-century biology (Lynch and Bogen 1994).[25] In both cases what was emphasised was the need for careful, detailed *description* of phenomena.

25 It should be mentioned that there were, in fact, important parallels between positivism and phenomenology in the early twentieth century. And these were brought to a sophisticated synthesis in Felix Kaufmann's *Methodology of the Social Sciences* (1944; see Huemer 2003), a book to which Garfinkel makes frequent reference. It is also worth noting that Husserl was himself influenced by the neo-positivist work of Avenarius and Mach: see Moran 2012: 187.

Also influential for some ethnomethodologists have been the philosophical writings of Wittgenstein, and of other philosophers belonging to what is sometimes referred to as the tradition of 'ordinary language philosophy' (two other early key figures were Ryle and Austin). There are, of course, tensions amongst these models and sources, but it is of significance that both Husserl and Wittgenstein challenged conventional philosophy in ways that are not entirely dissimilar to the manner in which ethnomethodology challenges conventional social science.[26]

So, ethnomethodology insists that rigorous analysis of the social world must focus on description of how phenomena come to be constituted in and through processes of social interaction, as phenomena of particular kinds that have determinate relations with one another. While the parallel with phenomenology is clear, it should be underlined that Garfinkel's motive for adopting this orientation did not stem primarily from philosophical concerns: it resulted specifically from his identification of fundamental problems in the practice of conventional social science. He argued that these derived from the fact that the meanings of social actions are context-dependent, and therefore in an important sense *ad hoc*. And he set out to investigate this 'indexicality' of action-meanings, and how this was practically remedied, doing so through empirical investigation of what is publicly observable, rather than by employing phenomenological investigations of personal experience.

This emphasis on the indexicality of meaning led to a further sense in which ethnomethodology was radical, what might be referred to as ontological occasional-ism.[27] In the account provided by Zimmerman and Pollner (1970), and even more in Garfinkel's later work, social phenomena – indeed all phenomena – are treated as generated *entirely* through processes of social interaction *on particular occasions*; having no existence independent of these processes, and deriving their character entirely from them. Thus, in a later article, Pollner (1979: 249) writes that 'social meanings are continuously created and recreated through the situated praxis which presupposes, preserves, and uses those meanings. Thus, "table" is a gloss for the cognitive, practical, and interactional work through which "table" is enacted.'

26 The influence of Wittgenstein seems to have derived to a considerable extent from the work and teaching of Wes Sharrock at Manchester. It can be seen particularly strongly in the writings of one of his early students, Jeff Coulter, and in that of some of his other colleagues. Wittgenstein has also been a particularly important influence on the work of Mike Lynch.

27 There are only a few parallels with the traditional philosophical doctrine of 'occasionalism' (on which see Pyle 2003: ch. 5; Lee 2016), but it is a convenient term in this context. The most obvious parallel is the emphasis on how events are produced through action on specific occasions. Another, I suggest, is the offering of an account that stresses a single source of experienced events, and one that is fundamentally at odds with what is routinely assumed by most participants involved in those events. This is a contentious claim I will discuss in the Conclusion.

There may also be a further, related, sense in which ethnomethodology is radical. Rawls (2006: 82) has claimed that it undercuts virtually the whole of Western philosophical thought, challenging its focus on individual, collective, or transcendent minds as the source of knowledge and morality. She writes that

> Instead of treating logic and reason as the starting points for a theory of social order, theory of knowledge, or conception of justice, beginning with the individual mind, or shared conceptual structures (culture), Garfinkel argues that logic and reason are characteristics of situated orders and depend entirely on the details of these orders for their production. On this view, the mutual commitment to constitutive orders of practice is at the heart of everything that is considered essential to the human being: reason, self, and sociality. Garfinkel offers the study of social interaction as the key to unlocking the great philosophical questions. As he says, 'once we get beyond Kant', reason, will, and moral reciprocity are revealed as questions of social order. They are not characteristics of the mind, however transcendental, and they are not values.[28]

In effect, the claim is that ethnomethodology represents a 'Copernican Revolution' to trump that of Kant, in the sense that not only is thought grounded in action but the relationship between actor and action is reversed: it is social practices that constitute the actor, rather than their being produced by decisions on the part of individual actors in light of intentions, motives, norms, values, etc. In other words, the identities of actors, and mental phenomena generally, do not precede action but are a product of it.[29] On this interpretation, ethnomethodology entails a whole philosophy, one that is at odds with the assumptions about the social world built into what Husserl (1965, 1983) calls 'the natural attitude'. There is a parallel here, perhaps, with the work of Heidegger, who argues that human being should not be understood 'primarily as a site of mental activity or a metaphysical substance, but rather as a "unity of living-through [Er-lebens]" whose fundamental relation to the world [is] activity, not theoretical contemplation' (Gordon 2010: 73).[30]

---

28 Rawls (2002) makes a similar claim, in more general terms in her introduction to Garfinkel's *Ethnomethodology's Program*, presenting him, along with Wittgenstein and Wright Mills, as confronting 'the problematic legacies of empiricism and neoKantianism', all three writers insisting that 'treating intelligibility and social order as fundamentally a matter of matching concepts with reality or logic was the problem', and independently embracing 'the social as an alternative approach to the great philosophical questions of knowledge and meaning' (p. 3).

29 There is, of course, a parallel here with some versions of structuralism and post-structuralism that announce 'the death of the subject'.

30 The quote within this quote is from Heidegger 1962: 73. See also McHoul 1998. This radical philosophical interpretation seems to be confirmed by Lynch (2016a: 1) who writes: 'Harold Garfinkel and Harvey Sacks emphasized that ethnomethodology and conversation analysis differed fundamentally, not only from sociology but also from intellectual traditions dating back to ancient Greek philosophy.' However, for many ethnomethodologists, including Lynch, Wittgenstein would be a more appropriate reference point than Heidegger.

It should be clear from this discussion that ethnomethodology's claims to radicalism are beyond question, albeit in epistemological and ontological rather than political terms. Of course, whether such radicalism is desirable, and whether ethnomethodologists' arguments are justified, is another matter. I will address this question in later chapters.

Ethnomethodology and research methodology

Perhaps not surprisingly, ethnomethodology is sometimes assumed by those first coming across the word to represent a new social research methodology; or, alternatively, it is confused with ethnography. While some ethnomethodological work has been ethnographic, a great deal has not been, and the two terms certainly do not have the same meaning.[31] The issue of whether ethnomethodology offers a new methodology is less clear-cut. On the one hand, ethnomethodologists would certainly resist the idea that their work offers a new method of doing what mainstream social scientists attempt to do, for reasons already explained. Furthermore, they would deny that ethnomethodological research amounts to following a single method or set of procedures. In fact, it has taken a variety of forms, and has used diverse kinds of data. These include: Garfinkel's (1967a, 1967b) breaching experiments; participant observation (Bittner 1967a, 1967b; Sudnow 1965, 1967; Zimmerman 1970a, 1970b; Wieder 1974; Anderson et al. 1989); the detailed analysis of audio or video recordings of naturally occurring social interaction (Heath and Luff 1992; Sacks 1992a, 1992b; Goodwin 2000; Schegloff 2007), and the work of many other conversation analysts; self-description of social experience (Sudnow 1978; Robillard 1999; Anderson and Sharrock 2018); the use of documents (Anderson 1978; McHoul 1982; Davies 1995; Watson 2012) or some combination of these (see, for instance, Sormani 2015).

More fundamentally, many ethnomethodologists resist the idea that their work employs specialised techniques at all: they insist instead that their task is simply to *document* the observable ways in which social phenomena are generated, and that the primary requirement for this is a suspension and explication of the natural attitude. However, this should not be taken to mean that the task is easily achieved. There are now quite a lot of introductions to ethnomethodology and conversation analysis, many of which are specifically concerned with assisting readers in carrying out this type of research themselves (for example Leiter 1980; Benson and Hughes 1983; Livingston 1987; Francis and Hester 2004; Hutchby and Wooffitt 2008; ten Have 2008). Moreover, in the case of conversation analysis, this has usually been treated as involving the production of audio or video recordings, and the use of technical transcription conventions to represent social interaction, as well as learning a distinctive form of analysis; one which requires

---

31 For a discussion of their relationship, see Pollner and Emerson 2011.

viewing social interaction in ways that are significantly different from how it is treated by participants – not least, paying attention to what they largely take for granted.

Despite many ethnomethodologists' coolness towards research methodology (see, for instance Sharrock and Anderson 1986: 107–8), it is important to remember that, to a large extent, it was methodological concerns that were the driving force behind Garfinkel's work. His starting point was a recognition that sociological research was failing to live up to its methodological ideals (Garfinkel 2006). And this also seems to have been the stimulus for Sacks (1963), who is undoubtedly the second most important figure in the movement. Moreover, as we have seen, ethnomethodologists often claim that their work is rigorous in a way that con- ventional social science is not.

Perhaps not surprisingly, given its history, there have been relatively few sustained efforts on the part of outsiders to understand the assumptions that underpin ethnomethodology, and to take seriously their implications for social science.[32] This is the task I have set myself in this book. While I stand 'outside' ethnomethodology, I am sympathetic to the spirit of the movement, and I have endeavoured to understand its principles as well as I can. Engaging with it is important because, as I indicated earlier, the problems it has identified in mainstream social science are genuine and serious ones that deserve more attention than they are typi- cally given. Writing about the work of Harvey Sacks, Silverman (1998: ix) has commented: 'Whether or not we follow the path that Sacks sets out is perhaps less important than whether we respond to the questions that [he] poses about social science'. He goes on to suggest that 'after more than twenty years, they are … still vitally important and still largely unanswered'. Another twenty years on, this remains true. At the same time, I have not hesitated to criticise what I find to be weaknesses in the case for ethnomethodology, and to identify problems with the alternative approach(es) to studying the social world proposed and practised. I believe that this sort of critical engagement is essential if we are to have any chance of resolving the divisions within sociology, and within social science more generally.[33]

Overview of chapters

The chapters in this book largely take the form of separate essays, examin- ing various aspects of ethnomethodology and its sources; though they reflect a consistent stance towards it, and towards social science more generally (a

32 For one previous example, see Atkinson 1988, and the response: Watson and Sharrock 1991. See Hammersley 2019a.
33 Few of my criticisms are new – most can already be found in the literature – but I have sought to spell them out clearly and fully, and to show how they relate to one another.

broadly neo-Kantian one). The fact that they are separate essays means that there is occasional overlap, but I hope that this will be, at most, only mildly irritating for any resolute reader who starts at the beginning and persists to the end. I found that writing the book in this manner was the only hope I had of completing it.

In Chapter 1 I try to clarify the views of Alfred Schutz, who was a major influence on Garfinkel's development of ethnomethodology, and more broadly on what came to be called phenomenological sociology in the 1960s and 1970s. I note the reception of his work by Garfinkel and others, but suggest that in important respects its purpose and nature have been misinterpreted. I examine the context in which Schutz began his studies in Vienna in the 1930s, and in particular his relationship to Austrian economics, along with the influence of logical positivism, notably through his friend Felix Kaufmann. Schutz's aim was to resolve a problem that had been at the heart of this economic tradition: to ground its basic theoretical principles. And he identified much the same gap in the interpretive sociology of Max Weber. He argued that Weber's development of the concept of ideal types was an effective way of understanding economic theory, and a sound basis for sociological analysis, but that Weber had failed to secure its roots. Schutz drew on the work of Bergson and Husserl in an attempt to clarify the nature of the lifeworld that underpins social and economic action. In this chapter I consider whether his work represented a fundamental challenge to what widely came to be seen in the 1960s as the positivism of the dominant sociological tradition; or, alternatively, whether it should be regarded as displaying strong elements of positivism itself, as has sometimes been suggested. I also address the question of whether Schutz regarded his work as part of social science or of philosophy, and therefore whether he was, in fact, aiming to build a phenomenological sociology, as seems to have been assumed by Garfinkel and many others.

The next chapter compares the orientations of Garfinkel and Goffman. They were contemporaries who knew one another, and their work is often regarded as similar, being concerned with the study of mundane patterns of social interaction. Some have suggested that their work is complementary and could be integrated into a more comprehensive approach. However, ethnomethodologists have usually insisted that there are fundamental differences between the two. Against this background, I examine both the similarities and differences, doing this via a comparison with the work of a third sociologist, Georg Simmel. It has often been noted that Goffman seems to have been strongly influenced by Simmel. By contrast, there are few signs that Simmel influenced Garfinkel, or ethnomethodologists more generally. Nevertheless, there are some interesting parallels. In particular, they share a concern with the constitutive role that social interaction plays in social life. While recognising that there are important similarities between the orientations of Garfinkel and Goffman, I argue that the suggestion that their work is complementary and could be integrated fails to take proper account of fundamental differences, and that these shed light on the radical distinctiveness of ethnomethodology. These differences focus not just on the sorts of data used but more particularly on what they are used *to do*. For Goffman, the aim is to generate conceptual frameworks that illuminate everyday behavior, whereas ethnomethodologists resist the bringing in of new concepts, being concerned instead with explicating, in their own terms, the processes by which social phenomena are produced. Other differences relate to what is taken to be the *context* of social interaction, with Goffman treating the interaction order as mediating the effects of outside factors, whereas ethnomethodologists insist that the context of any process of social interaction can only be what is constituted as context within it.

Chapter 3 considers the ambiguous disciplinary status of ethnomethodology, and especially its problematic relationship with the parent discipline: sociology. Sometimes ethnomethodology is presented as a radical internal reform movement, aimed at re-specifying the focus of the discipline and its mode of operation. On other occasions, it is put forward as an 'alternate' or supplement to mainstream sociological work, and as having an 'indifferent' attitude towards it, treating it as simply another kind of members' practice that can be studied by ethnomethodologists. Or, again, particularly in the form of conversation analysis, ethnomethodology is sometimes treated as if it were a discipline in its own right, independent not just of sociology but also of the various other disciplines with which it has a relationship, such as linguistics. Finally, some have suggested that it is anti-disciplinary in character, as regards social science, holding that ethnomethodology can best serve as a complement to other forms of practice, including the work of natural scientists and of those developing new technologies. I examine the cogency of each of these positions, arguing that ethnomethodology's critique of social science, while salutary, seems to imply abolition rather than reform; and I suggest that the proposal of its complementary relationship to conventional social science or forms of practice leaves open the question of why such a supplement is required. I acknowledge that there are strong grounds for claiming that conversation analysis has provided a significant cumulative development of knowledge, but I note questions about whether its ethnomethodological character was essential to its success in this respect, or is even compatible with it. Less successful in developing a cumulative body of knowledge has been the tradition of 'studies of work', but this can, like conversation analysis, reasonably claim to have made a practical contribution to some fields, for example to system and software design. Once again, though, it is not clear that this stems from the ethnomethodological character of the investigations. In conclusion, I suggest that the ambiguous status of ethnomethodology is built into its very nature.

In Chapter 4 I present a fuller assessment of what seem to be the key theoretical presuppositions of ethnomethodology. It treats social order as the central focus of sociological (and perhaps even of all social scientific) inquiry, but reinterprets this concept, transforming the way it was understood by Parsons. Indeed, Garfinkel redefines it as the intelligibility of coordinated patterns of action. He also breaks with Parsons' 'analytical realism', and the stance of other sociological approaches that emphasise the need for a theoretical framework if the causes of social order, and of disorder, are to be investigated effectively. Ethnomethodology insists, instead, that order is observable routinely in everyday situations, and that how it is constituted can only be discovered once the natural attitude (and, along with this, the theoretical attitude adopted by social scientists) is suspended so that processes of social interaction can be carefully examined in their own right. Another core element of ethnomethodology is the idea that the meanings of social actions are locally variable and context-dependent ('indexical' and 'reflexive'), rather than being determined by a semantic code, and that they are intelligible because they are self-identifying – their meaning is displayed and recognised by actors via shared methods or practices, in other words they are 'accountable'. Ethnomethodology also involves some important *methodological* commitments. As I noted earlier, it often seems to assume that for inquiry to be rigorous it must avoid reliance upon unexplicated resources, appealing only to what is observable or intersubjectively available. Finally, ethnomethodology appears to treat the aim of rigorous social analysis as literal description, rather than explanation or the production of explanatory theory: the task should be to 'make visible' members' methods for the production of social phenomena. I assess each of these claims in detail, concluding that, while they relate to significant issues for social science, the intractability of these problems has been exaggerated. Moreover, ethnomethodology itself does not escape them.

In the final chapter before the Conclusion, I consider the influence of ethnomethodology on qualitative research methodology, which is one of the main areas of mainstream social science where it has had an impact. I focus particularly on the reception of Cicourel's (1964) book *Method and Measurement in Sociology*, and also on how conversation analysis has shaped the work of many discourse analysts, and some ethnographers. I outline Cicourel's argument that sociology needs to be re-founded methodologically on an empirical theory that respects the complex and contingent character of human action and communication, along the lines suggested by ethnomethodology. He claims that this would facilitate resolution of the fundamental methodological problems that have plagued sociology. The effects of his early work were to support the rise of qualitative research and to encourage reflexive attention to the processes by which data are produced. However, these developments often subsequently went in directions that were at odds with his conception of rigorous analysis. As regards the influence of conversation analysis, I note how this encouraged the use of electronic recordings and transcriptions as data, raised doubts about the traditional uses of interviews, and encouraged the micro-analysis of patterns of social interaction. Furthermore, like Cicourel's work, it facilitated the spread of social constructionism. I argue that these effects have been beneficial in many respects but more negative in others.

The book ends with a Conclusion that summarises and elaborates on my evaluation of ethnomethodology, and considers its implications.

1 Was Schutz a positivist? Was he even a sociologist? Comparing the reception and inception of his work

My aim in this chapter is to clarify the nature and implications of the work of Alfred Schutz, the Austrian philosopher/social scientist who is often regarded as the founder of phenomenological sociology, and who had a significant impact on ethnomethodology. He began his work in Vienna in the 1930s, and continued it in the United States after emigration. While it had rather little influence on Anglo-American sociology during his lifetime, after his death in 1959, and the publication of his *Collected Papers* (Schutz 1962, 1964, 1966), his work became very influential in some quarters. Though references to Schutz have declined since the 1980s – he has been largely replaced in the sociological pantheon by other figures – some strands of sociological work on which he had a major influence continue to be important today.[1]

I will suggest that while Schutz's work – being phenomenological – is usually seen as anti-positivist, in fact he was influenced by positivism.[2] Of course, whether this is true depends heavily upon what the term 'positivism' is taken to mean. A loose, and misleading, sense that is now frequently used conflates it with 'realism', with the idea that the phenomena social science investigates exist and have the character they do independently of it. In these terms, there could be little challenge to the claim that Schutz was a positivist.[3] 'Positivism' is also sometimes taken to

1 He is included in Ritzer's (2010) *Classical Sociological Theory*, Ritzer and Stepnisky's (2011) *Companion to Major Sociological Theorists*, Vol. 1, and Scott's (2007) *Fifty Key Sociologists: The Formative Years*. Furthermore, there are still references to him in some dictionaries of sociology; though, interestingly, he is not included in Stones' *Key Sociological Thinkers*, while Garfinkel is. It is also worth noting that since 2009 there has been an annual review entitled *Schutzian Research*.

2 In some respects this parallels the claim that Comte was no positivist, despite inventing the term: see Scharff (1995).

3 He argues that all facts are 'interpreted facts', and they carry along with them 'their interpretational inner and outer horizon', but insists that 'this does not mean that, in daily life or in science, we are unable to grasp the reality of the world. It just means that we grasp merely certain aspects of it, namely those which are relevant to us either for carrying on our business of living or from the point of view of a body of accepted rules of procedure of thinking called the method of science' (Schutz 1962: 3). It seems that, while learning much from the later work of Husserl, Schutz adopted the 'realist' position characteristic of his early

mean the belief that social science should be value-neutral, adopting a detached or disinterested perspective on social affairs. In these terms, too, Schutz's position would be labelled 'positivist' by many today.

However, in this chapter I intend to adopt a more specific sense of the term, taking the Vienna Circle philosophers as the key exemplars – not least because this was the main sense given to 'positivism' in the context in which Schutz began his work in the 1930s. In fact, even in these restricted terms, the accusation of positivism has been made, notably by Lynch (1993: 135), who claims that Schutz 'adopted aspects of the Vienna Circle's philosophical version of a unified science'. And, indeed, I will argue that there are important respects in which Schutz, though a phenomenologist, employed methodological arguments that paralleled those of logical positivists of the 1920s and 1930s.[4] However, my main purpose is not classificatory, or to provide a critique of Schutz's work, but rather to highlight significant respects in which I believe it has been widely misunderstood (albeit perhaps productively), and to outline the important issues and distinctions that this has obscured.

Schutz wrote the only book he published in his lifetime, translated as *The Phenomenology of the Social World*, in Vienna, around the time when Schlick, Carnap, and others were developing and publishing their ideas. Schutz did not belong to what we now refer to as the Vienna Circle, but he did participate in two other intellectual circles in that city: that around the economist Ludwig von Mises, and also the *Geist Kreis*, a seminar on science and philosophy founded by Friedrich von Hayek.[5] Moreover, Schutz's close friend Felix Kaufmann was a participant not only in these two circles but also in the Vienna Circle, and his philosophical approach strongly paralleled that of its members: he was, if you like, one of their fellow travellers (others included, in different ways, Wittgenstein and Popper). At the same time, he had studied the work of Husserl; indeed, he introduced Schutz to this. The two of them engaged in close and sustained discussion during the period when Schutz produced his book, and this was also the time when Kaufmann was writing his book on the *Methodology of the Social Sciences*.[6]

The second question in my title, concerning whether Schutz was a sociologist, specifically relates to whether his aim was to develop a phenomenological sociology

writings. On Husserl's shift towards a more idealist or transcendental approach, see Ingarden 2005; Speigelberg 1960; Moran 2005.

4 Lynch attributes this, in large part, to the influence of Felix Kaufmann, on which see below. Schutz certainly argued that there were methodological features that were essential to both natural and social science, but both he and Kaufmann insisted that there were also distinctive features. See Schutz 1962: 48–66.

5 For brief characterisations of these circles, see Wagner 1983: 12.

6 This appeared in 1936 in German, but has only recently been translated (Cohen and Helling 2014). See also Kaufmann 1936b. Garfinkel cites Kaufmann 1944 quite heavily, a work in English produced after Kaufmann's arrival in the United States, which covers some of the same ground, from much the same angle, but has a different structure.

or to contribute to philosophical understanding of the foundations of sociology. At the time he set out on his inquiries, sociology was only beginning to emerge as a distinct discipline in German-speaking countries, and there were significantly different views regarding its character (Käsler 1983). One area of dispute concerned the boundary with philosophy; and this was, for example, a far from simple matter in the case of the work of Simmel, who was at the time the most prominent German sociologist. Of course, the nature of sociology as a discipline was no more a matter of consensus in the Anglo-American world of the 1960s and 1970s, when Schutz's work started to attract wide attention. Furthermore, at this time, questions about the discipline's relationship to philosophy were also raised by Winch's (1958) *The Idea of a Social Science*; though his position was significantly different from that of Schutz, drawing on Wittgenstein and Ryle rather than phenomenology.

As background to my argument, I will begin by exploring three significant strands within sociology in the second half of the twentieth century, and continuing today to varying degrees, that drew on Schutz's arguments, two of them claiming the title of ethnomethodology. I will then consider the original context in which Schutz developed those arguments, before outlining what I take to be the nature of his project. Finally, I will address the question of whether his work is best seen as sociological or philosophical, as well as in what respects it might be labelled 'positivist', along with the implications of this.

The reception of Schutz in Anglo-American sociology

In the 1960s and 1970s Schutz's work had an important influence on emerging trends in sociology: on ethnomethodology, on 'phenomenological sociology' more generally, on the field of qualitative research methodology, as well as that broad but influential stream of ideas often referred to as social constructionism (see Psathas 2004; Burr 2015; Weinberg 2014). The predominant effect of Schutz's writings in these contexts, often, was to undermine previously dominant approaches that had treated sociological analysis as documenting the objective character of the social world, where any discrepancy between this and actors' perceptions or beliefs was presented as a product of their ignorance and/or of ideology. A contrast had routinely been drawn between subjective and objective conceptions of social phenomena, for instance of the origins and functions of institutions, and of the nature of social class. This was a mode of argument common in Marxist work but equally so in the 'structural functionalism' that was influential in mainstream Anglo-American sociology during the 1950s and 1960s, and even in much of what came to be labelled 'conflict sociology' (Collins 1975). Indeed, that actors were ignorant, misled, or mistaken about significant aspects of their world was often taken to provide the very rationale for sociological work, its central task being to replace ignorance and/or to identify and explain ideological misconceptions (see Rock 1979: Preface).

A key message that was taken from Schutz's work in the 1970s, and from some other sources as well, was that social phenomena, rather than existing in much the same manner as physical objects, are constituted in and through human action, this itself structured by processes of interpretation or practical reasoning. Previously, most forms of sociology had assumed that social phenomena exist largely independently of the perceptions and intentions of individual people; indeed, these phenomena had been treated as acting on people so as to produce stable societal patterns; and perhaps also social divisions or conflicts. By contrast, what Schutz's work was taken to show was that it is the actions of participants, based on their understandings of particular contexts, that make social phenomena what they are.[7] This was frequently seen as undermining the idea that social structures or institutions exist independently of the orientations of participants, or that they are a product of forces – material or ideational – working 'behind people's backs'. Indeed, this was often taken to imply rejection of the whole notion of social causation and perhaps also of objectivity – of the idea that sociology can establish what is *really* going on, as against what people believe or say is happening. The central task now, for many, was to document common-sense knowledge, social meanings, or understandings, and their constitutive role in social life.

So, a substantial proportion of younger sociologists in the 1960s came to regard the social world as necessarily constituted in and through the particular assumptions, methods, etc., that are deployed by actors; and they took these to be the proper focus of inquiry. Along these lines, Gubrium and Holstein (1997: 39) report that Schutz

> introduced phenomenology to sociology, pointing out the constitutive nature of consciousness and interaction. He argued that the social sciences should focus on the ways that the lifeworld – the experiential world every person takes for granted – is produced and experienced by members.

Moreover, this lifeworld was frequently held to consist of 'multiple realities', rather than as involving a simple contrast between objective existence and subjective perceptions (see Schutz 1945). This involved a significant shift in focus, but also raised questions about the epistemological status that could be attributed to sociological accounts: to some it seemed that it was not just the claim to a superior form of knowledge that was undermined but also any relationship to the world being studied; in these terms, social science sometimes came to be treated as constructing its own distinctive reality, as do other forms of life (see, for instance, Mehan and Wood 1975).

7 There is, of course, a strong parallel here with symbolic interactionism.

However, there were also significant variations in the specific implications derived from Schutz's work. Some sociologists drew the conclusion that it is necessary to refocus sociology, so as to engage in rigorous analysis of how social phenomena are ongoingly constituted as recognisable features of the world, and as having determinate relations with one another. Here the key example is Garfinkel's ethnomethodology. A rather different, but not unrelated, approach was to examine the implications of Schutz's arguments for the methods employed by empirical sociology and its claim to scientific status. The primary example of this is the work of Cicourel (especially his 1964). A third response was to apply Schutz's ideas to the sociology of knowledge, and here the source text is, of course, Berger and Luckmann's *The Social Construction of Reality*.[8]

An alternative to sociology: Garfinkel and ethnomethodology

It is clear that Schutz was a very important influence on the early thinking of Garfinkel.[9] But equally significant was the work of Talcott Parsons, and of US sociologists more generally in the 1940s and 1950s. From Parsons, Garfinkel took the focus of sociology to be the problem of social order: how it is established and maintained. But he approached this issue in a more empirically minded manner than Parsons, drawing on contemporary forms of sociological and social psychological research. A crucial element of this was rejection of Parsons' analytical realism (Treviño 2001: xxv–xxvi), in favour of the idea that social order can be discovered in concrete social processes, without any need for an external theoretical framework.

Garfinkel seems to have taken Schutz's work both as pointing to a fundamental failing in conventional forms of sociology *and* as opening up an intriguing new empirical field of investigation concerned with practical reasoning itself; in other words with the methods that ordinary people use in making sense of the world, including how they deploy values and norms in order to engage in action that displays itself as 'rational in the circumstances'. The basic failing of conventional sociological work, by implication, was that, while there is reference – implicitly or explicitly – to the sense that people make of their environments, in other words to the meanings they generate, how they develop and deploy this understanding was largely taken as given. And this suggested that sociological analyses were, at the very least, incomplete in scientific terms; certainly, they did not live up to their claims to provide determinate causal explanations for social actions.

8 For a rather different approach to the reception or influence of Schutz's work, see Psathas 2004. See also Wagner 1988.

9 See Psathas 1980, 1999, 2009, 2012. Lynch 1988 and 1993 has argued that Garfinkel subsequently broke with Schutz's underlying philosophy: for discussion of this see Dennis 2004; Lynch 2004; Sharrock 2004.

Garfinkel's argument here amounts to a further development of Parsons' deployment of Durkheim's critique of social contract theory (see Durkheim 1933: 215–16; Parsons 1937: 311–12), emphasising the 'tacit' conditions on which contracts necessarily rely. Durkheim had pointed out that contracts cannot be entered into without people already sharing background understandings; not least about what a contract is but also about other relevant matters, such as the types of situation to which the contract would and would not apply. And he emphasised that all attempts to put every consideration that might be relevant explicitly into a contract would necessarily fail. In short, contracts cannot emerge out of, or operate on the basis of, nothing: they always rely upon prior understandings and commitments. Along the same lines, Garfinkel emphasised that their meaning is determined in particular cases – in other words, they are always accompanied by (often unstated) etcetera clauses, and they are applied through the deployment of other *ad hoc* practices, such as 'wait and see', 'let it pass', 'unless', and so on.

Garfinkel pointed out that neither Durkheim nor Parsons had provided a detailed account of the nature of the understandings underpinning contracts, and how they operate. In this respect, their own theories about how social order is established and maintained suffer from much the same problem as social contract theories. At the same time, Garfinkel deepened the problem by arguing that the meaning of all words, not just those in contracts, is indexical or context-dependent. This means that *work* always has to be done by people in order to recognise what others are saying or doing, and to make what they themselves say or do intelligible. While this work goes on routinely, and for the most part without being given attention by participants, it is essential to the existence and operation of any form of social order.

In this way, Garfinkel seems to have concluded from Schutz's notion of the reciprocity of perspectives (Schutz 1962) that the orderly character of the social world is created by methods, or accounting practices, that are used both to display meanings and to 'read' the displays produced by others. This, he argued, is how social order is achieved. Of course, as already indicated, here the concept of social order has been reinterpreted to refer to the intelligibility and coordinated character of social action, rather than the avoidance of conflict and violence, which was Parsons' Hobbesian starting point.

Thus, for Garfinkel, the task of sociology became to document how people behave in ways that are intelligible (or 'rationally accountable') to others, thereby creating the social world that each of them takes for granted in deciding how to act on particular occasions. Rather than assuming that actors simply respond to perceived reality via a form of rationality analogous to that presumed to be employed by scientists, or by following procedural rules that specify which type of situation demands which type of response, Garfinkel argued that artful practices of sense-making are necessarily involved. And by 'artful' he meant precisely that they are '*ad hoc*': designed to make sense of what is going on, retrospectively and prospectively, as action proceeds, according to the exigencies of particular situations. So the task of ethnomethodology is to describe these practices, so as to reveal the nature of the local practical rationality that characterises human social action.

On this basis, Garfinkel and his students set about identifying multiple examples of practical reasoning and action, such as the application of legal, bureaucratic, or informal rules (Zimmerman 1970b; Wieder 1974); the construction of orderly conversations through turn-taking (conversation analysis); the establishment and maintenance of queues (Schwartz 1978; Garfinkel 2002: ch. 8); the production of mathematical proofs and demonstrations (Livingston 1986); scientific discovery and the teaching of science (Garfinkel 2002: chs 7, 9); and Buddhist debates (Liberman 2007).

An obvious, but important, question that arises here concerns the relationship between ethnomethodology and conventional forms of sociology. Garfinkel's position on this issue has always appeared ambivalent. On the one hand, it is quite clear that criticism of conventional sociology is implied in some of what he writes. In effect, he argues that its commitment to a conception of rigorous inquiry, frequently modelled on (a positivist conception of) natural science, is at odds with its inevitable reliance upon common-sense practices and knowledge. Moreover, it thereby fails to take proper account of how the very phenomena with which it deals are constituted ongoingly in the process of social interaction. In this he was not rejecting social science but arguing for a reconceptualisation of what a scientific approach to social phenomena would entail, using the 'rigorous' philosophical work of Husserl as one model (Moran 2005). At the same time, Garfinkel sometimes denies that his work carries any critical implications for conventional sociology. Instead, he treats the latter as simply one more 'members' practice' that could be studied to reveal how it is intelligibly produced through routine practices.[10]

A foundation for conventional sociology: Cicourel and cognitive sociology

Cicourel drew heavily on Schutz's work, and was strongly influenced by Garfinkel (Cicourel 2016), but he reached somewhat different conclusions. One important difference was that he placed primary emphasis on what he took to be the methodological implications of Schutz's and Garfinkel's work for conventional forms of sociological research, seeking to address the question of how the problems they highlighted could be remedied. His starting point was the extent to which conventional sociology, of all kinds, tends to *assume* correspondences between its concepts, its data, and the social phenomena these are taken to represent.

10 For examples of such studies, see Houtkoop-Steenstra 2000; Maynard et al. 2002; Greiffenhagen et al. 2011, 2015. For Garfinkel's view of such research, see Maynard 2012.

In relation to quantitative research, he repeated the longstanding criticism that what is actually measured in much experimental and survey research is often different from what it is claimed is being measured. He argues that 'the typical problem of measurement in sociology is ... one of implicit theories with vague properties and operations tied in unknown ways to measurement procedures which ... have explicit quantitative properties' (Cicourel 1964: iii). He argues that the mismatches involved here have been largely ignored in practice, resulting in what he calls 'measurement-by-fiat', rather than genuine or 'literal' measurement.[11]

Cicourel also argues that much the same problem arises with qualitative sociology (Smith and Atkinson 2016): that there is a failure to show that the evidence employed actually represents the phenomena concerned accurately, in ways that articulate with the concepts embedded in the research questions addressed. What go unmentioned are the processes of editing and reformulation that take place in 'collecting', processing, and analysing data, as well as the errors that may arise from a failure to probe whether the data produced actually mean what they are taken to mean. What is involved here is not just a concern about errors in the analysis but also an insistence that the process of research should be transparent, so that readers of research reports can assess the likelihood of error.

Equally important, Cicourel argued that researchers' interpretations of what other people do and say is usually *ad hoc*, rather than being the product of a rigorous theory dealing with basic social, and especially communicational, processes, as he believed it should be. So, what is required, he suggested, is investigation of how social meanings are generated, both on the part of the people being studied and by researchers themselves. He suggested that this could produce a 'theory of data' which would place sociological research on a much sounder footing.[12]

In the course of a number of research projects, Cicourel sought to show what would be required to make the process of inquiry transparent, and at the same time to build a theory of basic social processes, thereby providing a more secure foundation for sociological work. Thus, in his empirical research he pays particular attention to issues such as the relationship between the summary accounts of social processes that people provide via questionnaire responses and in interviews, for instance about the institutional processing of 'delinquents' or of decisions relating to fertility (Cicourel 1968, 1974), and the complex and dynamic character of these processes as they actually occur. He also gives attention to the question

11 He derives the term 'measurement-by-fiat' from Torgerson (1958: 21–2).
12 Others had sought to provide a 'theory of data' (for instance, Coombs 1953), but along very different lines. Interestingly, there is a parallel here with the demand on the part of some conversation analysts that the analytic process be subject to control by an explicit methodological apparatus (Maynard 2006: 64). In arguing for this, Maynard treats this apparatus as analogous to what Felix Kaufmann (1944) calls 'inquiry-specific rules of scientific procedure'.

of whether interviewer and interviewee rely upon the same or different concepts, and the implications of this for the nature of the data produced. His research demonstrates that there can be serious discrepancies between accounts in these respects, whether amongst those of informants or between these and the account of the sociologist. He suggests that research relying upon data from questionnaires or interviews must be supported by a more ethnographic approach that inspects what people say and do outside the formal data-collection process – as a means of providing background information that can serve as a basis for checking the validity of the data or inferences from them. Through these studies, and also by studying sign-language communication among people with hearing difficulties (Cicourel 1973: ch. 5), he sought to develop a more adequate understanding of processes of communication than can be derived from linguistics and cognitive psychology. In doing this, he emphasised the role of the cultural resources on which people draw, the social as well as psychological nature of memory, and the necessarily situated character of all sense-making.

Much more clearly than Garfinkel, Cicourel accepts the value of traditional kinds of sociological work. While he insists that there have been serious failings in the ways in which it has pursued its goals, he seeks to diagnose the problem and offer a solution. The implication is that an effective remedy can be found, and that sociology can thereby become truly scientific. What is proposed could be characterised as a strong dose of reflexivity (using that term in a different way from Garfinkel),[13] so that the focus in any research project must include how accounts of the social world are being generated, including by the researcher her or himself. Equally important, as already noted, is development of theory about basic social processes so as to provide a sounder foundation for sociological work. This parallels the project of Schutz, but differs from it in important respects, not least in involving empirical sociological investigation rather than reliance upon phenomenological analysis of the researcher's own experience of social life.

In short, Cicourel treats Schutz as mounting a methodological challenge to conventional kinds of sociological work, and as highlighting the need for this work to have a more rigorous grounding. However, unlike Garfinkel, he does not propose a radical respecification of the discipline's goals.

A new sociology of knowledge: Berger and Luckmann

For Berger and Luckmann (1966), too, Schutz's work did not imply the need for a fundamental re-specification of sociological inquiry, but unlike Cicourel they were not concerned with its methodological implications. Rather, they saw Schutz's

13 On different meanings of 'reflexivity', see Lynch 2000a; Czyzewski 1994.

phenomenological analyses as offering a fruitful way of reconstructing a particular sociological field: the sociology of knowledge. The content of that field was to change, and it was to take on a more central role within the discipline.

Prior to the work of Berger and Luckmann, the sociology of knowledge had been primarily concerned with the ideas produced by intellectual elites, of various kinds, especially political ideas recorded in published documents. This is true, for example, of the work of Mannheim, the most influential figure in the field. However, Berger and Luckmann argued that the sociology of knowledge should focus, more generally, on 'what passes for knowledge' within a society, and how this comes to be established and maintained. Moreover, they emphasised that this knowledge plays a central role in all social action, even the most mundane. Thus, the focus of the sub-discipline was expanded to include the ideas of ordinary people, as these inform and shape everyday social interaction. In the process, Berger and Luckmann developed a complex theory concerning how ideas are objectified as institutional practices of various kinds, and how they are internalised by individual actors. In doing this they drew on the work of other writers besides Schutz, notably Durkheim, Mead, and Gehlen. In effect, Berger and Luckmann see the sociology of knowledge in its new form as providing an understanding of how the distinct social worlds characteristic of different societies, and indeed of groups within those societies, are created and reproduced. In other words, they insist that ideas and knowledge are central to human social life, and therefore to the study of social order.

Right at the start of their book, Berger and Luckmann draw a sharp boundary between the sociology of knowledge and epistemology, insisting that they are simply suspending questions about what is and is not genuine knowledge. This is done in order to facilitate specifically *sociological* investigation of how what is taken to be knowledge is produced, recognised, and used in the course of social life. Subsequent versions of constructionism, despite often appealing to Berger and Luckmann's landmark text, have frequently eroded or ignored this boundary between empirical inquiry and philosophy. Drawing on two other strands of work, on Kuhn's (1970) account of the development of natural science, and/or on French poststructuralist ideas and other sources, it has come to be argued by some sociologists that all knowledge is not just artefactual but, in effect, fictional (for an example, see Denzin 1997). In other words, all accounts create what they claim to represent, and as a result multiple realities exist whose relationship to one another is incommensurable; in the same way as are the different paradigms in the history of physics described by Kuhn. Furthermore, the implication has sometimes been drawn from this that sociological accounts must themselves be treated as constructions, and should be presented in ways that indicate this fact; indeed that they perhaps ought even to be self-subverting (see, for instance, Woolgar 1988; Ashmore 1989). These conclusions are very different from those of Berger and Luckmann, as well as from the position of Schutz; and it has also been argued that they are at odds with Garfinkel's ethnomethodology (Button and Sharrock 1993).

From this discussion of three kinds of work that have been inspired, in large part, by the writings of Schutz, we can identify several themes that need to be picked up. These include the relationship between philosophy and social science, whether conventional forms of sociological work are viable from a Schutzian perspective, and the methodological implications of Schutz's project. I will examine these later, but first it is necessary to describe the context in which he began his work.

The initial context

In order to understand Schutz's writings, it is necessary to have some familiarity with his early intellectual context, since this was very different from that of Anglo-American sociology in the 1960s. Schutz was educated at the University of Vienna, studying international law. As part of this, his studies included economics, and he subsequently secured a job as executive secretary of the Austrian Bankers' Association. Alongside this, he participated in the von Mises circle, whose focus of discussion covered economic theory and policy, but also philosophical issues relating to the social sciences more generally.[14]

Ludwig von Mises was a key figure in the distinctive Austrian tradition of economics that had been founded by Karl Menger, in explicit opposition to German historical economics. Where the latter was primarily concerned with analysing the development of economic institutions and their role in the national economy, as this relates to economic policy, Menger argued that the central task of economics is to produce theoretical understanding of universal economic processes, and he is usually identified as one of the key figures involved in the development of the marginalist interpretation of economic value that transformed economics at the end of the nineteenth century.[15]

14 At this time economics was not taught as a separate subject in most universities, and there was a close relationship between law and economics in German-speaking countries. On the distinctive significance of this relationship, see Hennis 1987. Furthermore, disciplinary boundaries were weak and conceptualised rather differently from today (see Cohen and Helling 2014: 48–9). Schutz's taking of a non-academic job, as with his friend Kaufmann, stemmed largely from the fact that there were few academic posts available in Vienna at the time.

15 On Schutz's relationship to Austrian economics, see Prendergast 1986, Ebeling 1999, and Wilson 2005. I have followed these authors in emphasising this aspect of his intellectual context, but there is a danger of underplaying his interest in Kelsen's legal theorising and in Weber's sociology. For detailed background on other aspects of Schutz's life see Wagner 1983 and Barber 2004. It is important to recognise that Menger did not reject the value of historical work or more practical economic concerns. He included these as part of the discipline, but tended to see them as subordinate to theoretical analysis (see Menger 1985).

The central tenets of this Austrian tradition were that economic agents act on the basis of subjective interpretations of their own and others' needs, goals, intentions, etc., rather than by responding in some fixed causal fashion to either background or situational factors. In effect, what is involved here is the core of what has come to be referred to as rational choice theory. A second element is that social action generates spontaneous forms of social order, often unintended by the actors involved. These two assumptions imply a commitment to methodological individualism, and this was in explicit opposition to various sorts of collectivist or organicist approaches in social science, not just Marxism but also much of German historical economics and sociology.[16]

The Austrian approach viewed the central goal of theoretical economics as to identify universal laws that operate in the economic sphere, and these were often taken to have the same formal structure as the laws of physics. At the same time, in opposition to empiricist views, economic theory was regarded as a logical construction based upon deduction from self-evident first principles. On the basis of this theory, practical empirical conclusions could then be drawn. However, it was argued that these could never refute the basic principles.

In some respects, Menger and the Austrian tradition followed the formalist approach that had come to be central to British political economy in the nineteenth century. Hutchison (2000: ch. 1) describes how this emerged in the work of Ricardo, though it was spelt out in methodological terms by Nassau Senior. And, within the Anglo-American world, the subsequent influence of this vision of the discipline can be traced through the remainder of the nineteenth and into the twentieth century, despite the rise of Keynesian macro-economics. It was exemplified, for example, in the influential essay on the nature of economics by Lionel Robbins, first published in 1932 (see Hutchison 2009). Moreover, after the Second World War, much the same basic conception of economics was retained alongside increasing mathematisation in the form of econometrics.

The Austrian tradition generally maintained a commitment to a non-mathematical version of formalism, and it had distinctive features in other respects too. The most important of these, for my purposes here, was a concern with the epistemological status of the basic propositions of economic theory. This was central to the conflict with German historical economists, who criticised the assumptions underpinning the economic theory developed by British and Austrian economists as empirically false, and rejected what they took to be its political implications.

The nature of German historical economics and the *Methodenstreit* generated by Menger's work is more complex than I have been able to indicate. For a somewhat different view from that presented here, see Tribe (1995: ch. 4).

16 Hayek, perhaps the best known representative of Austrian economics in the Anglo-American world, developed this line of argument into a political philosophy, for instance in Hayek 1967. However, this involved a significant break with Mises' position: see Hutchison 2009.

At the same time, there was disagreement amongst members of the Austrian School about the character of the basic principles of economic theory, in particular about how they could be validated; and uncertainty about this issue seems to have been one of the initial stimuli for Schutz's work.

In addressing this question, Menger, the founder of Austrian economics, drew upon a neo-Aristotelian approach that was influential in Austria at the time. This was exemplified by the 'descriptive psychology' developed by Franz Brentano (see Speigelberg 1960). It proposed that there are truths about the world – in this case the world of psychological phenomena – that are neither matters discoverable by conventional empirical investigation (since they are prior to any such investigation) nor simple logical truths or tautologies (the 'analytic' truths of logical positivists). The model here was, to some extent, that of mathematics. For example, Menger (1985: 70) writes that

> To want to test the pure theory of economy by experience in its full reality is a process analogous to that of the mathematician who wants to correct the principles of geometry by measuring real objects, without reflecting that the latter are indeed not identical with the magnitudes which pure geometry presumes or that every measurement of necessity implies elements of inexactitude.

Following Aristotle, Menger seems to have argued that, on the basis of direct experience of the world, insights about the necessary relations among types of phenomena can be derived, enabling the construction of 'exact' models of economic behaviour that are not open to empirical falsification because they relate to an abstracted world that does not correspond to concrete reality, yet at the same time underlies it. Moreover, he did not see the production of such models, specifying necessary relations, as marking a difference between the social and the natural sciences, since he held that models of this type are also central to the latter.[17]

Later figures in the Austrian School offered rather different accounts of the origin and nature of the basic principles of economic theory. For example, Wieser, one of the second generation of Austrian economists, argued that economic first principles could be grounded in psychological introspection (see White 1977: 11). Von Mises, who is usually regarded as belonging to the third generation, offered a different interpretation. Like Menger and Wieser, he saw economic laws as exact, not probabilistic, and as not open to refutation by observation. However, he adopted a more Kantian position, arguing that the basic principles of economics are *a priori* in character because they represent 'the logical structure of the human

---

17 There is a parallel here with the views of Husserl: see Gurwitsch 1974. It is perhaps worth noting a later similar disagreement about whether the features of talk-in-interaction documented by conversation analysts are empirical regularities or logical relations: see Coulter 1983b.

mind' (von Mises 1949: 4).[18] He also deviated from the position of Menger in drawing a sharp distinction between the natural and the social sciences (see also Hayek 1952); for methodological reasons, mind and matter are to be treated as distinct realms. He argues that, currently at least, we cannot explain people's subjective preferences in scientific terms, and must therefore simply treat these as givens. He writes:

> Reason and experience show us two separate realms: the external world of physical, chemical, and physiological phenomena and the internal world of thought, feeling, valuation, and purposeful action. No bridge connects – as far as we can see today – these two spheres. Identical external events result sometimes in different human responses, and different external events produce sometimes the same human response.
>
> We do not know why. ... We may or may not believe that the natural sciences will succeed one day in explaining the production of definite ideas, judgments of value, and actions in the same way in which they explain the production of a chemical compound as the necessary and unavoidable outcome of a certain combination of elements. In the meantime we are bound to acquiesce in a methodological dualism. Human action is one of the agencies bringing about change. It is an element of cosmic activity and becoming. Therefore it is a legitimate object of scientific investigation. As – at least under present conditions – it cannot be traced back to its causes, it must be considered as an ultimate given and must be studied as such. (von Mises 1949: 18)

Interestingly, von Mises sought to extend the scope of his analysis beyond the field of economics to embrace human action comprehensively. Initially he labelled the discipline concerned with this wider field 'sociology', but later switched to the term 'praxeology' because what he was proposing was very different from most of what was labelled as sociology at the time.[19] In the course of his discussion of methodological issues, von Mises compared his approach with that of Max Weber, particularly the latter's development of ideal types. Weber (1968) had explicitly treated the concept of rational action directed towards a goal, the core of Menger's economics, as an ideal type; and von Mises shared many assumptions with him. However, unlike Weber, von Mises regarded economic ideal types not simply as convenient devices for practical analysis but as representing an idealised model, *a priori* in character, underlying the complexities of concrete human activities. He writes that 'Praxeology is *a priori*. It starts from the *a priori* category of action

18 However, in an account from near the end of his life, von Mises (1962: ch. 1, section 2) puts forward an un-Kantian naturalistic explanation for the *a priori* knowledge possessed by human beings, appealing to biological evolution.

19 Some ethnomethodologists have used the term 'praxeology' or 'praxiology', and associated adjectives. For example, Garfinkel (2002: 115) refers to 'the praxeological validity of instructed actions'. However, it is not clear whether the term, or the idea, was derived from von Mises.

and develops out of it all that it contains' (von Mises 1962: 41). He argues that Weber's position on this issue derives from the fact that he had remained committed to historical analysis, subordinating the development of sociological concepts to this (see Crespo 1997).[20] Nevertheless, von Mises seems to have welcomed Schutz's attempt to use Weber's concept of ideal type to provide a more satisfactory grounding for economic analysis.

Schutz's project

Von Mises' proposed solution to the problem seems to have been no more widely accepted than earlier ones. Moreover, it was a form of argument that was increasingly subjected to criticism with the growing influence of the logical positiv-ists.[21] Schutz believed that a more solid philosophical foundation for economic analysis, and for social science generally, was required; and, as already noted, he set out to achieve this by drawing on Weber's notion of ideal types, but also on the work of Bergson and subsequently on Husserl's phenomenology.

Weber had seen ideal types as devices that were essential for producing singular causal explanations of social actions and processes. They were developed on the basis of familiarity with the sorts of phenomena that they were to be used to explain, as well as on experience of human social life more generally – rather than being derived solely from psychological or social scientific investigation, on the one hand, or from *a priori* reasoning, on the other. They were not in themselves hypotheses, nor were they intended to be accurate representations of the social world. Indeed, they were deliberately selective and exaggerated, and while concrete action could sometimes approximate to them, one of their purposes was to provide a basis for detecting deviations from the simplified models of behaviour they encapsulated. Hypotheses could then be developed and tested in order to discover the factors that explained this deviation. More or less following Menger, but not adopting his neo-Aristotelian philosophical approach, Weber drew a distinction between theoretical work, concerned with the development of ideal types, on the one hand, and, on the other, analyses of concrete situations, historical and contemporary, concerned with producing substantive value-relevant explanations for particular phenomena. For him, the term 'sociology' seems to

20 This is validated by Marianne Weber's comment that her husband 'could have no use for [the arrangement of ideal types] into a system for the sake of an integrated conception of the world. For those types were not intended to be definitive fixations but only temporary stopping places in the flow of a constantly changing process of historical cognition' (quoted in Tenbruck 1987: 266).

21 It is, for example, rejected by Kaufmann. A major part of Kaufmann's (1936a) German language book on methodology was concerned with establishing the conventional character of mathematics, as against claims that it offered *a priori* knowledge of the world. See Cohen and Helling 2014.

have referred primarily to theoretical work concerned with clarifying ideal types, though it is possible he also sometimes took it to cover the more concrete kind of work concerned with historical and contemporary actions and events.

What Schutz found in Husserl was an insistence that all scientific knowledge requires clarification of its foundations, plus the argument that this can be achieved by careful descriptive analysis of how the central phenomena in the relevant scientific domain appear within experience. Husserl intended phenomenology to be a *via media* between empiricism and rationalism, and to serve as a counter to the materialism and positivism that were influential at the time, not least in the emerging discipline of experimental psychology. Husserl's concern, above all, was that these tendencies undercut the very basis of Western thought, on which philosophy, and indeed the sciences themselves, depend; ultimately leaving only scepticism and relativism. A key element of this was his rejection of psychologism in the field of logic. Like some other philosophers, mathematicians, and logicians at the time, he insisted that logic is an independent discipline that identifies what is necessary in the realm of thought if conclusions are to be valid, rather than a naturalistic description of 'the laws of thought'.

So, Husserl claimed to have discovered a new route to *a priori* knowledge through suspending the presuppositions characteristic of what he called the 'natural attitude', the plethora of assumptions we routinely take for granted in acting in the world, and by focusing on how phenomena appear in experience. He argued that, through a series of 'phenomenological reductions', knowledge of what necessarily belongs to the essence of the various types of phenomena studied by the sciences can be disclosed.

Unlike the empiricists, including logical positivists, Husserl insisted that experience is not a sequence of atomistic givens, passively received. As Schutz explains:

> Even the thing perceived in everyday life is more than a simple sense presentation. It is a thought object, a construct of a highly complicated nature, involving not only particular forms of time successions in order to constitute it as an object of one single sense, say of sight, and of space relations in order to constitute it as a sense-object of several senses, say of sight and touch, but also a contribution of imagination of hypothetical sense presentations in order to complete it. (Schutz 1962: 3)[22]

On the basis of Husserl's work, Schutz claims that the processes of constitution built into experience display inherent structures, and these are treated as the foundation on which the epistemological status of scientific knowledge can be justified. It is these structural features that form the essential character of the

---

22 Interestingly, perhaps in order to appeal to his new American audience, Schutz underpins his argument here by referring to the work of Whitehead rather than Husserl, though the latter is his main point of reference in the remainder of his discussion.

types of phenomena that constitute the various domains with which the sciences deal.

Schutz argues that while Weber had made a major contribution in his efforts to clarify and define many of the concepts used in interpretive sociology, and in socio-historical analysis more generally, he had not carried this work far enough: in particular, he had taken for granted the concept of action, and how actions can be meaningful. In his book, published in German in 1932 (whose title, literally, was 'The Meaningful Construction of the Social World: A Prelude to Interpretive Sociology', but was translated as *The Phenomenology of the Social World*), Schutz (1967) seeks to clarify how meaning arises out of the constitutive features of the lifeworld, the world corresponding to the 'natural attitude' that we all share and take for granted in our everyday lives.[23] From this, he goes on to try to show how social science is able to produce objective accounts of actions that are subjectively meaningful. He argues that the typifications, or ideal types, that social scientists employ are derived, but at the same time distinct, from the typifications that we all use in everyday life in understanding others' behaviour – specifically, those relating to people whom we do not know personally.

For Weber, the development of ideal types was an auxiliary discipline to the task of social explanation, whether in historical work on the past, for example on the rise of capitalism in the West, or in seeking to understand contemporary social phenomena, such as economic conditions east of the Elbe, or the emergence of the Soviet Union. An important implication of this is that ideal types are to be judged in formal terms – as regards internal consistency, clarity of terms, etc. – and above all by their usefulness in highlighting value-relevant causal processes in historical and contemporary social life. So, Weber did *not* see them as capturing the true nature or essence of particular social or economic phenomena. As von Mises recognised, this reflected his continuing commitment to the tenets of German historical economics and to the kind of neo-Kantianism exemplified by Rickert (Weber 1927; Oakes 1990).

By contrast, Schutz's approach adheres more closely to Austrian economics and to von Mises' conception of sociology or praxeology as concerned with understanding the essential nature of social phenomena, this formulated in terms of basic propositions that are prior to empirical investigation. Schutz came to the conclusion that the work of Husserl could provide a more effective grounding for these propositions than was offered by von Mises' Kantian approach, or the neo-Aristotelianism of Menger.[24] And, indeed, there is a clear parallel between

---

23 Schutz took over the concept of the lifeworld from Husserl. For explications of this and other terms in Husserl's phenomenology, see Moran and Cohen 2012.

24 There is, however, an important link between Schutz and Menger here, in that Brentano's descriptive psychology, which influenced Menger, was also the starting point for Husserl's phenomenology.

Austrian economics and Husserl's phenomenology, in that they both treat knowledge of what might be called ideal objectivities as of value in itself, irrespective of its usefulness in addressing any particular issue. A related feature is that, where Weber emphasises that there are always different value-relevant perspectives that could be used to investigate the same phenomenon, Austrian economics tends either to treat the economic as a distinct domain in which the model of rational choice operates, or to apply this model to all human action, even while recognising that it is an idealisation. Moreover, there was an important sense in which, for the economists, 'ideal' meant not just a product of idealisation (the sense intended by Weber), but also 'desirable'. While they argued that people's goals were non-rational in character, they often treated rational pursuit of those goals as not just to be expected, other things being equal, but also as in the interests of the individual agent and of everyone else. Markets were believed to operate spontaneously, generating overall benefits that would not be available with a state-controlled economy, because no one can have knowledge of all the needs that are to be met or of how this can be achieved.[25]

Like the Austrian economists, and indeed like Parsons, Schutz seems to have regarded social science as primarily concerned with developing 'a body of logically interrelated "general concepts" of empirical reference' (Parsons 1937: 6), whereas for Weber the central task is to produce singular causal explanations for particular value-relevant actions, events, or outcomes. These very different orientations led Schutz and Weber to interpret the purpose, and perhaps nature, of ideal types differently. For Schutz, following Husserl, they are parallel to the idealisations to be found in natural science, for example in the work of Galileo. They represent determinate relations amongst a set of variables that have been abstracted from the complexity of concrete reality but that nevertheless capture the truth about what causes what in a particular domain, for example economic behaviour.[26]

So, Schutz largely took over Husserl's argument about how a foundation for the sciences could be achieved; though, unlike the early Husserl, his primary focus was on the lifeworld and how it is constituted. He highlighted the role of typifications, of what he called 'recipe knowledge', and of constitutive assumptions about the reciprocity of perspectives, in how people ongoingly constitute the environment within which all their experience and their actions take place. And he emphasised the temporal character of action, and indeed of the processes by which we make sense of the world. He also argued that experience is structured

25 See Hayek 1967. Weber shared the Austrian economists' opposition to Marxism and communism, but differed from them, like many of the German historical economists, in regarding the state as properly playing a large role in economic, as in other, matters.
26 On the similarities and differences between Weber and Schutz as regards social science typifications, see Eberle 2010.

by 'multiple realities': besides the world of everyday life, there are those of dreams, art, religion, children's play, and scientific inquiry. He claims that each of these 'finite provinces of meaning' is characterised by a distinctive 'cognitive style' (Schutz 1962: 230), and that a sense of shock is experienced (p. 231) in moving from one to another.[27]

Schutz argued that two clear distinctions needed to be drawn if we are to understand the relationship between social science and the lifeworld. First of all, there is the contrast between, on the one hand, the 'natural attitude' – oriented to pragmatic concerns – and, on the other, the attitude required for philosophical investigation, which demands phenomenological suspension of what is normally taken for granted. Both Husserl and Schutz treated the practice of science as adopting a theoretical rather than a practical orientation, but nevertheless as still operating *within* the natural attitude.

A second important distinction is between the knowledge that is available to us of 'consociates', with whom we are in close contact, and that which we can have of 'predecessors', 'contemporaries', and 'successors': people with whom we have only fleeting relationships or no direct communicative relationships at all. In other words, here he was pointing to the variable nature of the sense-making procedures involved in ordinary actors' understanding of other people's actions, and of social processes more generally. He argues that while interaction with consociates relies on knowledge derived from a 'we-relationship', by its very nature this cannot be the kind of knowledge produced by social science. Instead the latter must rely upon typifications, in just the way that we do in our everyday dealings with contemporaries, predecessors, and successors.

Schutz argues that, through the use of ideal types of this kind, social scientists can understand social actions in an objective manner, while at the same time taking account of the origins of these actions in subjective concerns, motives, perceptions, etc. Through showing how this is possible he hoped to clarify the foundations of, and thereby validate, abstract economic analysis of the kind carried out by the Austrian School, and also the kind of interpretive sociology practised by Weber. It also seems likely that he saw it as correcting those forms of social and psychological science that mistook the nature of the social world in seeking to understand it in terms of causal laws of the same kind as those to be found in the natural sciences; though, apart from some references to behaviourism (Schutz 1964, 1996: ch. 15), he does not spell out this critical aspect of his argument. Nevertheless, he does endorse Husserl's (1989) proposal that the study of human social life must adopt a personalistic rather than a naturalistic

---

27 It was this part of his work, only briefly sketched here – but extensively developed in his later writings (see for instance Schutz and Luckmann 1973) – that was most influential on Garfinkel and others in the 1960s and 1970s.

perspective, focusing on reasons as motivation rather than causes (see Schutz 1966).[28] In this respect, then, he seems to be criticising some approaches to social science, while treating economics (as conceived by the Austrian School) as the model for the proper form that it should take.

Was Schutz a sociologist?

I want to turn now to one of the two questions from which I began this chapter: the disciplinary status of Schutz's work. Despite the common tendency, discussed earlier, to treat his aim as developing a form of phenomenological sociology, it seems likely that he saw his work as a contribution to the philosophy of the social sciences. He offered a 'constitutive phenomenology of the natural attitude' (Schutz 1962: 138), and, as we have seen, like Husserl he regarded all the sciences as operating *within* the natural attitude, albeit with a theoretical rather than a practical orientation. Schutz (1962: 132) writes that 'the transcendental constitutive phenomena, which only become visible in the phenomenologically reduced sphere, scarcely come within the view of the cultural sciences'. This suggests that he did not see himself as operating within the cultural sciences, and that he believed there to be a clear distinction between the task of phenomenological philosophy and that of those sciences. In these terms, Schutz was seeking to use phenomenology to provide a more secure foundation for conventional social science, and in particular for economic analysis and Weber's interpretive sociology.[29]

In this respect, there is a clear contrast between Schutz, on the one hand, and Weber and Parsons, on the other. The latter do not seem to have felt any need for such a philosophical foundation in order to validate their work, even though both recognised that philosophical assumptions were necessarily involved in it. As we saw, for Weber ideal types were not intended to capture reality and were to be judged in terms of their internal consistency and usefulness. For Parsons, sociology could provide its own foundation; it did not need a further, philosophical underpinning. He suggested that the sciences and philosophy stand 'in a relation of mutually corrective criticism' (Parsons 1937: 22). There is no implication here, in the manner of Husserl and Schutz, that all assumptions need to be made explicit and philosophically appraised in order to render knowledge fully rational;

---

28 This is in line with von Mises' (1962: 7) position: 'The natural sciences are causality research; the sciences of human action are teleological.' Confusingly, though, von Mises recognised that causality is involved in teleology: he writes that 'among these elements of teleology is also the category of causality' (p. 8), and later that 'Whatever philosophers may say about causality, the fact remains that no action could be performed by men not guided by it' (p. 20). There seems to me to be a similar ambiguity in the work of Schutz.

29 This is very much the interpretation promoted by Luckmann, and even in Srubar's interpretation of Schutz's work a boundary is maintained with empirical sociology; see Eberle 2012.

though he does suggest that there is an 'immanent tendency of reason to a rational integration of experience as a whole' (pp. 26–7). Comparing himself with Schutz, Parsons wrote: 'I do not want to be a philosopher – I shy away from the philosophical problems underlying my scientific work. By the same token I don't think he wants to be a scientist as I understand the term until he has settled all the underlying philosophical difficulties' (quoted in Treviño 2001: 41). This difference in orientation is perhaps the reason for the largely fruitless character of the dialogue between the two of them in their personal correspondence (Grathoff 1978; Coser 1979; Wilson 2005).

At the same time, there are some places in Schutz's writings where he seems to present his work as a contribution to interpretive sociology, through deepening Weber's analysis of meaning and action. Furthermore, he draws a distinction between the natural and the social sciences in a relevant respect, suggesting that while natural scientists can leave the task of clarifying the foundations of their work to philosophers, social scientists cannot: 'it is a basic characteristic of the social sciences to ever and ever again pose the question of the meaning of their basic concepts and procedures' (Schutz 1996: 121). Moreover, we should remember that von Mises initially defined sociology as concerned with providing a theory of social action, and offered his own neo-Kantian account of the origins of its first principles as part of this. Even in these terms, however, it does not seem plausible to assume that Schutz was seeking to found a new venture called phenomenological sociology.[30]

Part of the problem here is the way in which various disciplinary labels were used at the time. For example, while their meanings were sometimes distinguished, the terms 'philosophy', 'logic', 'methodology', and 'science' were employed in a variety of ways that produced overlaps as well as differentiations. To take just one example, we can note Husserl's insistence that philosophy is a science, but he presents it as an eidetic rather than an empirical science. There are also the different interpretations of what 'logic' means, from its restriction to deductive reasoning to treating it as concerned with how scientific knowledge can be produced, where it clearly overlaps in meaning with 'methodology'. If we add to this von Mises' use of the term 'sociology' to refer to the abstract theory of human action of which economics is the most developed part, along with the ambiguities surrounding whether or not Weber was a sociologist, then it is perhaps not too surprising that Schutz does not clearly indicate what he takes to be the disciplinary location of his work.[31]

---

30 The closest I can find to this phrase in Schutz is a reference to sociology as 'based on phenomenological principles' (Schutz 1967: 249), but this is compatible with the idea that phenomenological philosophy supplies the principles on which interpretive sociology, of a Weberian kind, relies.

31 It has been argued that Weber's sociology was modelled on the 'anthropology' outlined by Eduard Meyer. Tenbruck (1987: 251) describes Meyer as having provided 'a universal

Nevertheless, as I have suggested, in terms of current conceptions of sociology and philosophy, it is probably safest to assume that Schutz saw his work as contributing to the philosophy of social science. There is of course quite a close relationship between this and scientific methodology, in the sense given to that term by his friend Kaufmann. The latter saw this as grounded in accurate description of the norms by which scientists operate, but also as drawing on philosophy in order to clarify those norms, to identify inconsistencies, and to resolve these.[32]

Was Schutz a positivist?

As I noted at the start of this chapter, how we answer the question of whether Schutz's approach was positivist will depend a great deal on how we define that contentious term, and I indicated that I would address it by treating logical positivism as its key exemplar. One aspect of this form of positivism Schutz takes over is viewing, and valuing, empirical science as the pursuit of theories stating 'determinate relations between a set of variables in terms of which a fairly extensive class of empirically ascertainable regularities can be explained' (Schutz 1962: 52), and that propositions must be 'subjected to controlled verification and must not refer to private uncontrollable experience' (p. 62). This reflects the sharp distinction he drew between scientific and practical rationality, despite recognising what they share. Furthermore, like the positivists, Schutz does not see *Verstehen, in the sense of a psychological process of empathy*, as playing a key role in social science. This is because social science must rely upon typifications of contemporaries (not on knowledge gained in a 'we-relationship'). In these terms we can perhaps conclude that Schutz's position is positivist. And another respect in which his position may be categorised in this way is that he sees the scientific explanation of human action as necessarily relying upon formal models of the kind exemplified by economic analysis: some sociologists today tend routinely, albeit misleadingly, to treat economics, and rational choice theory more generally, as 'positivist' – despite

historical theory of general forms of human life and of human development that was empirically worked out and, therefore, a "sociology" devised by a historian'. Weber was himself a historian by training, albeit primarily in the field of law and economy, and Tenbruck suggests that Meyer's work provided a model for what came to be published as *Economy and Society*. Meanwhile, Hennis (1988, 2000a, 2000b) has explicitly denied that Weber was a sociologist.

32 Kaufmann claimed that his work began where Schutz's left off, since he was concerned with providing a formal analysis of scientific method: see Reeder 2009. Wagner (1970: 47) characterises Schutz's work as including 'metasociology' (as well as methodology and substantive sociology), this being concerned with questions that are 'logically prior to sociology', in particular the 'establishment, delineation, and interpretation of the subject matter of sociology, the nature of "social reality"'. However, as far as I am aware, 'metasociology' was not a term in use during Schutz's early career, or one used by him.

the fact that this obscures important differences from other approaches categorised in this way.[33]

However, if 'positivism' is defined as demanding that social scientists measure and control variables, experimentally or statistically, then Schutz was no positivist.[34] Like most Austrian economists, with the exception of Menger, he drew a sharp distinction between social and natural science, and therefore did not regard the latter as a viable methodological model in this respect. Nevertheless, it should be clear that his position is significantly at odds with those of many who appealed to his work in Anglo-American sociology in the 1960s and 1970s. In large part, this reflects the fact that he is drawing on a very different non-positivist tradition from those which were influential in sociology at that time. The methodological implications of this Austrian tradition were later spelt out in detail in Hayek's (1952) *The Counter-Revolution of Science*, a book that seems to have had little influence within sociology.

As noted earlier, there was a direct quasi-positivist influence on Schutz, coming from his friend Felix Kaufmann. The latter was a frequent participant in the meetings of the Vienna Circle, and while he did not subscribe to all of their doctrines, and was a student of Husserl, his conception of the nature of science shared much in common with theirs.[35] Furthermore, it is worth noting that, contrary to what is widely assumed today, there was some common ground between Husserl's phenomenology and the work of logical positivists, particularly that of Carnap, partly derived from the influence of Mach (see Lübbe 1978; Smith 2010). For Kaufmann, social science was distinct from natural science in that it needed to take account of the meanings generated by human beings in the context of which their actions take place. Furthermore, he criticised empiricism for its failure to examine the nature of experience, and to recognise that it is *structured* rather than simply being a collection of atomistic sense-data – a lesson that could be learned from Husserl's phenomenological analyses. He argued that attention to this structure revealed the necessarily fallibilistic character of any process of verification. But while, in these respects, Kaufmann differed from the

33 Garfinkel appears initially to have taken over Schutz's distinction between ordinary and scientific rationality (see Garfinkel 1967a: ch. 8), but later to have abandoned it (see Lynch 1993). Much phenomenological sociology, and psychology, has treated *Verstehen*, in empathetic form, as central to social research.

34 At one point, Schutz (1962: 49) acknowledges, in opposition to Ernest Nagel, that 'social psychologists can successfully use laboratory experiments at least to a certain extent', questioning the claim that 'neither measurement nor experiment is practicable in the social sciences'. However, the social scientific mode of operation he outlines later in this chapter – in which second-order typifications are built upon common-sense ones – takes economic theorising as its model, in which experimentation had played little role.

35 On Kaufmann's semi-detached relationship to the Circle, see Helling's Introduction to Cohen and Helling 2014, and Kaufmann 1950. On his relationship to Schutz, see Schutz 1996: ch. 16; also Helling 1984, 1988; Reeder 2009; Kawano 2009.

logical positivists, he nevertheless insisted that all science depends upon the same basic rules of procedure. Taken together, these rules determine what should and should not be included in the body of knowledge that makes up a science.[36] Kaufmann (1944) argues that these rules are analytic and regulative, rather than being *a priori* or simply empirical in character. This too is an idea he shares in common with the logical positivists, though his later work was also strongly informed by pragmatism, especially Dewey's (1938) *The Logic of Inquiry* (Reeder 1991: 10–12).

The influence of Kaufmann on Schutz's thinking can hardly be exaggerated: he introduced him to Husserl's writings and they discussed these intensively together, at a time when they were each writing books concerned with social science. While what they aimed at achieving in those books was very different, they saw their work as complementary, despite some disagreement about the relationship between the two projects. It is not hard to see that many of the features in Schutz's position that could be labelled as positivist are shared with Kaufmann.

Conclusion

My main aim in this chapter has been to show that, in significant respects, Schutz's work has been misinterpreted by many sociologists who have claimed to build on it.[37] And I believe this is true of Garfinkel. Schutz pursued his analysis of the lifeworld in order to consolidate the foundations of conventional social science: in the form of Austrian economics and Weberian interpretive sociology. By contrast, those who have drawn on his work have usually treated it as mounting a critique of conventional sociology, and have sometimes even taken it to offer a replacement for this, or regarded it as opening up a new field of empirical inquiry, whether in the context of the sociology of knowledge or as an 'alternate' to 'formal' sociology or 'constructive analysis', as with Garfinkel's ethnomethodology.[38] While I do not want to imply that these misinterpretations have been unfruitful, my suggestion is that they obscure the issues Schutz was addressing. They also take attention away from the arguments he put forward, as regards the character of social science explanations, and how these can be objective and scientific despite the fact that they rely upon the typifications that people employ for practical purposes within the lifeworld.

36 Interestingly, this was one of the specific parts of Kaufmann's work on which Garfinkel drew.

37 Long ago, Helling (1984) argued that his 'radical disciples' misinterpreted him in significant ways, but this judgement seems to have had little influence.

38 In fact, Garfinkel actively recommended misreadings of various authors, designed to serve his purposes: see Lynch 1993: 117.

2 Garfinkel and Goffman via Simmel: parallels and divergences

Garfinkel's ethnomethodology and Goffman's investigations of 'the interaction order' have often been treated as very closely related, for example as each contributing to 'the sociology of everyday life' (Jacobsen 2009), as representing contemporary forms of 'micro-sociology' (Martin and Dennis 2010), and/or as 'sociologies of interaction' (Dennis et al. 2013). They have frequently been regarded as investigating more or less the same set of phenomena, particularly in the case of Goffman's final book *Forms of Talk* (1981), which shares its focus with conversation analysis. Indeed, they have sometimes been seen as complementary, perhaps even as open to integration into a single general theory (Denzin 1969; Giddens 1984; Rawls 1985, 2003; Manning 1992; Smith 2003). Yet ethnomethodologists have usually emphasised the fundamental differences between the orientations of Garfinkel and Goffman (Watson 1983, 1984, 1992, 1999; Sharrock 1999; Schegloff 1988a; Wieder et al. 2010: 134–8). For instance, Watson (1992: 2) insists that their approaches 'are, in terms of their inner reasoning, quite distinct and indeed irreconcilable'. In this Chapter I want to explore the similarities and the differences, in order to throw further light on the ways in which ethnomethodology constitutes a radically distinctive approach to studying the social world.

However I will adopt a rather indirect approach to this task – in the spirit of those who argue that in order to reveal the underlying dimensions of a comparison it is fruitful to compare not just two items but three (Kelly 1955). Indeed, I believe that systematic comparisons among multiple sociological approaches are a fruitful way of highlighting parallels and problems. Thus, I will compare Goffman and Garfinkel with an earlier sociologist who is often seen as sharing their interest in the study of everyday life, and whose work influenced at least one of them: Georg Simmel.[1]

Simmel and Goffman

The close relationship between the work of Simmel and Goffman has often been noted. In a personal reference that was probably instrumental in securing Goffman

1 I am not the first to have used this triadic tactic in examining the work of Goffman and Garfinkel; Rawls (2003) has compared them via Durkheim.

a job – in the Department of Sociology at University of California, Berkeley – Everett Hughes described him as 'our Simmel' (Winkin 1991: 8, cited in Chriss 1993: 469). Much later, Rock (1979: 27) suggested that Goffman may become 'the unacknowledged reincarnation' of Simmel. And Smith (1989) and Gerhardt (2003) have provided detailed comparisons of the work of these two sociologists, stressing the similarities. While Goffman only makes quite limited reference to Simmel in his writings, it is clear that he would have come into contact with this predecessor's work when a student in the department of sociology at Chicago.[2] Smith (1989: 6) notes that 'Simmel's sociology constituted a significant element of the intellectual milieu at the University of Chicago during Goffman's apprenticeship there between 1945 and 1954.' Indeed, there had been a long tradition of respect for Simmel's work: Albion Small (or, perhaps Charles Ellwood: see Turner 2007) had translated some of his writings for the *American Journal of Sociology*; Park had studied with Simmel in Berlin; and Hughes had a deep knowledge of Simmel's work (see, for example, Hughes 1955, 1958, 1965).[3]

It has been argued that there is a danger of exaggerating the influence of Simmel on Goffman. Howard Becker, who knew Goffman well, has argued that he represented a different sociological genealogy from what he calls the 'pure Hughes lineage', which 'could be said to start with Georg Simmel, and to go from there to Simmel's student Robert E. Park, and from Park to his student Hughes'. Becker argues that 'Goffman's lineage … begins with Emile Durkheim, and goes from there to pioneer social anthropologist A. R[adcliffe] Brown, from him to his student W. Lloyd Warner …, and from Warner to Goffman, who worked very closely with him' (Becker 2003: 659). And it is certainly true that the influence of Durkheim and Radcliffe-Brown on Goffman's work is important. However, it seems to me that Becker underplays the parallels between Simmel and Goffman, and probably thereby the influence of Hughes.[4]

Simmel is perhaps best known for defining sociology as concerned with social *forms* that are generated out of processes of social interaction (see Wolff

2 In fact, Goffman makes relatively scarce references to the work of other sociologists, even those who had a direct influence upon him such as Everett Hughes.

3 Hughes was one of Goffman's dissertation supervisors, though Goffman by no means simply followed in his footsteps. Burns (1992: 11) writes that: 'talk of "influences" is misleading where, as in this case, it is the positive effort to take up ideas and develop them in entirely new ways which counts'.

4 By contrast, in my view Gerhardt (2003:144) overplays the other side of the argument in claiming, for example, that Goffman and Simmel adopted 'one and the same approach in sociology'. Smith (1989) has argued that – while Goffman worked on at least a couple of research projects directed by Warner – Hughes, and thereby Simmel, were a far more important influence upon his work. Jaworski (1997: ch. 2) has provided a careful and illuminating analysis of key respects in which Goffman's work was influenced by Simmel, Park, and Hughes, specifically as regards the role of ceremony and etiquette in social life.

1950: 40–1). He argued that it should not focus on the *content* of those processes – on the particularities of the situations and individuals involved in specific events, their personal motivations, etc.; he suggested that these phenomena belong to the provinces of other social sciences. One example of what Simmel means by a social form is sociability – which he refers to as 'the play-form of sociation' – a topic on which he chose to speak when invited to give the welcoming address at the first meeting of the German Sociological Society in 1910. He argues that, under certain conditions, such as at a successful house party, a distinctive pattern of social interaction will emerge, in which the content of talk becomes less significant than its mode, in particular its playful and/or entertaining character, where external differences in status and position (and also, he suggests, personality and individuality) are downplayed, and where some of the normal constraints regarding truth and propriety are suspended (Wolff 1950: ch. 3). As part of this, Simmel discusses the characteristics of conversation – 'the most general vehicle for all that [humans] have in common' (Wolff 1950: 51) – treating 'sociable conversation' as its purest form, where people 'talk for the sake of talking' (p. 52).

Other forms whose character Simmel documented were more central to the topics dealt with by other sociologists: notably superordination/subordination, competition, and conflict. However, he was interested in these general types of social relation, not in particular instances for their own sake. As a result, he discussed these forms as instantiated in a wide variety of situations. He writes that

> social groups which are the most diverse imaginable in purpose and general significance, may nevertheless show identical forms of behavior toward one another on the part of their individual members. We find superiority and subordination, competition, division of labor, formation of parties, representation, inner solidarity coupled with exclusiveness toward the outside, and innumerable similar features in the state, in a religious community, in a band of conspirators, in an economic association, in an art school, in the family. … And on the other hand, a contentually identical interest may take on form in very different sociations. Economic interest is realized both in competition and in the planned organization of producers, in isolation against other groups as well as in fusion with them. The religious contents of life, although they remain identical, sometimes demand an unregulated, sometimes a centralized form of community. The interests upon which the relations between the sexes are based are satisfied by an almost innumerable variety of family forms; etc. (Wolff 1950: 22)

Simmel saw the relationship between form and content as interactive, but at the same time insisted that there is independence – this is why the same form can be found in the most diverse settings, while the same substance can take on a variety of forms, with different results. He also believed that forms could come to constrain or distort processes of interaction; though he thought that, eventually, the latter would generally undermine them, creating new forms. So, forms can lead to both order and conflict.[5]

It seems clear that Goffman was also concerned with documenting social forms, rather than particular situations. This is reflected in the fact that, as Atkinson (1989: 60) comments, even those contributions that 'draw most closely on Goffman's "fieldwork" make little in the way of concessions to the conventions of "ethnographic" reportage'. For example, in the book that is closest to being an ethnographic study of a particular setting – *Asylums* – rather than providing a straightforward account of the lives of the inmates of St Elizabeth's hospital in Washington, DC, where he did fieldwork in the early 1950s, Goffman's discussion is focused on the character of this hospital *as a total institution*, what this involves, and how inmates respond to it. Moreover, much of the data that he uses in the book is not from St Elizabeth's, and is not even about mental hospitals, but relates to other types of total institution.

Even more obviously, Goffman's other work is focused on forms of behaviour and social relationship that are widespread, rather than on particular groups of people in particular situations at particular times. He is concerned, for instance, with the dramaturgical techniques and everyday rituals to be found in face-to-face encounters. In his books *Frame Analysis* and *Forms of Talk* his focus on social forms is made explicit in their very titles. In this respect, with the partial exception of his PhD thesis and a couple of early research reports carried out for Lloyd Warner, Goffman's work differs significantly from that produced by fellow Chicago students, who generally used Hughes' ideas in producing substantive accounts of particular occupational and other types of group (see Becker 2003).[6]

There is also a parallel between Simmel and Goffman in that both focus on the implications or consequences of particular forms of social organisation for people's identities or sense of self (see Smith 1989). This was a central theme in Simmel's classic essay 'The Metropolis and Mental Life' (Wolff 1950: Part 5, IV), for example, where he was concerned with the psychological effects of living in the very large cities that were then emerging in Western countries – not least

5 There is a direct parallel here, one that is no accident, with Marx's idea that a dominant mode of production generates forms of social relation, institutions, patterns of belief, etc., which eventually come to constrain the development of new modes of production, this conflict usually resulting in a revolution, in which a new 'superstructure' emerges that is more in tune with the emergent mode of production. In his early career, especially, Simmel had considerable interest in socialism and Marxism.

6 Too much should not be made of this contrast: in his studies of particular occupations and groups, Becker is concerned with generating and deploying theoretical ideas, for example about the concept of commitment (Becker 1960). But, generally speaking, his approach is more substantively focused than that of Goffman, and for that matter even than that of his teacher Hughes. For illuminating accounts of the Chicago Department at the time, see Strauss 1996: 24; Winkin and Leeds-Hurwitz 2013: ch. 1.

Berlin, where he spent most of his life, 'the Chicago of Europe' as it came to be called. Similarly, his *Philosophy of Money*, far from being a study in economics, is concerned with the effects of the rise of a money economy on the identities and experience of modern individuals. Meanwhile, in *Asylums*, Goffman's (1961) focus was on the attempts of total institutions to define the selves of inmates so as to exercise control over them and/or to shape them psychologically. In addition, he investigated the forms of adaptation adopted by inmates, designed to preserve elements of their previous identities and/or to protect some sense of self-worth and a degree of leeway for autonomous action. His concept of 'role distance' encapsulates this interest too. And in another influential book he examined the threats of various forms of stigma to one's sense of self, and how attempts are made to manage these (Goffman 1968). More generally, his discussions of 'face work' in encounters also reflect this interest.

Besides similarities in their focus of inquiry, there are also parallels in the character of their work. The writings of both Simmel and Goffman are often seen as having a fragmentary quality, addressing a range of specific topics and employing a diverse array of concepts with little attempt at integration. This perhaps reflects, in part, the fact that, for both, the default mode of writing was the essay; a tendency that was also characteristic of Hughes. Furthermore, neither Simmel nor Goffman provides much guidance about the overall direction of his work and how it relates to that of other sociologists, certainly less guidance than many readers would want (Smith 1989: 7). In the case of Simmel, the most striking example is his book *Soziologie*, which, rather than providing a systematic introduction to the discipline, appears to comprise a series of essays on apparently unrelated topics: sociability, quantitative aspects of the group, spatial aspects of sociation, superordination and subordination, secrecy, the poor, etc.[7] Moreover, while Simmel offers a characterisation of the nature of his sociology at the start of this book, in doing so he emphasises the difficulties involved, requiring that readers must learn gradually to discern the coherence of his focus through reading his investigations of specific topics (Simmel 1908: Preface and ch. 2; see in particular p. 13, quoted in translation in Wolff 1950: xxxiii). Simmel's argument here, as I understand it, is that we must start from investigating particular topics with a view to identifying forms, and build up understanding gradually, so that the result and its value will only become clear later (see Wolff 1950: xxvi).

Similarly, while Goffman provides a rationale for his focus on the interaction order in two influential articles (Goffman 1964, 1983a), for the most part he

---

7 See Coser 1958; Axelrod 1977. Frisby (1984: 112–20) has proposed that, contrary to first impressions, there is a clear structure underlying the various topics that Simmel discusses in this book. But, even taking account of this, the sense of a fragmentary *oeuvre* remains; and, indeed, elsewhere Frisby (1981) has acknowledged this in portraying Simmel as a 'sociological impressionist'.

seems systematically to have avoided accounting for himself in theoretical and methodological terms.[8] Becker (2003: 660), again writing on the basis of first-hand acquaintance, emphasises Goffman's

> disinterest in questions of method. I don't remember, though I haven't made an exhaustive search through his works to verify this, Goffman ever writing about any of the standard questions that inevitably arise in doing field research, such questions as access to research sites, relations with the people studied, ways of recording or analyzing data, problems of reliability. All of these were much discussed at the time, and many of us (I was among them) wrote about them, in an effort to clarify for ourselves what we were doing. Goffman never did. This was a principled refusal, which he and I discussed a number of times. He felt very strongly that you could not elaborate any useful rules of procedure for doing field research and that, if you attempted to do that, people would misinterpret what you had written, do it (whatever *it* was) wrong, and then blame you for the resulting mess. He refused to accept responsibility for such unfortunate possibilities.[9]

In much the same way, Goffman did not provide much indication of how he saw the theoretical enterprise in which he was engaged: what its goal was, how it related to the approaches adopted by others, and so on.

There are also some more specific similarities between Goffman and Simmel in writing style. Smith (2006: 3) has described Goffman's writing as involving the 'subtle and skilful use of a range of metaphors (dramaturgical, ritual, game theoretical, ethological)' and noted 'his flair for sardonic witticism and ironic observation'.[10] Some of this stems from the influence of Hughes, who relied heavily on what Burke (1935) referred to as 'perspective by incongruity' for the purposes of sociological analysis. Interestingly, this was a device also used by Simmel. It involves, for example, contrasting high and low status occupations, or what goes on in the public, 'front region', of venues, as against what goes on in hidden 'back regions'. And Simmel also employed a style that relied heavily on the use of metaphors, this leading Durkheim to complain that his writing had a literary or artistic character that lacked the precision and clarity necessary for scientific work (Durkheim 1902).

Furthermore, both Goffman and Simmel employ examples from diverse sources, these relating both to mundane life experiences and to esoteric realms. These are employed to highlight features of the forms of interaction being discussed.

8 In his reply to Denzin and Keller (Goffman 1981b), he does, however, provide a useful sketch of his orientation and of the resources on which he drew in his work.

9 In fact, there *is* an article in which Goffman deals with some of these topics, but this is transcribed from a conference talk he gave: Goffman 1989. Its brevity and isolation from the rest of his work underlines Becker's point.

10 There has been quite a bit of commentary on Goffman's style of writing; see, for instance, Atkinson 1989.

Indeed, emphasising the value of analysing particular instances, Simmel writes of 'the possibility of finding in each of life's details the totality of its meaning' (Simmel 1907/1978: 55). While, in this use of examples, some evidential role is also implied, in the work of both authors there is little systematic testing of the fit between theory and evidence, or of the typicality of the instances employed. Writing about Simmel's *Philosophy of Money*, Durkheim (1979: 326) charged that it contained 'many ingenious ideas, lively observations, interesting, even sometimes surprising, comparisons, a wealth of historical and ethnographical facts, yet unfortunately put together without accuracy of proof'. Very similar criticisms have been made of Goffman's work (see, for instance, Argyle 1969). And the response to this criticism, on the part of Goffman at least, would probably have been that the concepts generated are intended as tools whose value is to be discovered through use, rather than constituting hypotheses that needed testing.[11]

Despite these similarities, there are also several significant *differences* in orientation between these two sociologists. Simmel's work was carried out within a socio-philosophical perspective concerned with the implications of the distinctive character of modern societies for human identities and lives, in particular the effects of the process of social differentiation (see Frisby 1984). In this respect, his analyses were located within a macro-historical framework. As part of this he identified what he labelled the 'tragedy of modern culture': while social differentiation had opened up the possibility of greater individuality, at the same time the sheer range and diversity of objective culture, and the need for specialisation, meant that no individual could grasp it all, so that what tended to be generated were fragmented rather than rounded and coherent selves. He also saw in modernity a tendency to 'turn life into a technical problem' (Simmel 1995: 176). Most fundamentally, Simmel was concerned with the ways in which social forms constrain the life forces that originally gave rise to them. This reflects the fact that he was at least as much a philosopher and a cultural critic as he was a sociologist – indeed, towards the end of his life Simmel offered a *Lebensphilosophie* strongly influenced by Goethe (see Giacomoni 2002; Bleicher 2007). Here there is a sharp contrast with Hughes as well as with Goffman.

Also striking is the range of topics Simmel addressed. Smith (1989: 19) notes that: 'In the years up to 1890 [he] published articles on Dante, pessimism, the freeing of the Prussian peasantry, Goethe, social ethics, Michelangelo, money, women and Rembrandt. He lectured on Kant, ethics, pessimism, Darwin, theories of science, and problems of social science.' This breadth of philosophical and

---

11 Of course, it could be argued that their *validity* is also tested through use. This seems to have been the position adopted by Blumer: see Weller 2000. There is also a parallel with Weber; see Chapter 2.

cultural interest is reflected in the fact that, besides its legacy within sociology, his work has also been influential in the fields of aesthetics and cultural studies, shaping the thinking of such writers as Lukács, Benjamin, Kracauer, and Adorno.[12]

By contrast, Goffman does not locate the phenomena he studies socio-historically, to any great degree. In this respect he is perhaps truer to Simmel's formal sociology than was Simmel himself. In most of his work, Goffman treats the social forms he identifies – by implication, at least – as more or less universal in character. Moreover, he focuses on a smaller range of social topics than Simmel, and primarily on those relating to the micro-level of face-to-face interaction. Indeed, Goffman tended to return to the same topics, almost starting again each time, developing new concepts to pick up previously neglected aspects of these phenomena. At one point he writes of 'repeated approaches from different angles and the eventual retracing of practically everything' (Goffman 1981a: 1). Goffman also generally provides more detailed illustrations, drawing on ethnographic fieldwork and a range of contemporary documentary sources, where Simmel relied much more informally on his own knowledge and on wide reading in philosophy, history, and aesthetics, as well as familiarity with contemporary literary, artistic, and political debates. Moreover, Goffman does not offer any broader philosophy, he saw himself very much as a sociologist or anthropologist.

I will turn now to my second comparison, one that may appear likely to offer less similarities and more differences.

Simmel and Garfinkel

By contrast with the case of Goffman, there are no explicit signs of the influence of Simmel on Garfinkel; as far as I can tell he makes no reference to Simmel in his published work.[13] Moreover, his sociological training would not have brought him into contact with the latter's work to the same extent as Goffman, even though Parsons, his doctoral supervisor, was, of course, familiar with Simmel's writings – indeed, he had originally written an extensive section on Simmel for his first book, *The Structure of Social Action*, which was not included in the published version (see Levine 1989, 1991; Jaworski 1990).

We can also note that Simmel's and Garfinkel's modes of writing are very different. Garfinkel's early published work takes the standard form of social science research articles, by contrast with the more essayistic, less technical character of Simmel's writings. There is also a sharp contrast if we look at his thesis and his other writings from the late 1940s and early 1950s, which are made up of

---

12 On this aspect of Simmel, see Davis 1973; Frisby 1981, 1985.
13 Sacks *does* refer to Simmel, albeit very briefly, in at least one place (1992b: 132).

research memos and reports.[14] And even his later writings, while distinguished by an increasingly idiosyncratic style, are not close in character to those of Simmel.

There is also little similarity in topics addressed: Garfinkel did not write about a very wide range of topics, focusing for the most part on situations where formal or informal rules are being applied, for instance in playing games, coding records, behaving gender-appropriately, or examining how queues form. Furthermore, like Goffman, Garfinkel does not share Simmel's concern with the consequences of modernity or with the ways in which forms come to constrain the forces of Life or the development of individuality. He is interested instead in fundamental social processes that are assumed to be more or less universal in character – ones that underpin all activities in the social world.

For all these reasons there is no obvious sense in which it might be said that Garfinkel built, or drew, on Simmel's legacy. Nevertheless, there are a few significant parallels that are worth mentioning.[15] One is that they were both concerned with the *constitution* of society: in other words with the processes that generate the very possibility of human social life. Simmel wrote an essay entitled 'How is society possible?' (Simmel 1971: ch. 2), a question that few other sociologists had raised, and he answered it by drawing on Kantian ideas about how our experience of the world is constituted through a framework of *a priori* ideas. Similarly, in his later work especially, Garfinkel was centrally concerned with how it is that the familiar, intelligible social world that we experience is generated through the practices in which we all engage. In this sense, it would not be misleading to say that he was concerned with 'how society is made possible'. Furthermore, Simmel insisted that both historical and sociological work *constitute* the phenomena they investigate by adopting distinctive disciplinary perspectives (see Simmel 1971:Part I), and this is an idea that can also be found in some of Garfinkel's early writings (1952/2008: 116–17): he argues that different perspectives – religious, political, occupational, etc. – involve rules that give emphasis to some matters and not others, as well as selecting and formulating relevant data. Garfinkel also applies this idea in contrasting Parsons' orientation with that of Schutzian phenomenology.[16]

14 As regards Garfinkel's style in his early writings (unpublished at the time), there is a broad similarity with some published articles by contemporaries, such as Selznick 1948, with which Garfinkel was almost certainly familiar: Selznick recruited him to the jurors' study, and was instrumental in his obtaining a post at UCLA.

15 It is possible that these similarities were the result of a mediation of Simmel's influence through the work of Schutz and Mannheim, with which Garfinkel was very familiar. Mannheim was strongly influenced by Simmel (see Kettler 2012) and Schutz certainly knew his work (see Schutz 1962: 18). For a discussion that relates the work of Garfinkel (though with more emphasis on that of Schutz and Goffman) to Simmel's approach to sociology, see O'Neill 1973.

16 Curiously he treats this perspectivism as a feature of phenomenology, and then contrasts a 'neo-Kantian phenomenology' with a 'Husserlian phenomenology'.

Over and above this, like Simmel, and Goffman, there is an important sense in which Garfinkel is concerned with identifying social forms, rather than with examining the contents of social life.[17] In some of his earlier writings he identifies methods of practical reasoning or sense-making as invariants that lie behind, or underneath, the contingent occasionality of social process. Later the status of these methods is less clear, indeed he sometimes seems to deny their existence, which would signal a move away from the formalist orientation of Simmel and Goffman. Even so, it is clear that his concern is with how particular types of intention, action, outcome, or institution are signalled and constituted in and through processes of social interaction – he does not believe that sociology should focus on the distinctive perspectives or experiences of individual people, their motives, etc. His concern is with *how* social life is constituted, rather than on why it is constituted in one way rather than another. In this respect he is more or less in line with Simmel, who insists that sociology is not primarily interested in people's purposes or goals but rather in the forms of sociation through which these are pursued (see Frisby 1981: 52).[18]

Another parallel between Simmel and Garfinkel is that, while both were concerned with identifying forms, albeit of different kinds, they also emphasised the key generative role of social interaction. Both resist the idea that the character of social life is a simple product of human nature, or of independently existing institutional structures, social systems, or cultures that impose their character on actors. Simmel (1907/2004: 107) writes that

> society is a structure that transcends the individual, but [one] that is not abstract. Historical life thus escapes the alternative of taking place either in individuals or in abstract generalities. Society is the universal which, at the same time, is concretely alive.

Garfinkel similarly stressed the role of social interaction as a process – as against accounts of the social world that treat it as determined by fixed structures, whether institutionalised values and norms, on the one hand, or the psychological characteristics of individuals, on the other. For him, contingency is the characteristic feature of social experience; whatever predictability it displays comes out of how people orient to one another's actions. So, for example, he emphasises the *ad hoc* character of rule use.

Indeed, Garfinkel's term 'reflexivity' – referring to the way in which actions and their contexts reciprocally define one another – is similar in some respects to

---

17 It is perhaps of significance that there is a parallel between Simmel's concern with forms and Husserl's focus on essences, so that Simmel may be characterised as concerned with developing an eidetic social science: see Backhaus 1998.

18 However, Garfinkel, unlike Simmel, insists that any forms identified must be ones that are oriented-to by participants, rather than being 'imposed' by the analyst. Watson (2016: 37) takes this to signal a fundamental difference between these two sociologists.

what Simmel means by *Wechselwirkung*, often translated as 'reciprocal interaction'.[19] In both cases what was involved here was an attempt to overcome the dichotomy between individual and society (Wolff 1950: xxvii–xxxi; Sharrock and Anderson 1986: 54). Simmel attached great significance to this concept, regarding reciprocity as a 'regulative world principle': 'everything interacts in some way with everything else, that between every point in the world and every other force permanently moving relationships exist' (cited in Frisby 1981: 41).[20] And his message is that in this process of interaction each element redefines the others (see Lichtblau 1991). He treats '*Vergesellschaftung*', which is usually rendered as 'sociation' (see Wolff 1950: lxiii–lxiv), as a special case of reciprocity, one that is illustrated, for example, by the mutual dependence involved in authority relationships. Simmel insists that the relations involved do not represent causal sociological laws but rather propositions which have the status of 'a phenomenological formula that seeks to conceptualize the regular outcome of regularly coexisting sequences of events' (1971: 257).[21]

Garfinkel's insistence that actions and their contexts reciprocally define one another seems to have arisen in particular from the work of Gurwitsch (1964) on perception, which was strongly influenced by Husserl. Reliance on this source signals another similarity with Simmel: a strong interest in philosophical ideas and their relevance for social inquiry; though in the case of Simmel the resources on which he drew were primarily Kant, Goethe and Hegel (see Bleicher 2007), rather than primarily phenomenology. Of course, Simmel had a much wider and deeper interest in philosophy than Garfinkel: indeed, he seems to have regarded sociology as a subfield of that discipline. By contrast, Garfinkel's interest in philosophical ideas was in the sociological uses to which they could be put.

19 Or 'dialectic'. Giacomoni (2002) traces the source of this concept back to Kant, read under the influence of Goethe.

20 This idea is also at the heart of structuralism. For example, Piaget (1971: 8–9) writes that what he calls 'operational structuralism' 'adopts from the start a relational perspective, according to which it is neither the elements nor the whole that comes about in a manner one knows not how, but the relations among elements that count. In other words, the logical procedures or natural processes by which the whole is formed are primary, not the whole, which is consequent on the system's laws of composition, not the elements.' Also relevant here is the kind of relational philosophy developed by the neo-Kantian philosopher Ernst Cassirer (1953).

21 Gerhardt (2003) argues that the principle of reciprocity is also central to Goffman's analyses of interactional order in face-to-face encounters, and to his work more generally. In face work, for example, efforts are made to preserve the 'face' of others because, as it were, one's own face is in their hands. Similarly, team work involves reciprocal relations among members, and there is a reciprocal relationship between teams and audiences. Of course, reciprocality here, and in the work of Simmel, remains significantly different from what Garfinkel meant by 'reflexivity'. Rawls (1989) builds on this difference in her development of Goffman's notion of 'the interaction order', specifically distinguishing it from Simmel's position. See also Fuchs 1989.

A final point is worth making: a crucial element of the process of interaction for Simmel was that it involved people acting 'as if' certain things were the case, in ways that often brought those things into existence.[22] For example, certain pieces of paper or metal become money solely because people treat them in this way. Something similar is built into Garfinkel's notion of accountability, where actions, situations, etc., are what they are only because this is the meaning given to them in and through processes of social interaction: actions are designed and read as being of particular kinds, and their status is confirmed or challenged via the responses of others. This, according to Garfinkel, is how reality is constituted.

Having taken a detour via Simmel, in the remainder of this chapter I will compare the work of Garfinkel and Goffman directly.

Garfinkel and Goffman: similarities

Garfinkel and Goffman began their sociological careers at more or less the same time: they were both doctoral students in the late 1940s. Furthermore, they were in contact with one another in the 1950s. Wieder et al. (2010: 134) report that Goffman gave Garfinkel an early draft of *The Presentation of Self* (Goffman 1956b), and that they met and discussed it in 1953. Furthermore, Garfinkel thanks Goffman for 'criticisms and editorial suggestions' relating to his paper on 'Conditions of successful degradation ceremonies' (Garfinkel 1956b; see also Garfinkel 1963: 187), and in the acknowledgements to his 1967 book he includes Goffman among a list of 'old friends' (Garfinkel 1967a: xi). Garfinkel also cites Goffman's work on a few occasions, notably in his early article 'Some sociological concepts and methods for psychiatrists' (1956a) and in the chapter on Agnes in *Studies* (Garfinkel 1967a: ch. 5), where there is some criticism. There is less evidence of contact, or of influence, on Goffman's side, but it is quite clear that he was aware of Garfinkel's work and was in contact with him (see Smith 2003: 256; Rawls 2003: 236, 2008: 8, 57).[23] At the same time, he was undoubtedly critical of ethnomethodological work in private (Hymes 1984). Furthermore, *Frame Analysis* looks as if it may have been partly stimulated by Garfinkel's ethnomethodology (Goffman 1974: 5; Smith 2003: 256–7); and, of course, *Forms of Talk* amounts, in many respects, to a critical dialogue with conversation analysis.[24]

---

22 This was a common theme in German philosophy at the time, see, most notably, Vaihinger 1924.

23 Letter to Dell Hymes, 26 Oct. 1967: http://cdclv.unlv.edu/ega/documents/hymes_eg_corr.pdf.

24 Much earlier Goffman had initially blocked the award of PhD to Sacks, eventually being persuaded to withdraw from the panel: see Schegloff 1992a: xxiv.

There are certainly some important similarities in orientation. It is striking, for example, that both these sociologists formulate the focus of their early work as being concerned with processes of communication and social order. In a prospectus for his thesis (written in 1948, though only published in 2006) Garfinkel presents his primary interest as the 'communicative effort' that is involved in processes of social interaction; and he sees this as central to the constitution of social order. Garfinkel's work for the Organizational Behavior Study at Princeton in the early 1950s also focused on processes of communication (Garfinkel 1952/2008). Meanwhile, Goffman's doctoral thesis of 1952 centres on the communicational patterns to be found in the Shetland community he studied, these being treated not as culturally specific but as universal in character. Moreover, he describes 'conversational order' as one species of social order, citing Parsons' *The Social System*.[25]

More broadly, the similarities between the work of Goffman and Garfinkel relate, of course, to a joint concern with the mundane features of everyday social interaction. While their approaches to this topic were different, the work of both was shaped by the contemporary literature on small groups, in both sociology and social psychology (Strodtbeck and Hare 1954). Garfinkel was also familiar with research on information processing and theories of communication more generally (Garfinkel 1952/2008), while Goffman (1953) appeals to anthropological and sociolinguistic studies of communication.

In more specific terms it could be argued that Garfinkel's concept of 'account-ability' overlaps significantly with Goffman's 'impression management', in which projected selves are either credited or discredited by audiences, and this is particularly true of Goffman's later conceptual re-workings of this idea. When he writes that 'we find ourselves with one central obligation: to render our behaviour understandably relevant to what the other can come to perceive is going on' (Goffman 1983b: 51), he is almost paraphrasing Garfinkel. Their work also seems close when, in *Frame Analysis*, Goffman presents impression management as operating within frames that largely impose themselves on actors. After all, Garfinkel's (1967a: 173–5) objection to Goffman's earlier dramaturgical treatment of social interaction – that it implies too much conscious agency and portrays it as directed at personal goals, rather than treating the accountability of actions as effectively enforced through processes of social interaction, and as underpinning all aspects of social life – seems to be rather less applicable to Goffman's later work; though significant differences remained, notably the latter's emphasis on the ritual aspects of social interaction and their relationship

---

25 It seems to me that this concern with communication and language led to a focus on the part of both Goffman and ethnomethodologists on explicating member competence, and this indicates an important difference from much symbolic interactionist work, and indeed from the rest of sociology (see Hammersley 1981).

to the preservation of 'face'. We also find in Goffman an emphasis on the self-organising character of social settings that parallels the position of Garfinkel in some respects. In both cases, what we have here is a decidedly sociological orientation. Goffman (1967: 2, 3) writes that: 'the proper study of interaction is not the individual and his psychology, but rather the syntactical relations among acts of different persons mutually present to one another ... not, then, men and their moments. Rather, moments and their men' (Goffman 1967: 3). Garfinkel could have agreed.

There is also a common inheritance from Durkheim. Burns (1992: 25) argues that Durkheim's definition of a 'social fact' 'is the foundation of Goffman's own method. A "social fact" is "every way of acting, fixed or not, which is general throughout a given society, while existing in its own right, independent of its individual manifestations".'[26] Burns continues as follows:

> [Goffman's] indebtedness to Durkheim is anchored in this proposition. If the objects of sociological study, being impossibly abstract or impossibly large or impossibly numerous, are out of reach of empirical observation, then we have to make use of something which we treat as if it were a kind of Leibnizian monad, a constituent particular which both reflects and prehends the cosmos of which it is a constituent particle. Most sociologists have plumped for individual persons, taking their circumstances and their relationships to others, and what they are asked, or choose, to tell about their attitudes, beliefs, ideas and opinion, as representations of the society whose members they are. Goffman's monad was the social act itself – the encounter between individuals.[27]

Again, there seems to be a close parallel. Take, for instance, Garfinkel's attitude towards Durkheim's (1894: 15) principle that the fundamental principle of sociology is 'the objective reality of social facts'. In *Studies* Garfinkel rejects 'versions of' this principle (Garfinkel 1967a: vii), but he adopts a rather different attitude in *Ethnomethodology's Program*, which carries the subtitle: 'working out Durkheim's aphorism'. He objects to the term 'principle (principe), but he nevertheless claims that while Durkheim has been interpreted as advocating what mainstream sociology has set out to do, in fact ethnomethodology is closer to what he intended, insisting that 'the objective reality of social facts is sociology's fundamental phenomenon' (Garfinkel 2002: 66; see also Hilbert 1992). And the facts he is interested in are patterns of social interaction, much like Goffman.

More specifically, Rawls (2002: 20–1) has claimed that the roots of ethnomethodology are to be found in Durkheim's sociology of religion, and it is worth

---

26 The quotations here are from Durkheim 1938: 13.

27 I am not sure this is entirely true. Goffman, like Simmel, focuses on human beings, noting that they exist independently of the roles they play, as exemplified in his concept of role distance. By contrast, it seems that Garfinkel's focus, following Parsons' (1951), was on role-playing, with 'members' being defined as those in possession of the methods that make up the competence required for 'collectivity membership' (Garfinkel 1967a: 57).

noting here that Goffman's (1956a) discussion of interaction ritual in 'The nature of deference and demeanor' draws on Durkheim's chapter on the 'soul' in *The Elementary Forms*, identifying the respects in which personhood is treated as sacred. Indeed, he even follows Durkheim (1915: 37) in distinguishing in this context between negative rituals (keeping away from topics that might be 'sensitive' for the persons present) and positive rituals (the offering of compliments, for example) (see Goffman 1967: 73; Smith 2006: 52; Winkin and Leeds-Hurwitz 2013: 43). Here, what is taken from Durkheim, by each of these authors, is rather different, but they draw on some of the same ideas.

Another Durkheimian parallel relates to the role of non-contractual aspects of social relations. Writing about Goffman, Burns (1992: 26) notes that for him:

> the world of contractual and quasi-contractual relationships and power struggles coexists with – indeed, is founded on – an implicit, substructural "moral" order on which each and every individual relies, if only as a guarantee of the rational order based on contract, if only as the repository and source of the rituals which guide behaviour and govern relationships.

However, whereas Durkheim assumed that this underlying moral order was 'durable, consistent and all-sustaining', Goffman treats it as 'fragile, impermanent, full of unexpected holes, and in constant need of repair'. Of course, this notion of a non-contractual infrastructure underpinning social life is also a central theme in ethnomethodology; but, where Durkheim and Parsons formulate it in terms of shared informal rules, Garfinkel insists that it takes the form of *practices*, and ones that cannot be rule-*governed*. So for him, as for Goffman, moral order is a contingent matter: both Goffman and Garfinkel emphasise that people do not, and indeed could not, simply act out role obligations in a programmed fashion. Rather, in fulfilling institutionalised obligations they must act in ways that are sensitive to the particular situations in which action is taking place: they interpret and elaborate rules, and manage contingencies that arise. Furthermore, they may flout obligations, or use them for unofficial purposes. At the same time, for Garfinkel this does not mean that social order is liable to break down at any moment.

A rather different kind of similarity between these two sociologists was their emphasis on empirical investigation rather than on programmatic statements about the purpose and rationale of, or methods employed in, their work. Goffman is reported to have insisted that 'sociology is something you *do*, not something that you read' (cited in Smith 2003: 257). Along the same lines, Garfinkel criticised much social science as concerned with 'shoving words around' rather than actually carrying out careful investigations (Garfinkel et al. 1981: 133). Neither was engaged in building a theoretical system, in the manner of Parsons, but rather with exploring a new field of phenomena they had discovered. This might be viewed as indicating an empiricist orientation; though neither writer fits the mould of what would normally be implied by that term.[28] Of course, neither neglected theoretical issues completely. As I noted earlier, Goffman did offer a justification for focusing on the interaction order in two of his articles, and he was clearly concerned with developing a theoretical framework for understanding patterns of everyday social interaction. Meanwhile, in his early writings, Garfinkel explicitly set out a theory about the constitution of mundane social reality, derived from Schutz and Parsons. It is not true, therefore, that either of them was indifferent to theoretical and methodological concerns, but it is nevertheless the case that their primary focus was on empirical investigation.

A final similarity worth noting is that both Goffman and Garfinkel took a delight in subverting normal expectations as a way of putting into sharp relief what is normally taken for granted. Garfinkel did this most obviously through his breaching experiments. In the case of Goffman this kind of 'trouble-making' seems to have been confined to his personal relations with other people, and especially with colleagues. Smith (2006: 3) writes of Goffman's 'sociologically-inspired mischievousness', noting that 'acquaintances of Goffman tell of how he enjoyed testing the limits of the rules and understandings shaping face-to-face conduct in restaurants, cinema queues, lecture theatres and living rooms'.[29] This complemented the focus in much of his fieldwork on the occurrence of offence and embarrassment, since the otherwise taken-for-granted rules are highlighted where these occur, along with the strategies used to avert or deal with them (see Winkin and Leeds-Hurwitz 2013: 34, 35, 40–2). Even his investigation of a mental hospital can be viewed from this point of view: he writes that total institutions are 'forcing houses for changing persons; each is a natural experiment on what can be done to the self' (Goffman 1961: 12). His later investigation of errors in 'radio talk' is an even more obvious example (Goffman 1981a: ch. 5). Here, Garfinkel and Goffman, like Simmel, recognise that disorder can illuminate how social order is achieved and sustained.

As I noted earlier, the similarities between Goffman's work and that of Garfinkel and ethnomethodologists have sometimes led to proposals or attempts to integrate the two. In his detailed examination of the relationship between Goffman and ethnomethodologists, Smith (2003) concludes by suggesting that

28 Becker (2003: 668) writes that 'It is not often appreciated to what degree Goffman was a serious empiricist, even perhaps what might be called (in some meaning of the term) a positivist. ... He believed that there was an empirical reality and was wary of anything that ... could not be verified empirically, or was overly speculative.' In his reply to Denzin and Keller, Goffman (1981b: 62) refers to 'the crude empiricism I was raised with'.

29 See some of the 'biographical materials' in the Erving Goffman Archives: available at http://cdclv.unlv.edu/ega/.

there is compatibility, and indeed complementarity. He argues that Goffman generated fruitful concepts, but, for these to be tied down empirically and made to work in documenting what is happening in particular situations, the techniques of conversation analysis are an essential resource. On the other side, he insists that, while extremely fruitful, conversation analysis, in the form promoted by Schegloff, has adopted a very narrow focus on sequential patterns, failing to explore the ritual aspects of human social interaction that shape these patterns, which Goffman highlighted. Meanwhile, Heritage (2003: 2) has suggested that, in fact, conversation analysis was the result of: 'a synthesis of the perspectives of two highly original social scientists, Erving Goffman and Harold Garfinkel, both of whom directly influenced Sacks and Schegloff'.

However, while (as I have indicated) there are certainly important similarities between the work of these two sociologists, in my view these claims about compatibility and complementarity overlook or underplay some fundamental differences in orientation.

Differences

Despite belonging to more or less the same generation of American sociologists, there were, as I noted, significant differences in intellectual background between Garfinkel and Goffman. To a large extent Garfinkel was shaped by his contact with Parsons, with empirical sociological and psychological research of a mainly quantitative kind, and with the writings of Husserl, Gurwitsch, and Schutz. By contrast, Goffman was influenced initially by social anthropology, particularly the work of Radcliffe-Brown and his American students, and by the ideas of Ray Birdwhistell (who later went on to develop kinesics: Birdwhistell 1970), both of which he came into contact with when studying as an undergraduate at the University of Toronto. During his postgraduate training at Chicago he was influenced by Lloyd Warner and Everett Hughes. The former seems likely to have reinforced the Durkheimian influence coming via Radcliffe-Brown, while Hughes exemplified the approach of Park, which was in turn influenced, as we have seen, by the work of Simmel. Of course, both Garfinkel and Goffman departed in significant ways from the sources that influenced them – in an important respect both were mavericks, creatively appropriating and using what was available to them. While this may have brought them closer together in some respects, particularly in terms of a deep interest in the empirical study of mundane social interaction, significant differences remained.

While Goffman made little public comment on Garfinkel's work (it is briefly mentioned in *Frame Analysis*), or even on conversation analysis (he uses some of its findings, and makes some criticisms, in *Forms of Talk*), Garfinkel did occasionally register differences between his own work and that of Goffman. Moreover, as I noted earlier, there have been criticisms of Goffman by ethnomethod-ologists, who have insisted that fundamental differences in orientation are involved.[30]

One of the main criticisms that ethnomethodologists have made of Goffman's work concerns his use of data. While he draws examples from his own fieldwork, he also employs illustrative material from a variety of documentary sources, including newspaper reports and magazines, and he occasionally even uses invented examples. In *Frame Analysis*, he reports that he has employed 'cartoons, comics, novels, the cinema' as well as writings about the stage (Goffman 1974: 15). While Garfinkel and other ethnomethodologists have deployed several kinds of data, these have usually been drawn from a much narrower, and less exotic, range.[31] Above all, though, how they use these data has been significantly different from Goffman's approach. One aspect of this is conversation analysts' emphasis on the need for rigour in handling data, limiting what they employ to recordings and transcripts of naturally occurring talk, and restricting inferences to what is 'observable' in these data.[32] By contrast, Goffman structures his discussion in such a way that the disparate data he employs are used to *illustrate* the concepts he is discussing, rather than to display what is going on in the data (Watson 1992, 1999). Watson (1983: 105) argues that his examples have a 'just so' character: that his empirical materials 'seem to be designed to deliver just the analytic point [he] wishes to make: no more and no less'.

I suggest these differences with regard to data reflect the fact that, for Goffman, the intended product was a *conceptual framework* that could be used to understand mundane features of social interaction. There is a direct parallel here with Hughes. Chapoulie (1996: 4) writes:

> [F]reely developing a small number of concepts, [Hughes'] work offers a collection of subtly elaborated ideas that outline an analytic perspective on social reality. ... [There is] frequent recourse to concrete examples, taken from the author's own experiences and from literary works as much as from research in the social sciences, [and] a breadth of perspective based on an anthropological and historical background much greater than that of most sociologists. ... Finally, his style – simple, direct, sometimes informal – risks hiding the subtlety of his analyses and the broad perspec-tive that inspired them.

30 For a detailed discussion of the responses of ethnomethodologists to the work of Goffman, see Smith 2003.

31 However we should note that, as a student of Goffman, Sacks wrote a paper based on police manuals: Sacks 1972c. And in his lectures he occasionally employs items from newspapers, etc.

32 For critiques of Goffman's use of data by ethnomethodologists, see Helm (1982); Schegloff (1988a:101); the latter claiming that it amounts to 'sociology by epitome', creating only the illusion of detailed empirical investigation.

Most of this could also be said of Goffman. He seems to have been concerned with providing the systematic and precise vocabulary which he believed was needed to make the conceptual distinctions necessary for understanding inter-personal processes from a sociological perspective. Indeed, Becker (2003: 659) argues that Goffman offered

> a solution to a major problem in the presentation of social science thinking and results: how can we describe concrete social phenomena without using the descriptive terms already in use in the organization studied? Existing terminology embodies the perspectives of participants in the organization and so accepts all of those people's conventional judgments. This makes it impossible to isolate a class of similar social objects about which generalizations can be made. Goffman avoided this trap by creating a neutral but specific technical language and by a rigorously comparative analysis.

The aim attributed to Goffman here could not be more different from that of Garfinkel and ethnomethodologists. For them the analytic task is to explicate the understandings by means of which people constitute social phenomena through their actions. And they specifically avoid putting forward new concepts that can be seen as offering a re-description of people's actions in sociological terms. Yet, as Becker suggests, this is precisely what Goffman's multiple arrays of concepts do. Furthermore, ethnomethodologists reject the use of ironic contrasts. Thus, Watson (1992: 10) complains that 'Goffman's analyses contain several stipulative and ironic elements. Insofar as he mobilizes a "perspective by incongruity", his analyses contain a built-in feature of irony ... . To present *all* actions as, say, forms of "play-acting", espionage, or whatever, is at the level of membership to downgrade or ironicize them.'

In fact, Goffman is quite explicit that his work involves the kind of abstraction that is involved in using metaphors of various kinds, that he is not aiming to describe any particular social scene simply 'in its own terms'. It has been argued that his analysis deploys a 'dialectic of opposites' (Winkin and Leeds-Hurwitz 2013: 50), for example of models of the actor as ritual participant, as manipulator of impressions, or as peg on which social selves are hung. This is one reason why what he produced did not take a conventional ethnographic form, even though he relied to a considerable extent on ethnographic data.

By its very nature the sort of framework aimed at by Goffman is perspectival, even though the focus is on social forms that are taken to be stable features of human social life. Williams (1983: 100) writes that 'it is rarely the case that any essay or book of Goffman's failed to contain some explicit announcement of its "arbitrariness", its "selectivity", its constitution by a specific form of "attention", its nature as a "framework", "set of assumptions", "points of reference" or equivalent expression. The analytic features thus announced were not to be understood as the essential features of the phenomena to be examined ... but as constitutive elements of the analysis'. This implies that the world is 'unknowable in its fullness' (p. 101).

There is a close similarity with Simmel here, who insists that reality is inexhaustible: no phenomenon within it can be represented 'in itself' by any account, since all accounts are selective and frame what is included within some conceptualisation. He argues that: 'in the last instance, there is no science whose content emerges out of mere objective facts, but rather it always entails their interpretation and ordering according to categories and norms that exist *a priori* for the relevant science' (cited in Frisby 1981: 37–8). Different perspectives can provide illumination of different kinds, capturing some aspects of reality, but no perspective captures everything, even everything that may be of human interest.

This is a view characteristic of the German neo-Kantians of the late nineteenth century (Beiser 2014), who sometimes even denied that there is any inherent structure in the world, insisting that knowledge is only possible *through concepts*.[33] By contrast, in its fundamentals, Garfinkel's approach seems to be closer to that of phenomenology: he does not regard the process of ethnomethodological inquiry as itself constitutive but rather as aimed at revealing the constitutive processes that generate the world we all experience. As with Husserl, this requires suspending the natural attitude, with the aim of producing literal description rather than conceptual analysis.[34]

A further significant difference is that whereas a central theme of Goffman's work is the disparity between appearance and reality (Smith 2006: 19), Garfinkel disattends the issue of whether there are factors behind the process of social interaction pushing or pulling it in one direction rather than another. He is interested in how people *constitute* phenomena as what they are, not with what motives people may have in doing this or whether there are constraints on how social phenomena can be so constituted – for him ethnomethodology necessarily remains (at the very least) agnostic about such matters, in much the same manner as does phenomenology.

In this sense, like Simmel, Garfinkel identifies a relatively narrow topic as the focus for sociological investigation; yet, while Simmel treats investigations into the *contents* of social reality as the proper concern of other social sciences,

---

33 This line of argument is very close to the stance of analytical realism that Parsons (1937: ch. XIX) adopted.

34 While I believe that this captures the predominant orientation of ethnomethodology, there are times when Garfinkel and some other ethnomethodologists seem to adopt a more constructionist conception of the process of inquiry (see for instance Garfinkel 1948/2008, 1952; Mehan and Wood 1975; Pollner 1987; Watson and Sharrock 1991; Anderson and Sharrock 2018).

ethnomethodology seems to throw doubt on the scientific status of studies beyond its own focus; even while recognising that these matters can be a legitimate topic for members' inquiries. Indeed, it adopts an 'indifferent' attitude towards professional sociological reasoning, effectively treating it as equivalent in epistemic status to lay reasoning.

By contrast, Goffman sees his work as complementing other kinds of sociological investigation. Thus, he presents the 'interaction order' as mediating the effects of the sorts of causal factor with which conventional social scientists are concerned; and this connects with the issue of the relationship between micro- and macro-levels of analysis that arises in much social science. For Garfinkel, and most ethnomethodologists, context can only be what is constituted as context in particular processes of social interaction: what the analyst takes to be 'the wider context' must not be brought into the account, because it would be an imposition. This is one of the key respects in which ethnomethodologists have frequently seen their work as standing apart from, or even as in opposition to, mainstream sociology. Goffman, on the other hand, appears to have regarded his work as continuous with, and complementary to, macro-sociology. So, for example, he treated 'the interaction order' as one of several orders operating in modern societies, the others including the political and the economic.[35] And in some of his work, notably *Asylums*, he was very much concerned with the effects of institutional structures on patterns of social interaction. Here there is a close parallel with Simmel, who regarded the 'microscopic-molecular processes' (*Soziologie* 1908: 327, quoted in Smith 1989: 69) that he studied as underpinning, but also as shaped by, the institutions and systems of the larger society (Smith 2006: 69). In this respect these two authors differ sharply from Garfinkel.

Perhaps equally significant is that whereas Goffman is willing to locate human social action in the wider context of animal behaviour, drawing on ethological studies (see Winkin and Leeds-Hurwitz 2013: 100), there is little sign of this in Garfinkel's work.[36] Instead, for him, both natural and social phenomena are constituted solely through the processes of human social interaction on which ethnomethodology focuses.

Conclusion

It is by no means straightforward to characterise the orientations of Goffman and Garfinkel, or that of Simmel. I have sought to do this by examining both

35 It is possible that these terms are intended to be analogous to Parsons' economic and political systems, so that in studying the 'interaction order', Goffman was offering a further system that Parsons had neglected.

36 Interestingly, Sacks (1992a: 98–9) does seem to acknowledge this possibility. See also Moerman 1988.

similarities and significant differences. Despite interesting parallels, what should have emerged clearly is the radically distinctive perspective of ethnomethodology. This is at odds not just with mainstream sociology, but even with other work concerned both with the sociology of everyday life and with communicational processes, including that of Goffman. I suggest that the fundamental differences in orientation I have identified mean that the work of Garfinkel and Goffman cannot be integrated into a single enterprise, at least not without serious distortion of one or the other.

3 On the disciplinary status of ethnomethodology

There is uncertainty in the writings of ethnomethodologists about the relationship of their work to the discipline of sociology, and to social science more generally. At least four formulations of this relationship can be identified, though they are not always as sharply distinguished as I present them here. The most common one treats ethnomethodology as a radical internal reform movement, proposing to re-specify the goal of sociology (Zimmerman and Pollner 1970; Button 1991) or to rebuild its methodological foundations more effectively (Cicourel 1964). These two proposals for reform are, of course, themselves very different (see Chapter 1).[1]

A second conception presents ethnomethodology as an 'alternate' (perhaps a supplement?) to conventional sociology, offering important reminders to sociologists, and also to the users of sociological knowledge, about what that discipline takes for granted or does not take into account. The kind of supplement intended is, for example, detailed description of the practices involved in particular forms of work, practices that are presupposed but never examined by most studies in the sociology of work (Garfinkel and Wieder 1992). This position is exemplified by Garfinkel's comments about Durkheim's 'aphorism': 'the objective reality of social facts is sociology's fundamental principle' (Garfinkel 1948/2005: 122). He seems to treat this as the pivot by which sociology and ethnomethodology are connected: that whereas the objective reality of social facts is 'constructivist sociology's' starting point, ethnomethodology is concerned with how that objective reality comes about in the first place (see, for instance, Garfinkel 1990; Anderson and Sharrock 2018). In these terms it could be seen as serving a similar function to Schutz's philosophical work.[2]

1 Anderson (2016) has suggested that there are further modalities involved here: he distinguishes between critique of sociology that is aimed at clarification, in which category he places the work of Cicourel, critical commentary with a corrective interest, and a more oppositional approach in which the founding premises of sociology are denied.

2 Following Rawls (2004), Garfinkel appears to claim that Durkheim was an ethnomethodologist *avant la lettre*. On Rawls' interpretation of Durkheim, see Schmaus 1998.

A third view is that ethnomethodology is a distinct discipline, and so it neither challenges conventional sociology nor serves as a necessary complement to it: it simply has a different focus, and therefore is 'indifferent' to it.[3] It is not uncommon to find ethnomethodology referred to as a discipline (see for example Wieder 1977: 1); though, of course, that word carries a variety of senses. But, even where the word is not used, this position sometimes seems to be implied. For example, Harvey Sacks declares: 'I want to propose that a domain of research exists that is not part of any other established science. The domain is one that those who are pursuing it have come to call ethnomethodology/conversation analysis' (Sacks, 1984: 21). What is at issue here is not simply ethnomethodology's relationship to sociology and other social sciences but also to neighbouring disciplines, such as linguistics and psychology, and to the various applied fields in which ethnomethodological work has been done.

Finally, some have suggested that ethnomethodology is *anti*-social science in character. For example, Button et al. (2015: 135) write that 'Ethnomethodology would do away with social science as it stands …, dispersing the study of the social into "innumerable hybrids" … or interdisciplinary endeavours, where studies of the social are built into other disciplines to shape their ongoing development … '.[4] So, the task of ethnomethodology is to assist practical disciplines (in the case of these authors, those concerned with system and software design), rather than to contribute to academic literature. They refer approvingly to Garfinkel's dismissal of the social sciences as 'talking sciences' 'essentially occupied with the business of "shoving words around"' (Button et al. 2015: 14). They also see them as imposing a misleading theoretical gloss on the nature of social activities. Along similar lines, Schegloff (1997: 165) has proposed that conversation analysis operates 'as a buffer against the potential for academic and theoretical imperialism which imposes intellectuals' preoccupations on a world without respect to their indigenous resonance'.[5]

There is evidence both *for* and *against* all of these interpretations of the relationship of ethnomethodology to sociology within the writings of Garfinkel. Thus, in various places he insists that no critique of mainstream sociology is intended, and that ethnomethodology is not a separate discipline. On one occasion, for instance,

3 In these terms, the work of sociologists can itself be studied by ethnomethodologists, just as much as can that of other 'members'. There has been some ethnomethodological study of sociological work, see for instance Greiffenhagen et al. 2011, 2015; Maynard et al. 2002; Maynard and Schaeffer 2006; Houtkoope-Steenstra 2000. Interestingly, earlier, McHoul 1982 and Anderson and Sharrock 1984 had studied conversation analytic work in this manner, the latter focusing on how a particular article by Schegloff establishes its claims.

4 Button et al. derive the idea of 'hybrids' from Lynch (1993: 274), and he attributes the idea to the later Garfinkel.

5 This echoes a longstanding complaint made against intellectuals, in general, and sometimes specifically against sociologists: see, for instance, Alpert 1938.

he describes ethnomethodology as 'incommensurable with and asymmetrically alternate to' the 'formal analysis' employed by the 'worldwide social science movement' (Garfinkel 2002: ch. 2), insisting that it 'is NOT a corrective enterprise. It is Not a rival science in the worldwide social science movement. EM does not offer a rival social science to the established methods of carrying on analytic studies ...' (p. 121). However, as Dennis (2003) points out, it is hard to see how its character can avoid at least *implying* a fundamental critique and a rival approach, and indeed this is how it is often presented (see, for instance, Rawls 2002; Hutchinson et al. 2008).[6] A similar conflict can be found in relation to the fourth interpretation. In contrast to Button et al.'s (2015) anti-academic stance, there is the following:

> The studies by Ethnomethodology's authors are academic enterprises through and through. Despite the variety of empirical subjects of EM studies, whatever their immediately practical consequences and mundane motives, there prevails a concern for university-level professional subjects whose priority of relevance is that they contribute to the renewal of the University. (Garfinkel 2002: 77)

That the relationship of ethnomethodology with sociology is not a settled or a comfortable one, on either side, is indicated by Lynch's (1993: 2) characterisation of the range of accommodations adopted by ethnomethodologists to their home discipline as being analogous to 'the different "stances" that inmates in an asylum take towards the institution and its staff: openly rebelling, going along with, or making the best of the situation'. And, to pursue this analogy further, accusations of insanity, in metaphorical terms, have come from both sides.[7]

In this chapter I want to assess these various proposals about the status of ethnomethodology in relation to sociology, and to social science more generally. I will begin by briefly examining Garfinkel's early career and what indications this might carry for that relationship. Then, given the influence of phenomenology on Garfinkel, I will examine *its* relationship with the natural and social sciences to see whether this can provide some illumination. I will then outline the ways in which Garfinkel's arguments carry a critical challenge to social science. Finally, I will assess the viability and fruitfulness of two influential forms of ethnomethodological work, since these characteristics would be essential for this work to operate as a distinct discipline, or to function as an adjunct to practical disciplines.

---

6 There are some interesting exchanges in the Purdue Symposium relating to this: Garfinkel insists that ethnomethodology is not a critique of conventional sociology, but Edward Rose states that it plainly is, and this is borne out by some of the contributions of Sacks and Sudnow: see Hill and Crittenden 1968: 20 and *passim*.

7 Indeed, Garfinkel himself described ethnomethodology as insane at first sight (Hill and Crittenden 1968: 122).

Garfinkel's early career

An apparently straightforward starting point would be to say that Garfinkel was trained as a sociologist and spent the whole of his career in departments devoted to that discipline. As part of his doctoral work, he engaged in careful study of the writings of Talcott Parsons, one of his teachers, and it is clear that these were a major influence on his thinking. Indeed, he explicitly presents his work as concerned with the problem of social order, which Parsons had treated as the core focus of the discipline. Garfinkel was also involved in empirical sociological research on various topics (Rawls 2013; vom Lehn 2014), though it seems clear that his primary interest was as much in what this could tell us about the nature of social order (and about social science) as in the topics themselves. We might think of Garfinkel as seeking to operationalise Parsons' concern with the problem of social order in empirical research terms (see Sharrock and Anderson 1986: 15–17), though his approach was more radical than this phrasing might suggest. At face value, at least, the implication seems to be that ethnomethodology falls *within* sociology; and, if it is part of that discipline, it cannot but be taken as offering a critical challenge to the predominant mode of work within it at the time (and later).

However, the context in which Garfinkel started out on his sociological career, during and after his PhD, was a more complex one than this implies. Besides championing sociology, Parsons was also involved in seeking to establish interdisciplinary connections, not least through his role in founding the Department of Human Relations at Harvard (Schmidt 1978). While he identified a clearly defined task for sociology, he wished to locate it in a systematic way within the broader field of social science, with each discipline making a distinctive contribution to the whole (Camic 1987, 1991). Furthermore, this was a time when there was considerable funding for interdisciplinary social science. And some of the research projects in which Garfinkel was involved brought him into contact with psychology, organisational theory, and studies of small group behaviour and decision-making. As a result, he came to be very much concerned with psychological and economic theories, and applied forms of work, as well as with sociological views about social organisation (see Garfinkel 1952/2008).

In addition, we must remember that, from early on, Garfinkel had an interest in philosophy, specifically phenomenology, and its implications for social science. This stemmed from his time at the University of North Carolina, but at Harvard he came into contact with Aron Gurwitsch, and with the writings of Schutz, whom he also met on several occasions for 'tutorials' (Psathas 2012). He took Schutz's work as providing a significantly different point of access in studying social order from that offered by Parsons (Garfinkel 1952/2008, 1948/2005; Anderson et al. 1985a; Heritage 1984: ch. 2). In his view, it highlighted Parsons' failure to take adequate account of how actors identify situations prior to evaluating them in terms of norms and values; and Garfinkel concluded that Parsons' assumption that socialisation into a shared symbol system would be sufficient for the achievement of social order is inadequate.[8]

Schutz's phenomenological orientation also relied upon very different *philosophical* presuppositions from Parsons: rather than the processes by which social order is produced only being discoverable through the analytic perspective of the sociologist, phenomenology implies that *order is to be discovered in the phenomena themselves.* In his early writings, Garfinkel (1952, 1952/2008: ch. 5) set up Schutz's approach as a sharply contrasted alternative to the framework that Parsons had elaborated, one that adopted a congruence rather than a correspondence conception of knowledge. Garfinkel seems to have drawn from Schutz's work the idea that order in the social world is constituted by actors in and through their activity, for instance via such 'methods' as assuming a reciprocity of perspectives, accepting appearances 'until further notice', and so forth (Schutz 1962; Garfinkel 1963: 210–14).

So, while Garfinkel was very much operating within the field of sociology, and his work was intended as a contribution to that discipline, he was, at the same time, engaging with a wider interdisciplinary field of ideas and practices.

Parallels with phenomenology

Given that the initial development of ethnomethodology was strongly influenced by Schutz's work, and by phenomenology more generally, it may help in understanding the disciplinary status of ethnomethodology if we examine briefly the character of that philosophical approach. This is because there are some significant parallels with *its* relationship to philosophy; and, more especially, its relationship with the natural and the social sciences (see Kockelmans 1983). I will look first at the case of Husserl, the founder of phenomenology, and then at that of Schutz.

It is clear that Husserl's aim was to reform philosophy, conceiving this discipline as properly concerned with explicating the foundations of our experience, and thereby of our knowledge of the world. While regarding himself very much as a philosopher within the mainstream Western tradition, he rejected what he saw as a strong trend towards materialism or naturalism, exemplified not least in the character of the scientific psychology emerging out of philosophy at that time, especially in Germany. He also questioned key aspects of the neo-Kantian versions of philosophy that were dominant. He saw both as stemming from Descartes' false dualism between matter and spirit, and phenomenology was intended to overcome this.

Husserl regarded philosophy as the primary intellectual discipline; but, at least in his early work, he did not see it as in competition with other disciplines (with

8 This is an aspect of the problem of 'double contingency', on which see Vanderstraeten 2002. See Chapter 4.

the partial exception of psychology), since these all had their separate and distinctive functions. Phenomenology's primacy derived from the fact that it suspended, and subjected to investigation, the range of assumptions that are characteristic of the 'natural attitude', and thereby constitutive of the 'lifeworld'; on which not only all practical human activity relies but also the *theoretical* work of the other academic disciplines, including the natural sciences. While this suspension of the natural attitude amounted to critique in the Kantian sense, it did not imply rejection or even criticism of reliance on the natural attitude by scientists and others; indeed, Husserl believed that such reliance was essential in the pursuit of both practical and scientific goals. Suspension of the natural attitude was required only for philosophical work.

So, in these terms phenomenology is concerned with the rigorous description of how all types of phenomena appear in experience, and of what can be learned from this about their character. It provides clarification of the foundations of human knowledge, and is thereby complementary to other disciplines. However, especially in his later writings, Husserl (1970) goes beyond this. He questions natural scientists' tendency to misrepresent, and perhaps misunderstand, the foundations of their own work, since they treat it as directly accessing reality *entirely through scientific procedures of observation, measurement, and logical inference* (see Moran 2005; Tieszen 2005). He argues that what is forgotten here is that science is necessarily rooted in the lifeworld and in subjective experience; and that its idealisations and abstractions cannot supplant our ordinary experience. He also criticises the 'naturalism' that follows from the influence of this distorted conception of natural science, particularly in the field of psychology, where the effect is to reduce human beings to no more than material objects, to be understood 'mechanically' on much the same basis as other physical phenomena (see Gurwitsch 1974: 78–81 and *passim*; Moran 2012).

As a result, Husserl proposed a quite different approach to psychology, one that was directly dependent upon phenomenological analysis. This was to provide an *a priori* foundation for the empirical discipline, in a parallel way to the manner in which he took mathematics or theoretical physics to supply an *a priori* basis for experimental physics (Gurwitsch 1974: 83–4). And he extends this to the social sciences, arguing that they require a 'personalistic' attitude that takes account of the distinctive features of human beings, without separating these off from their physical characteristics. This contrasts with what he regards as the dominant naturalistic attitude that stems from a desire to ape the natural sciences; which he believes is a threat to Western culture, one whose effects are exemplified by political developments in Germany and elsewhere at the time he was writing, in the 1930s (see Moran 2012).

By comparison, Schutz seems to have adopted a more limited view of the role of phenomenology in relation to the social sciences; though he shares both Husserl's commitment to the need for clarification of their foundations and his belief that phenomenology can provide this. Above all, he does not treat phenomenology as providing a form of social science that would *replace* existing forms; though it may indicate the need for modifications to social scientists' current ideas and practices. His criticism of Weber was simply that the latter had provided inadequate foundations for the enterprise in which he was engaged – he did not challenge the validity or value of that enterprise, or of its findings. Moreover, Schutz, like his friend Kaufmann, very much adopted economics as his model for the nature of social science, and in particular the Austrian version of this discipline with which he was most familiar (see Chapter 1).[9]

We can conclude, therefore, that there is some ambiguity about the relationships among phenomenology, philosophy, and the psychological and social sciences, not unlike that arising over ethnomethodology's to sociology. Husserl's phenomenology was certainly intended to be a reform movement within philosophy, and was designed to serve as an important reminder to scientists about the nature of the foundations on which scientific knowledge relies. Moreover, in his later work especially, Husserl saw phenomenology as offering a major corrective to European culture, in countering the influence of a distorted picture of natural science, arising from the manner in which it had developed since the time of Galileo. In particular, he treated phenomenology as implying a fundamental critique of current 'scientific' psychology and the other human sciences, as these had developed in the late nineteenth and early twentieth centuries. By contrast, Schutz appears to have assigned a more modest task to phenomenology as regards the social sciences, analogous in some respects to the 'underlabourer' role adopted by the logical positivists; in this respect complementing the methodological work of his friend Kaufmann.

Ethnomethodology as providing an internal critique of sociology

While there are clear continuities between previous sociological work and Garfinkel's early investigations, the discontinuities are *more* obvious, and these signal the ways in which ethnomethodology came to be regarded as posing a fundamental challenge to conventional sociology. Garfinkel not only abandoned Parsons' 'analytical realism' (Parsons 1937: chs 1, XIX; Treviño 2001: xxv–xxvi), in favour of an approach modelled on phenomenology, but also redefined the focus of sociological inquiry: away from Parsons' concern with social order in the traditional sense of an absence, or containment, of conflict and violence, and towards interpreting 'order' as intelligibility, this being a precondition for the coordination of social action within a particular setting, and beyond. Thus, for Garfinkel, the opposite of order is confusion or meaninglessness. Moreover, he

9 Lynch (1993: 117) argues that Schutz 'delivers a rather weak version of the Husserlian critique of the natural sciences'.

drew attention to the local and situated character of the sense people make of particular situations, and to the 'work' involved in this: he insisted that sense-making cannot be formulated in terms of abstract rules, compliance with which causally produces specific outcomes, in the manner assumed by Parsons and many other sociologists. To put it another way, social organisation is an achievement of practical, common-sense reasoning.

Central here is Garfinkel's claim that language-use is indexical: in other words, that the meaning of particular utterances is always sensitive to context rather than being decodable from linguistic rules and stock definitions of words, as assumed by formalist semantics as well as by Parsons. While any uncertainty of meaning is usually routinely remedied by actors in the course of their activities, this is done in ways that are situationally appropriate rather than conforming to standard patterns that could be incorporated into a formal model, especially one that would provide an analytical basis for automatically substituting non-indexical for indexical meanings. In this respect Garfinkel's work is in line with the anti-formalism that arose in English philosophy against the efforts of logical atomists, such as Frege and Russell, to produce a logico-mathematical language that would remedy the vagueness and ambiguity of natural language-use, this anti-formalism being exemplified in Wittgenstein's later philosophy (see Coulter 1989, 1991). It also shared something in common with the work of sociolinguists, such as Gumperz and Hymes (1972), who insisted that language must be studied *in use*, rather than as an abstract generative mechanism – in the manner of Chomsky (see Zimmerman 1978). In parallel terms Garfinkel's anti-formalism counted against the efforts of sociologists to build models of social processes intended to capture universal, albeit usually probabilistic, laws.[10]

Garfinkel's ideas here highlight a cluster of fundamental problems that face social science:

- How to deal with clashes between the accounts given by participants and those developed through sociological analysis. A not uncommon 'solution' was to treat lay accounts as providing supporting evidence where they agree with the analysis, and to dismiss them as the product of ignorance or ideology where they do not. This assumes that social science has a superior capacity to determine the meanings of actions, an assumption that is certainly open to question (see Winch 1958);

10 At the same time, there are places where he himself appears to be proposing a different kind of formalism, perhaps one modelled on the phenomenological notion of eidetic science (see Gurwitsch 1974) – see, for example, the reference to 'formal structures' in Garfinkel and Sacks 1970, and the very idea that understanding is generated by *methods*. And this notion of formal analysis was taken over by Schegloff and others: see, for instance, Schegloff 1997.

- How can actors' meanings be incorporated into sociological theories, as they must be given that social action is more than physical behaviour. This is a problem if these meanings are indexical, and therefore situationally variable, involving open-textured concepts only definable by means of family resemblance – in Garfinkel's (1967a: 40) terms, they are 'specifically vague'. Does not science require statements whose meaning is determinate, in the sense of being independent of local variation? An implication might seem to be that the meaning of any sociological analysis is itself necessarily indeterminate, and therefore fails to meet the requirements of science;
- Actors do not simply conform to or reject norms and values, but employ these flexibly, and this appears to undermine, or at least greatly to weaken, their explanatory force – yet these are the factors to which many sociologists appeal, by no means only Parsons. Indeed, much the same criticism could be directed against use of the concept of interests, which is probably the most common alternative type of causal factor employed in sociology; or that of preferences, which is central to economics;
- Ethnomethodology challenges the rigour of much sociological analysis, pointing to the gap between the claims made and the level and quality of evidence typically offered in support of them. It is argued that this stems from a failure to analyse social action *in detail*, and to provide the data for readers so that they can *inspect* the grounds for the analysis. It is argued that 'the chain of inference in sociological analysis' needs to be made much more explicit (Sharrock 2000: 536);
- Any scene, including the participants within it, can be described in innumerable ways that are not logically or factually incompatible with one another but that would be differentially appropriate on different occasions. As Schegloff (1997: 165) points out: 'it is not enough to justify referring to someone as a "woman" just because she is, in fact, a woman – because she is, by the same token, a Californian, Jewish, a mediator, a former weaver, my wife, and many others'. The question that arises here is: by what rigorous means can sociologists decide under what descriptions to present the phenomena they are studying?

An obvious consequence of ethnomethodologists' emphasis on these problems was rejection of the assumption, commonly made by sociologists in the 1950s and early 1960s (and perhaps still today), that, by comparison with the vagueness and error of 'common-sense knowledge', the conclusions *they* produce are rational and well-founded. Schutz (1943) had already raised questions about any such claim, by drawing a distinction between scientific and practical forms of rationality. While Garfinkel (1962) initially took over this distinction, later he seems to have come to the more radical conclusion that scientific reasoning is practical in character, in much the same sense as the reasoning in which all of us engage in the course of our lives; or, at least, that any fundamental difference remains to be discovered

(Lynch 1993). Furthermore, while he frequently refers to professional and lay sociological reasoning (in Garfinkel and Sacks 1970, and elsewhere), therefore apparently distinguishing between the two, he is not thereby validating a claim to distinctive analytic expertise on the part of professional sociologists.[11]

Given this, it is not surprising that ethnomethodology has often been presented as a radical reform movement within social science, or sometimes even as dissolving it (Hutchinson et al. 2008). At the very least, ethnomethodology promotes a refocusing of social scientific inquiry, away from the substantive topics that are its standard fare, and on to the local features of practical reasoning through which people constitute the social world via practical activity (see Button 1991). Moreover, these two foci are incompatible: 'Ethnomethodology's imperative (to examine the organisation of common-sense understandings and natural language use as its own topics) dislocates the possibility of making sociological studies of the usual kind' (Sharrock 2004: 33). Thus, even the argument that ethnomethodology is 'incommensurate' with social science, or is concerned with differentiating it into hybrid interdisciplinary endeavours that serve practical disciplines, represents a major challenge to the status of sociology. Only a little less radically, Cicourel (1964, 1968, 1974) saw ethnomethodology as providing a new and more rigorous theoretical and methodological foundation for conventional social research (see Chapters 1 and 5).

It seems clear, then, that ethnomethodology offered an internal critique of the predominant forms of US sociology in the 1950s and early 1960s, as well as of psychology and economics, pointing to key respects in which these had failed to live up to their own methodological ideals: in particular that the attempt to produce sociological explanations meeting the requirements of the covering-law model, held to be characteristic of science, had been unsuccessful (see, for example, Wilson 1970a, 1970b). Moreover, Garfinkel's work implied that this was not simply a technical failing but rather that this model could *never* be realised: that the whole project is vitiated by the impossibility of explicating human behaviour in terms of fixed, determinate meanings and laws. And it was shown that this was not just a matter of the failures of physicalism and behaviourism, as argued by Schutz, but also of those approaches, such as the work of Parsons, that took norms or rules into account as causal factors. Instead, ethnomethodology highlights the contingency, discretion, and judgement involved in human social life; and, thereby, the essential role of forms of artful practical reasoning that are not lawlike in terms of either process or outcome, but that *are* intelligible. It is this which undercuts any prospect of the kind of social science proposed, and

---

11 His attitude towards the distinctive knowledge and skills that natural scientists deploy is less equivocal, insisting on the need for 'unique adequacy' in investigations of these (Lynch 1985). This presumably reflects his distinction between 'discovery sciences' and 'talking sciences' (Garfinkel et al. 1981: 133). However, see Maynard 2012.

purportedly practised, by sociologists from Durkheim to Blalock, as well as more recent incarnations of the same approach. I will assess the force of this critique in the next chapter, and in the Conclusion.

The viability and fruitfulness of ethnomethodology

In the final section of this chapter I want to turn to the viability of ethnomethodology as a research programme: in other words, the question of whether it is a coherent and worthwhile enterprise that could operate as a distinct discipline or serve as a valuable adjunct to practical activities. Of course, there is an issue here about what criteria of assessment should be used. There is no incontestable way of dealing with this, but I will use a criterion that I regard as relevant to all social science: whether it can produce knowledge that is more reliable than that available from other sources, about topics that are of human relevance, and/or knowledge that is of immediate practical value. Another criterion I will employ concerns whether it occupies its own distinctive territory, which certainly would be a requirement if it is to be regarded as a separate discipline.

For the purposes of this assessment, I will look briefly at two influential, but very different, forms of ethnomethodological investigation: conversation analysis (CA) and 'studies of work' (sometimes also referred to as 'workplace studies').

Conversation analysis

As regards the first criterion, in my view CA clearly addresses important topics, even though – in the past at least – these were not rated highly by the 'news values' of mainstream sociology.[12] Furthermore, it offers a clear case of the *development* of knowledge in a new field. Indeed, it is one of the few areas of social science where a progressive cumulation of knowledge can be documented. As a result, we now have detailed understanding of the complex processes involved in turn-taking within various kinds of talk-in-interaction; of how preferences operate amongst responses to invitations and other initiatives; how the repair of errors, potential insults, etc. is managed; and so on.[13]

At the same time, it is not clear how much the development of this knowledge relied upon ethnomethodology, or indeed whether it is even compatible with it. This is because CA has increasingly been concerned with documenting general sequential patterns. This is often seen as stemming from Sacks, Schegloff and

12 Complaints by some sociologists that the knowledge ethnomethodology produces is about trivial matters (Coser 1975: 697) reflect these 'news values'. But it is worth noting that the topics investigated by CA are not trivial from the point of view of other disciplines, such as linguistics.
13 Schegloff (2007) has synthesised many of the main findings; see also Sidnell and Stivers 2013.

Jefferson's (1974) account of the 'speech exchange system', consisting of a hierarchi-
cally organised set of components with associated rules of use that generates
conversational turn-taking patterns.[14] Similarly, in Membership Categorisation
Analysis, a cognate area of investigation that Sacks initiated, the aim was to build
an 'apparatus' (Sacks 1974: 218) that can show how the sense that members
make of utterances is generated, in other words to display the 'machinery' (Garfinkel
and Sacks 1970: 355–8) involved (see Sacks 1972a, 1972b; Hester and Eglin 1997;
Fitzgerald and Housley 2015). Yet, even if the focus on identifying such generative
methods may have fitted Garfinkel's earliest conception of the task of ethnomethodology, it seems to be at odds with his later work, where the possibility is
rejected of identifying methods that are general, in the sense that they are
recurrently used on many occasions, even if always in ways that are contextually
sensitive (see Wilson 2003, 2012). And, in fact, Garfinkel, and some of his later
students, have been very critical of the way that conversation analysis has developed.
For example, Lynch (2000c: 521) reports a passage from an unpublished paper
in which Garfinkel lodges 'a series of complaints against recent (post-1975)
developments in conversation analysis' (see also Livingston 1987: chs 12, 13;
Hester and Francis 2001; Watson 2008).[15]

Sharrock (2001: 257) summarises the criticisms as follows:

> The work of conversation analysis was becoming more a matter of administering
> a developed and formal analytical scheme to the further study of conversational
> materials. The possession and use of the scheme seemed to engender a distinct,
> specialized and professional competence that distinguished the analyst from the
> participant. The phenomena in conversation that were being sought and found
> appeared to be those which could only be noticed and identified by those operating
> with the guidance of the scheme. Thus, there was a divergence from the initial
> concerns of conversation analysis with the identification of those phenomena
> which anyone (at least anyone who could carry on a conversation, preferably in
> the appropriate natural language) can find, into an interest in phenomena in
> conversation that can only be found through the use of a specialized investigative
> apparatus.

Thus, in one of the sharpest critiques, Lynch and Bogen (1994: 80) complain that
much conversation analysis invokes 'a principled distinction between professional
analysis and members' intuitions' (Lynch and Bogen 1994: 66). They write that

14 For interesting discussions of the character and place of this seminal article in the
history of conversation analysis, see Lynch 2000c; Sharrock 2000.
15 Heritage (2016: 41–2) has referred to 'the increasingly divergent and conflicted relationship
between CA and ethnomethodology'. And, from the other side of the argument,
Lynch (2016a: 4) declares that 'much of what passes for CA today, even when decorated
with citations to Garfinkel and Sacks, has reverted to what Garfinkel called "constructive
analysis"'. See also Lynch 2017, and responses to the criticisms: Heritage 2018; Maynard and
Clayman 2018.

> Schegloff has argued ... that a vernacular mastery of language does not entitle a speaker to the kind of analytic knowledge attained through the study of tape-recorded data. Although ordinary conversationalists presumably 'know' how to take turns, and conversation analysts rely upon evidences of 'participants' orientations' as a 'proof criterion' for specific analytic characterisations, Schegloff draws a fundamental distinction between an analytical understanding of the abstract components, rules and recursive operations that describe systems of talk-in-interaction, and a vernacular understanding of talk. According to this distinction, the societal member exhibits a naïve mastery of the techniques which the scientist describes formally. (p. 80)

In these terms, Lynch and Bogen (1994: 90) argue that, as it has come to be predominantly practised, CA is at odds with the principles of ethnomethodology. They insist that 'the naïve adequacy of *ordinary* practices is not grounded in context-free descriptions of ordinary methods, any more than the stable reproducibility of scientific activities is grounded in context-free descriptions of scientific methods'.

So, while CA meets the first criterion I outlined above very effectively, having developed a cumulative body of knowledge whose value can be recognised, there are grounds for arguing that this achievement does not arise from its ethnomethodological character and may even be incompatible with it. In other words, while it may be possible to regard CA as a viable discipline in its own right, or perhaps as a hybrid that takes an 'applied' form (see Antaki 2011; Stokoe and Sikveland 2017), the features that allow this are ones that raise questions about whether it is a form of ethnomethodology.

Furthermore, there are doubts about how well CA fares in relation to the second criterion I put forward: it is not clear that it has its own distinct intellectual territory, even though it certainly opened up a new set of topics for investigation and has provided detailed understanding of them. At the very least, the field is not well-bounded: there seems to be significant potential overlap with sociolinguistics (Gumperz and Hymes 1972), with some work in the social psychology of language use (for instance, Beattie 1983; Roger and Bull 1988), as well as with work in linguistics concerned with 'pragmatics' or 'discourse analysis' (see, for example, Levinson 1983, 2006; Stubbs 1983; Johnstone 2008). Of course, the extent and character of this overlap varies somewhat according to the version of CA adopted, as well as to assumptions about its relationship to ethnomethodology, and how that is conceived.[16]

16 For a more positive view of the connections and overlaps involved, see Schegloff 2005. It may be that what is required here, and what is happening, is a fundamental reconfiguration of the disciplines involved. The relationship between conversation analysis and linguistics seems to be especially close in the work of Heritage and his colleagues, and this has been a focus for criticism (Lynch and Macbeth 2016). It is perhaps necessary to say that all of the social sciences, and specialities within them, can make, at best, only contested claims to distinctive territories. What is at issue here is a matter of degree.

Studies of work

A considerable number of studies have been carried out under the auspices of ethnomethodology that are concerned with what would conventionally be regarded as work. There have also been investigations of other kinds of activity that would not normally be put under that heading but that involve work in the broader sense of the term frequently used in ethnomethodology: from this perspective, effectively, all action involves work (Garfinkel and Sacks 1970: 342; Button 2012; Lynch 2018). I will therefore include some of these other investigations under the heading of 'studies of work' here. Examples that focus on conventional forms of work would include those of natural scientists (Garfinkel et al. 1981; Lynch 1985; Sormani 2015), of controllers on the London underground (Heath and Luff 1992; Luff 1992), of optometrists (Webb et al. 2013a, 2013b), of an entrepreneur (Anderson et al. 1989), and of lawyers and quality assurance inspectors (Travers 1997, 1999, 2007). Also relevant is a body of work inspired by ethnomethodology in the field of Human Computer Interaction (HCI) (Button 1993; Heath and Luff 2000; Luff et al. 2000; Button et al. 2015).[17] Studies of what would *not* conventionally be included under the heading of work, but which are treated to much the same kind of analysis, include investigations of learning to play jazz piano (Sudnow 1978), of alchemy (Eglin 1986), and of learning kung fu (Girton 1986).[18] Some of these studies rely on detailed analysis of video recordings, while others employ self-study (Robillard 1999), or what might be called mundane ethnography (for instance, Zimmerman 1970a, 1970b; Bittner 1967a, 1967b; Anderson et al. 1989).[19] Equally importantly, some have been academic in orientation, while other work has been commissioned by commercial companies and has had a much more applied focus.

Despite the claims often made, for example by Garfinkel himself (1986: Introduction), it is hard to identify a coherent body of new knowledge cumulatively generated by these 'studies of work', analogous to that produced by CA. What knowledge has been produced often amounts to detailed descriptions of the activities concerned, and thereby of the knowledge and skills involved in them. Of course it could be argued that this constitutes a necessary complement to conventional sociological investigations, for example because, in Garfinkel's (1986: vii) words, the sociology of work 'without remedy or alternative' 'ignores' the 'massive domain of organisational phenomena' involved in each 'locally produced

---

17 See also the studies in Llewellyn and Hindmarsh 2010 and Rouncefield and Tolmie 2011.

18 There are further studies of diverse activities in Tolmie and Rouncefield 2013.

19 What I mean by this term is that, by comparison with much conventional ethnography, it displays resistance to the assumption that social scientists are able to provide a theoretical perspective that penetrates more deeply than the perspectives of participants.

order of work's things'. But Garfinkel does not explain why this supplement is required, or indeed exactly how it informs conventional sociological research. There may be respects in which such research relies upon false assumptions that lead it astray about the actual work with which its studies are concerned, but this does not imply the need for wholesale detailed description, only for selective attention to potential errors that are relevant to the analysis.[20] Garfinkel appears to assume that such description constitutes a necessary foundation if a *complete* account of the nature of human social life is to be provided. But it is left unclear what would count as a complete account, and why this foundation is essential. Alternatively, it sometimes seems to be suggested that the phenomenon of work as experienced by participants is entirely lost by the conventional sociology of work, and that the task of ethnomethodology is to capture it, so that what it produces is 'endogenously comprehensive' (Watson and Sharrock 1991: 13) rather than foundational (see, for instance, Randall and Sharrock 2011). This argument depends upon the theoretical presuppositions of ethnomethodology that I discuss in the next chapter.

In terms of general knowledge, many of these studies are designed to illustrate one or both of two theses. The first is that the various activities studied are not pursued by applying a pre-specified method or plan but rather involve ongoing, artful processes of judgement; that these are designed to cope with routine contingences which must be addressed, ongoingly, in the particular circumstances faced and with the resources available; and that they rely upon background knowledge and skills, often associated with the use of artefacts and technologies, that have been developed with, and/or are distributed across, various co-actants (see, for example, Suchman 1987). The second general thesis, effectively the obverse of the first, is that formal representations of any practice do not fully elucidate the practices themselves as they are displayed in the actual work of practitioners (Button and Sharrock 1995: 231). These are important points but, arguably, they do not require exemplification in every case, or need to be illustrated more than a few times. Nor are they uniquely generated by ethnomethodology: arguments that are analogous in some respects have been developed via more philosophical routes by Polanyi (1962; 1966) in the form of his notion of 'tacit knowing' and by those who have highlighted the implications of Aristotle's concept of phrónēsis for professional work (see, for instance, Dunne 1997; Hammersley 2018) or for life more generally (see MacIntyre's 1999: 92–3 discussion of practical reasoning).

So, whereas CA has developed a considerable body of general typological knowledge, applying to many forms of talk-in-interaction, these 'studies of work'

---

20 Some of what I have referred to as mundane ethnographies seem to verge on this approach, for instance, Anderson et al. 1989.

have been largely concerned with providing detailed descriptions of specific occupational activities and other forms of practice, albeit in ways that reinforce the general messages of ethnomethodology. Of course this work could still be justified in a manner similar to that of much conventional ethnography: as providing thick descriptions, and thereby understanding, of some of the multifarious settings and forms of activity that are to be found in societies; and perhaps also as illuminating, or correcting, some of the ways in which these are often misunderstood. But, even more than other kinds of ethnographic description, what these studies offer would probably be of very limited interest to most audiences. This arises from the fact that they specifically abjure the adoption of a theoretical angle that selects what is to be described, and formulates it in ways that relate to the sorts of personal troubles and public issues that most sociology addresses. While practitioners of the forms of work described may sometimes find the descriptions produced of interest, perhaps as offering reminders of what they had forgotten, or in drawing attention to what they were unaware of, much of the time this seems unlikely to be the case. Furthermore, non-practitioners are likely to find these detailed descriptions tedious and perhaps pointless. Commenting on a study of scientists, Atkinson (1988: 446) writes: 'The stance advocated by Garfinkel, Lynch, and Livingston [1981] is reminiscent of the French *nouveau roman* of authors such as Alain Robbe-Grillet: minute descriptive detail is assembled in a hyper-realist profusion, until the reader loses any sense of meaning. Livingston's [1986] mathematical reworking is likely to strike the sociological reader in precisely that way.' And in one place Garfinkel seems to acknowledge this: he writes that lay people would necessarily have no interest in, and no means of accessing, the findings of ethnomethodological studies, at least insofar as they remain within the natural attitude (Garfinkel 1967a: 7–9).

A partial exception to this judgement is provided by work in HCI, which was clearly found to be of value by system and software designers: because they needed to know how *other people* relate to the systems and machines which they produce. But, as Hughes (2001; see also Sharrock and Randall 2004) points out, what they found of value was the detailed ethnographic reportage itself, rather than the ethnomethodological character of the studies. This suggests that an ethnomethodological orientation facilitated the provision of descriptions that were found useful for the designers' purposes because these descriptions were not structured in terms of some sociological theory that was irrelevant to those purposes. However, while Hughes graces these accounts with the label 'ethnographic', it is open to question whether such descriptions (as opposed to their framing in ethnomethodological terms) could not have been produced by anyone who was able to observe carefully and record what is done by people involved in various tasks in relatively concrete terms, and who was capable of writing it up in a way that is intelligible to system and software designers. Indeed, this seems to follow directly from Lynch and Bogen's (1994) rejection of the distinction between analytic expertise and vernacular mastery of language. Furthermore, there has been non-ethnomethodological ethnographic work in the CSCW field that has also been found useful (see Blomberg and Karasti 2013).[21]

Overall, then, it appears that, as in the case of CA, here the value of ethnomethodology has been at most as a catalyst: while knowledge of practical value has sometimes been produced, it is not clear that ethnomethodology was even a necessary condition for this; and, for the most part, there has been no development of academic knowledge of the kind that CA has achieved. Furthermore, where such knowledge *has* been produced, this seems to have stemmed from links being made to key issues in social science in a way that is at odds with the radical re-specification of focus demanded by ethnomethodology.[22]

Conclusion

In this chapter I have been concerned with what I have called the disciplinary status of ethnomethodology, and especially its relationship to sociology. I argued that there has been, and remains, considerable ambiguity in the writings of ethnomethodologists about this issue. I identified four possibilities, each of which has been proposed or implied: that ethnomethodology is a radical reform movement within sociology; that it is designed to serve as a complement to ordinary kinds of social science; that it is intended to be a new discipline, with its own distinct field of inquiry; or that it is a hybrid whose task is to facilitate the work of practical activities.

In my discussion I sought to assess how far ethnomethodology can successfully fulfil each of these roles. As regards the first, I argued that it points to some important and difficult theoretical and methodological issues that sociology faces, and ones that have not been given sufficient attention. And, in a brief examination of the analogous case of phenomenology, I noted that Husserl came to view his work as offering a similarly fundamental critique not just of philosophy but also of psychology and the human sciences, though Schutz seems to have taken a rather more limited view of the role of phenomenology in this respect. Of course,

21 Button et al. (2015) insist that it was precisely the ethnomethodological character of this work that made it useful, and they dismiss other kinds of ethnographic investigation in the area as of little value, or even as 'harmful'; as well as insisting that what they offer could have been produced by anyone. However, they simply assert these claims, rather than providing detailed comparative analysis of what was found useful by designers and why, how it was produced, and what was not found useful or was even felt to be harmful, and why.

22 In discussing the relationship between ethnomethodology and conversation analysis, Sharrock and Anderson (1986: 61) appear to suggest that it is in the nature of the former to be a catalyst.

the question of how effective the ethnomethodological critique of conventional social science is remains open, and I will address that question in the next chapter and in the Conclusion.

In relation to the second option, I raised the question of why any alternate, or supplement, to conventional social science is required. This seems to rely on a foundationalist conception of science whereby conventional sociological explanations are incomplete because they do not include the practical reasoning that underpins such matters as the application of values and norms, or the operation of interests and causes. But Garfinkel does not provide any explicit justification for this foundationalism, and it does not seem convincing – unless we adopt the view that sociological accounts of social action must capture its *essential* nature, rather than answer specific questions about it. But this opens up a major question about the capacities and task of social inquiry, related to the conflict between neo-Kantian and phenomenological philosophies (see Chapter 2).

In order to address the third and fourth options it was necessary to try to determine whether ethnomethodological work is viable and justifiable, and I examined two major forms it has taken: conversation analysis and 'studies of work'. I argued that CA has been very successful in generating a cumulative body of knowledge about talk-in-interaction, and is clearly viable and worthwhile. However, it has been argued that, in precisely this achievement, it has departed from ethnomethodology, or at least from Garfinkel's later conception of it, since the latter rejects any prospect of such general knowledge (Wilson 2012). There are also questions about whether CA meets the second criterion I adopted: it is not clear that it occupies a distinct territory, since it overlaps significantly with linguistics, sociolinguistics, and semiotics.

In the case of studies of work, what has been produced is detailed knowledge about a wide variety of practices, in terms of exactly how they are performed. But it is not clear what *general* value this knowledge has, aside from reinforcing key ethnomethodological themes, and it does not seem to be cumulative. Furthermore, I argued that while the knowledge produced by some of these studies has been found to have practical value, for instance by software and system designers, this generally arises from the fact that the detailed descriptions it provides enable them to tailor their efforts more closely to how people use the machines or software they produce. And this value does not appear to have stemmed directly from the specifically ethnomethodological character of the investigations.

My conclusion, then, is a mixed one. There is no doubt that ethnomethodology has been of great value in drawing attention to important methodological issues, and in correcting mistaken but prevalent conceptions of the nature of social practices; and it continues to have value in these terms. Furthermore, at the very least it has been important in stimulating the production of new knowledge about talk-in-interaction. However, there is little evidence to suggest that it constitutes an essential complement to conventional forms of social science. In the case of CA it may represent a distinct and viable discipline in its own right, though there are questions about this. And what it offers to practical activities as an interdisciplinary hybrid may not differ sharply from what a reflective practitioner, or some lay observers, would be able to provide.

4 An assessment of the theoretical presuppositions of ethnomethodology

Ethnomethodologists often explicitly reject theory (see Lynch 1999; Button 1991: Intro; Sharrock and Coulter 2009; Hutchinson et al. 2008): they criticise the way that much social science aims at, or relies upon, theories; and insist that the proper task of social inquiry is, instead, to *describe* social practices. Of course, the term 'theory' carries several meanings.[1] One refers to a set of statements – universal, or at least quite general, in scope – that, along with information about specific situations, can be used to explain why something occurred in those situations, or what the consequences of some event or action in those situations are likely to be. Such theories relate to *types* of phenomena, and causal relations amongst them, identifying factors that, under certain conditions, tend to produce some type of outcome. Much social science has been aimed at discovering theories of this kind, and/or has used existing theoretical ideas to explain particular phenomena. At face value at least, ethnomethodology does not share either of these goals. The aim of its analysis is to describe how social phenomena are generated through processes of social interaction on particular occasions in particular locales, and perhaps also to identify trans-contextual methods that structure these processes. Like phenomenology, which as we have seen was an important early influence upon it, the aim is to describe how the world is constituted, not to document causal processes operating within it.

A very different meaning often given to the term 'theory' by social scientists, perhaps even more influential, refers to a framework of presuppositions within which research takes place.[2] Here theory is a starting point, rather than a product. Theoretical presuppositions relate to various aspects of the inquiry process: to its goal and why this is of value (what might be called axiology); to the nature of the phenomena being investigated (ontology); and/or to how these can best

---

1 For an outline of seven senses of the term, see Hammersley 2012. Lynch (1999: 212) offers a further one: 'constructing intellectual genealogies that commemorate notable authors and foundational writings'.

2 There is ambiguity in the meaning of the terms 'presupposition' and 'assumption', as to whether they imply conscious adoption. In my usage here I am not assuming this, as regards either term; and I will treat them as synonyms. It seems clear that many of our assumptions/ presuppositions are inherited, and for this and other reasons we may be unaware of them.

be understood (epistemology and/or methodology). And these assumptions may or may not form a systematic framework; some commentators reserve the term 'theory' for explicit *systems* of presuppositions.

Ethnomethodologists also often deny that their work rests on theory in this second sense. This is one of the key parallels with phenomenology. Husserl insisted that phenomenology employs a presuppositionless starting point: examining phenomena as they present themselves to consciousness, and seeking to describe these and their mode of presentation. However, I suggest that it is impossible for any form of inquiry (or for any other human activity) to avoid incurring *some* presuppositions. Moran and Cohen (2012: 261) write, without comment, that 'Husserl speaks of "presuppositionlessness" … as a central presupposition of the phenomenological approach.' As already noted, the aim of ethnomethodological work is to examine human social interaction with a view to describing how social phenomena are constituted, in and through it, as the types of phenomena they are. While this clearly involves suspending many assumptions that are commonly employed by other social scientists, and by ordinary actors in the world, it nevertheless presupposes that social phenomena are constituted in this way, that it is possible to describe their constitution, and that the knowledge produced thereby is worthwhile. As will become clear, some of these assumptions are open to question.[3]

So in this chapter I will outline what seem to be ethnomethodology's key theoretical presuppositions, and assess their cogency. They can be listed as follows:

1. As Parsons (1937) argued, social order should be the central focus of sociological (and perhaps even of all social scientific) inquiry. Of course, as I noted in the previous chapter, ethnomethodology re-specifies this focus: where, for Parsons, the opposite of order was conflict and violence, for ethnomethodology it is uncertainty and confusion. So, for Garfinkel, 'social order' means the intelligibility

---

3 Lynch (2013) seems to suggest that ethnomethodological inquiry can be presuppositionless, at least in terms of ontology. However, McHoul (2009) has acknowledged that there are 'field propositions' underpinning ethnomethodology, a term deriving from Heidegger. See also Pollner 1991; Liberman 2013: Intro; Anderson and Sharrock 2018: ch. 11. And if we look at Garfinkel's (1952) PhD thesis we find that he explicitly sets up a contrast between the presuppositions underpinning Parsons' approach and the phenomenological ones that he takes to underlie that of Schutz, which he recommends. However, Garfinkel also sometimes presents ethnomethodology as consisting of 'study policies' (Psathas 1999), which would suggest that at least some of its assumptions are simply adopted for working (or 'methodological') purposes. But this would require spelling out the grounds on which one study policy has been adopted rather than another, with these grounds necessarily being taken to be more than working assumptions. A study policy is an instrument, and the selection of any instrument assumes a worthwhile goal. It also relies upon some presuppositions about why it will serve that end, and these necessarily relate to the nature of the phenomena involved and the particular circumstances in which they are encountered. See Hammersley 2019b.

of patterns of action *to the people engaged in them and other 'members'*. In these terms, even social conflict is generally orderly: the various actions involved are often all too clear and highly coordinated. Thus, Garfinkel (1948/2005: 114) describes riots as orderly.

2. Parsons' (1937: ch. XIX) 'analytical realism' is misconceived, with its emphasis on the need for a comprehensive and explicit theoretical framework if the production of social order is to be understood. So too are similar commitments on the part of other sociologists. Garfinkel insisted that order is observable routinely in everyday situations, and that how it is constituted can be discovered once the natural attitude (and especially the theoretical attitude of social science) is suspended, and processes of social interaction are examined carefully.

3. The meanings of social actions are locally variable and context-dependent, rather than being determinable by means of some semantic code; in other words, they are 'indexical' and 'reflexive'. And actions are intelligible because they are self-identifying: their meaning is displayed and recognised by actors via shared methods or practices, in the course of ongoing processes of social interaction – what Garfinkel refers to as 'accountability'.

4. In order for inquiry to be rigorous it must *not* rely upon unexplicated resources, only on what is observable or intersubjectively available. In this sense Garfinkel's orientation is a radical empiricism or behaviourism, albeit very different in character from other forms (Lynch 1999: 226–7; Garfinkel 1948/2005: 140; Rawls 2006: 59–62), as well as from Husserl's phenomenology.

5. The aim of rigorous social analysis must be literal description, not explanation or explanatory theory: the task should be to 'make visible' members' methods for the production of social phenomena, or the processes through which this production occurs.

The first assumption is axiological, the third is ontological, while the others are, broadly speaking, epistemological in character.

The bold and radical character of Garfinkel's programme should be clear from these presuppositions. At the very least, they put in question the intellectual status of all the social sciences. I will assess each of them in turn.

A refocusing of sociological inquiry

For Parsons, in *The Structure of Social Action*, the central focus of sociology is how social order is achieved and maintained; its absence amounting to a Hobbesian war of all against all.[4] Contrary to Hobbes, he argues that, to a large extent, social

---

4 This problem had been all too evident in Western societies during Parsons' early life: see Gerhardt 2011.

order is generated and maintained by processes of socialisation into common values and norms. However, he recognises a problem of 'double contingency': that parties to any encounter know that they could act differently, that others could act differently, and that others know that *they* could act differently. This makes it difficult (on the face of it, perhaps impossible) for ego to anticipate what alter will do, in response to any action that ego might take (Parsons and Shils 1951: 16; see also Vanderstraeten 2002). At the same time Parsons seems to have assumed that this problem is solved through members of a society becoming socialised into the same symbol system, just as the motivational problem of social order is largely resolved by socialisation into the values and norms of a society.

Following Schutz (see Grathoff 1978), Garfinkel argued that Parsons had treated values and norms as if they were self-applying. In other words, he assumed that, so long as actors had been properly socialised, they would generally behave in the manner required, thereby preserving order; and that any tendency towards deviance would be largely dissuaded by the threat or use of sanctions. Garfinkel famously remarked that this amounted to treating people as 'cultural dopes' (Garfinkel 1967a: 66–75). What he found in working on the recordings of jury sessions was that jurors were, and had to be, 'artful' in how they assessed information about cases, and made sense of legal and other rules, in coming to their judgements. One aspect of this was reliance upon a considerable body of background, common-sense knowledge about the sorts of situation involved in the cases. And this was in line with Schutz's analysis of the essential features of intersubjectivity.

So, Garfinkel denies that socialisation into a shared symbol system can guarantee mutual understanding and the coordination of action; indeed, socialisation *presupposes* such understanding and coordination. In effect, Parsons assumes that people will simply recognise the nature of the situations with which they are faced, the identities of the others involved in them, what their actions mean, and therefore what must be done in order for a new action to articulate with a previous one. Again following Schutz, Garfinkel argues that this is to leave unexplicated the practical reasoning through which this ordering is achieved, and which underpins the explanations and theories developed by social scientists.[5] Moreover, in his early writings he treats Schutz's work as offering a radical alternative to Parsons' social theory and to social science generally. Schutz (1945) identifies various 'finite provinces of meaning' that effectively represent 'multiple realities', and Garfinkel asks what the conditions are for the existence and operation of one of these – the intersubjective world of practical action – since it is this which provides for the coordination of action and thereby the establishment and maintenance

5 Some ethnomethodologists have applied the label 'praxeology' to the study of such practical reasoning. The source of this is unclear. It may have been von Mises (see Chapter 1), Kotarbinski (Anderson et al. 1985a: 235), or Cieszkowski (Coulter 1989: 7).

of social order. And, initially at least, he uses Schutz's work as a means of identifying these conditions, and the processes through which the everyday world is constituted, whose existence and character is largely taken for granted by participants and social scientists alike.

In assessing this argument about what the focus of social inquiry should be, it is worth pointing out that while social order, in the Parsonian or in the Garfinkelian sense, may be a legitimate topic of investigation, in historical terms neither has been the main focus for sociologists most of the time. Instead, their predominant interest has been, at most, in threats to *particular forms* of social order. In the nineteenth century, the aim was, mainly, to explain the processes of social development that had produced modernity, the character of emerging modes of social organisation in the West, and their effects. So, sociologists have not usually been concerned with explaining social order/social organisation *per se* but rather with explaining why particular kinds of social organisation occur in particular settings, why they produce particular sorts of outcome, etc. This was certainly true of the work of Comte, Marx, Spencer, Durkheim, and Tönnies; and in many respects that of Simmel and Weber as well. Moreover, part of their focus was the variety of social problems that emerged in large, urbanised modern societies. And social problems, or public issues more generally, by no means *always* linked closely to the question of social order, became the prevailing focus of sociological inquiry during the twentieth century in the United States, and elsewhere. Moreover, this has continued in the twenty-first century. At one time some of these problems were conceived as signs of 'social disorganisation' (Carey 1975), thereby being linked directly to the issue of social order, but that view has been repeatedly challenged. Moreover, from early on there has also been sociological work of other kinds, for instance aimed at developing and testing 'middle-range' theories (Merton 1956) about particular types of social process, many of which are not directly related to social problems and/or to the issue of social order.

Indeed, the general problem of how social order emerges, or is established and maintained, has not only remained in the background for many sociologists – sometimes its importance has been challenged. Thus, there was explicit opposition to Parsons' approach in the mid-twentieth century, with critics insisting, for example, that conflict rather than order is the characteristic feature of modern societies, and that Parsons' theoretical framework is incapable of explaining social change, given that conflict is its motor (see Zollschan and Hirsch 1964; Demerath and Peterson 1967). It was also claimed, drawing on the work of Simmel, that conflict can be functional (see Coser 1956). At the same time, others argued, apparently along similar lines to Garfinkel, that Parsonian theory portrayed people as passive carriers of social system forces, and that instead we must recognise the active role they play in shaping the social world in which they live, this often being presented as an explicit rejection of 'sociologies of order' (see, for instance, Dawe

1970). However, the assumptions underpinning the arguments of these critics were very different from those characteristic of ethnomethodology.

It should also be noted that the concept of social order is by no means a simple one. Parsons seems to employ at least two rather different versions of it. As already noted, he starts from Hobbes, where the opposite of order is conflictual and violent relations amongst community members. However, later he seems to move towards a rather different (albeit related) notion, to do with the structural integration of the institutional sectors of a society, in such a manner that the basic functions required for this society to persist are fulfilled. There is also some uncertainty about what Garfinkel means by the term 'order'. One meaning he relies upon is the sort of orderliness that is required if social phenomena are to be open to scientific investigation, and he rightly ascribes a concern with this to Parsons. Another is that of their intelligibility to participants; he treats the first as dependent upon the second. Moreover, he seems to conflate the intelligibility of actions with whether they are coordinated; and with the question of whether they are judged to make *good* sense, in other words whether they are rational – a term that is necessarily evaluative.

While it can hardly be denied that the core sense Parsons gave to the term 'social order' is an important social issue, at least as it arises in concrete contexts (for example, the problem of 'failed states', 'domestic violence', etc.), it is less clear whether this is true of Garfinkel's re-specification of the concept. As he himself points out, most of the time most of us simply find that the patterns of social interaction we observe make sense: intelligibility is not usually an issue, even if rationality sometimes is. Given this, it is not clear why the processes that make intelligibility possible need to be explicated, or why this should be treated as the task of sociology rather than of, say, psychology or linguistics. Alternatively, the influence on ethnomethodology of phenomenology and of Wittgenstein's work could be taken to suggest that this task belongs to the field of philosophy. As I argued in Chapter 1, despite the way it has often been interpreted, the work of Schutz, on which Garfinkel drew heavily, seems to have been intended as a contribution to philosophy, as much as to social science. And the implications of Wittgenstein's thought for social inquiry have been interpreted by some as demanding a taking back of territory by philosophy from social science (Hutchinson et al. 2008: 31). In what might seem like a counter-move, Lynch (1993: 299–308) has suggested that ethnomethodology amounts to empirical investigation of themes in epistemology that were previously addressed by philosophy, advocating what he refers to as 'primitive epistopics'. However, ethnomethodology is not a version of social science for either Hutchinson and his colleagues or Lynch. Furthermore, both draw a sharp distinction between the discipline of philosophy as it currently exists and Wittgenstein's philosophical work. From this point of view, the disciplinary status of ethnomethodology remains uncertain, and therefore so too does the rationale for its focus on the intelligibility of social action.

From analytical realism to ethnomethodology

In the early part of *The Structure of Social Action*, and again towards the end, Parsons (1937) laid out what he took to be the nature of scientific investigation. His stance of 'analytical realism' places emphasis on the need for any science to develop an explicit and systematic theoretical perspective which *formulates* the objects with which it is to deal, and his first book was concerned with developing such a framework for sociology, as he saw this emerging out of the writings of four social scientists (Marshall, Pareto, Durkheim, and Weber). Most of his subsequent work was focused on refining and elaborating this theoretical framework, as well as locating sociology's task in relation to other disciplines.

Parsons' conception of science here was heavily based on the model of economics, as promoted by neoclassical economists, and on ideas about the nature of science found in the work of Whitehead and Henderson.[6] By contrast, as already noted, Garfinkel's approach was influenced by phenomenology, in particular its emphasis on careful observation of 'the things themselves' rather than reliance upon prior theoretical ideas. He argued that order, in the sense of intelligible patterns of social interaction, is ubiquitous. And how it is constituted is observable if we suspend many of the prior assumptions underpinning both conventional social science and the orientation of practical action – though this may need to be supplemented by various means of disrupting normal scenes. Indeed, he claims that the social world is constituted in and through an array of 'ordering practices' which are open to direct investigation.

Parsons was criticised for 'theoreticism' not just by ethnomethodologists but also by many other sociologists (a notorious example is Wright Mills 1959), and few sociologists followed him in operating at such a high level of abstraction (Luhmann is perhaps the main exception). Most of the US sociologists who came to be associated with 'structural functionalism' in the 1950s and 1960s developed, and applied, 'middle-range' theories, and often engaged directly in empirical investigation much more than did Parsons (for one example see Lipset et al. 1956). At the same time, their work was also significantly different in methodological orientation from that of Garfinkel.

So, there was a fundamental difference in attitude between Garfinkel and not only Parsons but also most of his fellow sociologists in the United States in the 1950s and 1960s, as well as most of the psychologists and organisational theorists with whom he came into contact. Where these others saw theory, in the sense of concepts generated within scientific disciplines, as essential for understanding social phenomena – serving the role of selecting and formulating phenomena

6 See Camic 1987. While this author downplays the influence of neo-Kantianism on Parsons, there are certainly parallels: see Hamilton 1983: 63–4. In a later retrospective discussion, Parsons (1978: 117) refers to 'the "neoKantian" point of view, which I take'.

for investigation out of the complex reality that is human social life – Garfinkel came to view such theory as an obstruction because it discourages analysts from attending to the ordering processes that are evident in processes of social interaction, *and that must be evident if these processes are to be intelligible to participants*. This is the basis for the fundamental switch in focus deployed by Garfinkel, away from the task of *explaining* social phenomena and on to that of *describing* them and the processes by which they are produced. Initially he appears to have seen his work as clarifying the basis for more conventional kinds of social scientific analysis, and thereby making it more effective, but subsequently he came to view ethnomethodology as a separate enterprise in its own right that could serve as some sort of complement, albeit one that inevitably raised doubts about the scientific status of conventional sociological findings.[7]

As I noted in Chapter 2, in some respects what we have here is a replay of the debates that took place within German philosophy and social science around the turn of the nineteenth into the twentieth century. Influential kinds of neo-Kantianism had tended to portray the sciences, and indeed rational understanding more generally, as necessarily *constituting*, rather than simply representing, the phenomena investigated. This derived from Kant's argument that in experience we only have access to appearances, not to 'things in themselves', and that these appearances are, to a considerable extent, the product of the categories that we necessarily use to make sense of the world. For example, that there are causal relations amongst physical phenomena is a constitutive assumption, on Kant's view, rather than something that has been discovered about the physical world. And while he had treated this process of constitution as necessarily working with what is simply *given* via the senses, many neo-Kantians downplayed the role of sense data, and rejected the idea that there are 'things in themselves' independent of our experience. Instead, they tended to assume that, if anything exists beyond appearances, it is an unstructured and infinite manifold.

Husserl's phenomenology was one of the most influential reactions against this neo-Kantian position. He argued that there had been an increasing tendency for natural science and philosophy to neglect the fact that their foundations necessarily lie in subjective experience. He did not deny that the phenomena we experience, and for the most part treat as unproblematic features of the world, are *constituted* in the process of understanding them, rather than being simple reflections of reality. However, he insisted that these processes do not consist of abstract ratiocination, exemplified in its purest form by scientific disciplines, but rather are pre-predicative and endogenous to our normal, everyday experiencing of the world. Moreover, like Kant, he argued that they are founded on what is given to the senses. But the most important point for my purposes here is that

7 There were parallels, of course, with some other approaches, notably symbolic interaction-ism and interpretive anthropology, but also significant differences.

he argued that these processes are open to direct investigation and representation in their own terms through phenomenological reflection, a possibility rejected by most neo-Kantians – since they denied that any understanding can involve unmediated representation of phenomena, even subjective ones.

Garfinkel adopts much the same position as Husserl here, albeit with an important twist.[8] Husserl began from analyses of his own experience, in the belief that these could reveal constitutive processes that are characteristic of all human (or rational) beings. While in his later work he came to see our experience of the world as *socially* constituted, developing the concept of the lifeworld (Husserl 1970; Moran 2012), the problem of intersubjectivity remained troublesome for him, precisely because he retained a commitment to grounding his analyses in individual experience. By contrast, albeit taking his cue from the phenomenological concept of the lifeworld, Garfinkel argued that meanings, rather than being anchored in individual experience, must be publicly displayed and accessible if people are to understand one another and to coordinate their actions; in other words, if there is to be intersubjectivity. However, he retained from phenomenology both the idea that meanings are constituted rather than being direct reflections of what is sensed in the world, and that these meanings, and the processes by which they are constituted, are *directly* available for investigation: that their understanding does not require the prior adoption of theoretical concepts in the way that much neo-Kantianism insists.

I suggest that there is a fundamental tension within phenomenology between the picture of our understanding of the world that it provides and the claims it makes about its own method. Moreover, the same is true of ethnomethodology. The problem can be formulated as follows: if it is true that even the perception of simple everyday objects – such as tables and chairs – is the product of complex processes of constitution, whereby they are recognised as stable objects (not fleeting appearances), actually existing objects (rather than mirages), objects of these particular types (rather than of some other kind), etc., how is it that the phenomenologist can identify and describe the processes of constitution involved in understanding the world in a manner that does not involve similar constitutive processes and the prior concepts that these entail?

---

8 In early work not published until much later, Garfinkel adopts what in my terms is a radical form of neo-Kantianism, whereby reality is not simply divided up in the process of understanding but is constituted as different realities by different forms of understanding. Some discussions by ethnomethodologists (see, for instance, Lynch 2013: 449, who cites Garfinkel 1960/1972) contrast this with neo-Kantianism, but this is misleading. The problem here stems from the diverse forms that neo-Kantianism took (see Beiser 2014) and the fact that Garfinkel treats Parsons' analytic realism as the defining form of neo-Kantianism. As I go on to argue, the position that Garfinkel adopted from phenomenology in his mature work is different from most neo-Kantianism, especially the radical form just mentioned.

Phenomenological method relies on the idea that we can have immediate access to our own subjectivity, and, of course, ethnomethodologists reject this. Nevertheless, ethnomethodology faces the same sort of problem. It portrays the accounts that both social scientists and lay people produce as constituted on particular occasions for particular purposes, and therefore as necessarily being 'glosses'. Yet, at the same time, the assumption is that ethnomethodological work can identify and describe the processes by which these phenomena are produced in a manner that *simply captures them as they are in their own terms*. In light of this, it could be argued that ethnomethodologists' appeals to the 'observable', 'inspectable' character of the meanings they study, and of the processes by which these are generated, obscure the fact that their own analyses *constitute* these phenomena. Indeed, this is precisely the criticism made early on by a group of 'Analysts', who broke away from eth-nomethodology (McHugh 1970; Blum and McHugh 1971: n. 1; McHugh et al. 1974; Raffel and Sandywell 2016). I will have more to say about this problem later, when I discuss the notion of literal description.

Action meanings as context-sensitive and locally variable, but also self-identifying

As I noted, one of Garfinkel's starting points was the problem of double contingency in Parsons' theory, and his insistence that the meanings of social actions are not simply given, even though that is how we experience them as everyday actors most of the time. His point becomes clear if we focus on the role of language in social interaction, where we find that the meanings of utterances often cannot be specified simply through appeal to a shared semantic dictionary and grammar; perhaps even if we include knowledge of grammar in the rather broader sense of the term used by Wittgenstein and Ryle. Rather, meanings are always contextually sensitive, and therefore can be locally variable – in the sense that the same set of words uttered in different situations will sometimes be taken to mean very different things. Similarly, if we look at how rules or norms operate: they do not *apply themselves*, their meaning has to be 'found' for particular situations; it, too, is context-dependent. This is what Garfinkel refers to as the '*indexical*' character of meanings.[9]

---

9 In linguistics and the philosophy of language, the term 'indexicality' had long been used to refer to the fact that there are certain words – I, me, here, there, etc. – that are sometimes referred to as deictic terms – whose specific meaning is dependent upon who is using them and/or on the context in which they are being used. There are two sources of this notion in an early article by Schutz with which Garfinkel was familiar: William James' discussion of the dynamic character of word meaning; and Husserl's notion of 'occasional expressions' (see Schutz 1943: 133, 140). However, as Heap (1975) points out, Garfinkel extended the meaning of 'indexicality' well beyond the way it is used in the main sources he cites: Farber (1943: 237–8) on Husserl (cited in Garfinkel 1948/2005: 151; 1967a: 4) and the influential

The implication of this argument is that situated or local 'work' is always involved in overcoming the problem of double contingency, in 'remedying' the intrinsically uncertain meaning of utterances and actions. This is precisely because there is no general way of doing this: how a rule is to be applied has to be 'determined' on each and every occasion, in the course of action. In other words, applying norms, or rules of any kind, depends on practical rather than scientific rationality (see Sharrock, 1977: 568–9, and *passim*).

More than this, sense-making is a *process* in which nothing is given or entirely fixed; for example, over time we make sense of an action in terms of its context *but also of this context in light of the action*. As Garfinkel (1967a: 78) puts it, elaborating on Mannheim (1952: 43–63): 'not only is the underlying pattern derived from its individual documentary evidences, but the individual documentary evidences are in their turn interpreted on the basis of "what we know" about the underlying pattern'. Each is used to elaborate the other. In short, a hermeneutic circle is involved (Watson 1997: 55). Garfinkel refers to this as '*reflexivity*', another key concept. However, he suggests that it is important to recognise not only that *work* is involved in making sense of others' actions, but also that actors design their actions in methodical ways so as to make the character of those actions evident. This is the '*accountability*' of action.

So, Garfinkel argued that the achievement of shared understanding and coordinated action is possible because people deploy common methods of practical sense-making, rather than through their immediately identifying objects in terms of a set of common substantive meanings that are simply given. Nevertheless, as a result of these methods, most of the time the character of people's actions is self-identifying for others. In short, then, Garfinkel's solution to the problem of double contingency was that, in the course of acting, people display the meaning of their actions in methodical ways, and they also 'read' the meanings of others' actions by reliance on the same set of methods, and display their readings in responses, these forming part of sequential processes of social interaction through which substantive meanings of actions become established. As a result, people not only make mutual sense of what is going on, most of the time, and can therefore coordinate their actions with one another, but when there are discrepant meanings they are often able to understand these and deal with the differences. Or it might be said that mutual understanding and coordination are generated through the process of social interaction, since Garfinkel sometimes

article by Bar-Hillel 1954 (cited in Garfinkel and Sacks 1970). (See also Abercrombie 1974; Phillips 1978.) This is certainly true, but my approach to the concept is very different from the phenomenological stance of Heap, who proposes what we might call a form of auto-ethnomethodology. A rather different approach, under the heading of 'third-person phenomenology', is offered by Anderson and Sharrock 2018. It should perhaps be noted that there is now a very considerable philosophical literature on indexicality: see Braun 2017.

seems radically to downgrade the agency of individual actors in favour of the constitutive power of situated practices or local orders (see, for example, Rawls 2002: 60). There is a strong, albeit partial, parallel with Durkheim in this respect.

There are several questions that need to be asked about these ontological assumptions, focusing on the three central concepts of ethnomethodology I have mentioned, and on the notion of methods as generating understanding.

Indexicality and reflexivity

While Garfinkel is not unique in pointing out that the meaning of utterances or actions is not simply the product of a set of abstract rules, indeed that any rules must always be applied in light of the particularities of situations, he adopts a very radical version of this view. Especially in his later work, he appears to treat meaning as entirely a product of occasioned processes of sense-making, effectively ruling out the role of pre-existing rules and other kinds of background knowledge. An early, and partial, version of this is spelt out quite clearly in an influential article 'The Everyday World as a Phenomenon' by two sociologists who were his students in the 1960s (Zimmerman and Pollner 1970).[10] They write: 'We underscore the occasioned character of the corpus in contrast to a corpus of member's knowledge, skill, and belief standing prior to and independent of any actual occasion in which such knowledge, skill, and belief is displayed or recognised' (Zimmerman and Pollner 1970: 94). And, later, they emphasise the point: 'for the purpose of analysis, a setting's features … are not independent of, and cannot be detached from, the situated work through and by which they are made notable and observable' (p. 96).[11] In effect, this seems to rule out completely the role of semantic and other kinds of rule, and even prior knowledge about particulars (such as the identities of the people involved): the implication appears to be that these have no existence apart from their invocation on particular occasions'.

---

10 For a discussion of this article concerned with many of the same issues, but approaching them from a slightly different angle, and coming to rather different conclusions, see Dennis 2003.

11 This is what I referred to in the Introduction as 'occasionalism'. Something very like this idea can also be found in some of Garfinkel's early writings: in a working paper developed for the Organizational Behavior Study, he wrote that 'I would prefer (though again only to take a stand on the problem) to regard information as something not recalled but re-created out of the resources of the available order of possibilities of experience, available sensory materials, actions, etc. Thus, preferred usage would be to talk of a communicant as knowledge-able rather than talking of his knowledge. What he knows he knows only in the moment of knowing and not otherwise' (Garfinkel 1952/2008: 158). In some later discussions, devoted to 'studies of work', the notion of an occasion is replaced by that of a 'work-site' that is 'local', in both spatial and temporal terms: see, for instance, Livingston 1986.

Implicit here is a dichotomy between two conceptions of how meaning is generated: by a semiotic system that produces meanings which are fully explicit and standardised across occasions; or by language-use that is indexical in the radical sense that meanings are constituted uniquely on each and every occasion, solely from the resources available within that occasion. The assumption appears to be that, in rightly rejecting the first option, the second must be adopted – the key point being that *work* is required in making sense, rather than meaning being generated simply through the automatic application of a rule. However, this is a false dichotomy; it involves the fallacy of the excluded middle, as I will go on to argue.

In some parts of *Studies in Ethnomethodology* Garfinkel recognises two kinds of context-transcendent resource that play a role in everyday understanding. The first is the *methods* of practical reasoning that he takes to be the central topic of investigation for ethnomethodology. The second is substantive common-sense knowledge, in the form of typifications about particular types of actor or situation. Wilson (2012: 217) has argued that in his early 'classical' phase, Garfinkel was not arguing

> that there are no such things as standard symbols and meanings or that these are irrelevant to understanding on concrete occasions. ... Though one cannot understand what is happening on a particular concrete occasion solely from a dictionary supplemented by a grammar book, it is by no means rare that one cannot understand what is meant without aid from a dictionary or, what amounts to the same thing, being told by someone what a particular phrase or gesture means.

Zimmerman and Pollner's (1970) influential article seems to mark a transition stage in the move away from this position. While they still acknowledge the role of context-transcendent *methods*, they appear to rule out the role of prior background knowledge. And Wilson (2012) points out that in his later work Garfinkel seems to reject the notion of invariant methods as well, this resulting in a very radical conception of indexicality indeed.[12]

The origins of this extreme position seem to lie in the argument that meaning is reflexive: that there is a hermeneutic circle integral to the documentary method of interpretation. In these terms, the meaning of particulars is assigned on the basis of some presumed whole to which they belong, and the meaning of the whole is determined by that of the particulars. So, the meaning of an act is determined by the situation in which it arises, and the meaning of the situation

---

12 Heritage (2016: 42–3) has argued that three phases can be identified in the development of Garfinkel's approach leading up to this position. Lynch sums up the implications of the final stage as follows: 'By calling a halt to the analytic movement from singular expressions to delocalized semiotic schemas, Garfinkel suspends a preliminary requirement of virtually every established program in the social sciences, including much of what rides under the banner of ethnomethodology' (Lynch 1993: 297).

is determined by the meaning of the act. However, it is important to insist that, while our understanding of both particulars and the wholes to which they relate undoubtedly shape one another, this does not necessarily imply a 'double-fitting' process that is entirely circular and arbitrary, in the sense of being unanchored by anything outside it (Krausser 1968; Føllesdal 1979).

As I noted, Garfinkel's notion of reflexivity seems to have been derived from Mannheim's discussion of the documentary method of interpretation (Mannheim 1952: ch. II; Wolff 1971: xvii–xxi). Yet while, at least to some degree, arbitrariness *does* seem to be a feature of the interpretations regarding *Weltanschauungen* with which Mannheim was concerned, it is necessary to remember that he derived the notion of the documentary method from Husserl's account of perception. And the latter denies that the complex processes by which our perception of, say, a table is constituted imply that it is a figment of our imagination, or only exists in and through our seeing it. There is a process of self-correction built into the perception of objects, grounded in sensual data. Furthermore, he insists on the role of invariant essences as necessary for us to recognise objects as what they are.

The second point I want to make about indexicality and reflexivity is closely related. What is primarily at issue in the problem of double contingency is not the theoretical question of whether there can be an ideal language – in other words one where meaning is fully explicit and standardised – but, rather, the practical matter of uncertainty or ambiguity of meaning. And this is also a matter of degree: in social life we are not faced *either* with complete clarity or with total bewilderment, but rather with varying degrees of uncertainty *about particular aspects of situations, courses of action, etc.* And indeed, most of the time, for most actors, making sense of what is going on is not problematic at all; even though there will be occasions when there is some puzzle about what is happening, and rare occasions when some feature of a situation appears unintelligible at first sight, and perhaps even subsequently.

There is a close link between the two points I have made here: the reason why the level of uncertainty or puzzlement varies is that our background knowledge sometimes fits closely with evidence from the situation, whereas at other times there are gaps or discrepancies. So, I suggest that the background knowledge we already have about the various roles people play in society, and the activities associated with them, as well as about the meaning of words, grammatical rules, etc., along with local knowledge about particular settings, play a key role in enabling us to understand what is happening in new situations, even though they cannot *guarantee* understanding. Furthermore, much of the time as practical actors, this background knowledge goes a long way in determining the sense of utterances on particular occasions. If this were not true, dictionaries would be useless. So, to repeat, what we have here is variable: a grunt is usually more uncertain in meaning, in the sense of being less interpretable by recourse to a semantic code, than use of the word 'I'; while non-deictic words that have specifiable ranges of meaning, provided in memories and in dictionaries, are even less dependent on context for their meaning (though what they mean is still not entirely determined by shared background knowledge).[13]

There is also a problem about the nature of the 'work' that ethnomethodologists claim is involved in producing the situated mutual sense that is achieved through processes of social interaction. At face value, we can say that much social interaction is routinised, rather than requiring a great deal of work to be done for meanings to be brought off.[14] It could be argued that this is a deceptive appearance: that much work nevertheless goes on subconsciously even in routine action – that this is necessary because of the radical indexicality of meanings. But, generally speaking, ethnomethodologists have been reluctant to engage in the ascription of such hidden cognitive processing. Instead, they have preferred to see social interaction as comprising self-organising practices that assign identities to participants, in terms of which they act, in the process displaying the appropriate intentions and motives, and thereby commitment to relevant norms and values (Garfinkel 1967a: 33–4; Sharrock and Anderson 1986: 67–9). Thus, Button et al. (2015: 98) report that 'Garfinkel ... described how actions are done so as to be accountable, that is they are done so as to be recognisable as what they are, and this recognis-ability resides in the organisation of the action *not* in the person performing that action'.[15] This is reflected in the way that the concept of 'member' is defined as possession of the methods that make up the competence required for 'collectivity membership' (Garfinkel 1967a: 57), or the ability to speak a natural language (Garfinkel and Sacks 1970: 342). Rawls (2006: 82–3) presents this as a revolutionary change, reversing the relationship between actor and action that is built into the

13 This is a point that seems to be recognised by Schegloff (1997: 174) when he describes the question 'What's he gonna do?' as '*thoroughly* indexical' (emphasis added), since it does not specify what course of action is being asked about. He contrasts this with 'What's he gonna do, take the first flight on Southwest, or take any airline he can get?', which he presumably takes to be 'less indexical', even though it still includes a deictic term: 'he'. There is a further issue that I cannot address here: the ethnomethodological emphasis on the context-dependency of meanings seems to conflate two rather different sources of situational variability: that coming from the orientation of whoever is engaged in making sense of a situation, and that arising from the way in which the different elements of a situation mutually define one another as being a situation of one type rather than another. See Hammersley 2019c.

14 See Coulter 1989: 65–7. This suggests that the problem of double contingency is, to a large extent, a pseudo-problem. Parsons is surely right that there is normally enough shared background, in terms of knowledge and commitments, for actions to be sufficiently intelligible for at least some coordination of actions to take place, with relatively little work required. What is more problematic is whether others will conform to normative expectations; which is, of course, his main focus.

15 One of the main models for this seems to be Gurwitsch's (1974) concept of gestalt contextures, derived from gestalt psychology as well as from the work of Husserl: see Embree 1972; Wieder 1974; Maynard 1996.

'action frame of reference' of Parsons, as well as the model of the actor built into economics and rational choice theory, or even that typical of symbolic interactionism. However, if the claim is that it is practices, 'local orders', or 'situated action systems' (Rawls 2006: 86) that do the work required to reduce uncertainty, there are challenging questions that must be addressed about the nature of the agency involved here, and how we can detect the work in which it engages. Or, indeed, whether there can be any 'we' to do this that is not itself the product of a self-organising local order.[16]

The accountability of action

The notion of accountability identifies something important about human actions: that much of the time we are aware of what sense others are likely to give to our actions – including those actions we *could* take – as well as the fact that we sometimes specifically design actions in such a way as to clarify what is intended, and/or why it is being done.[17] This was, of course, a central point made by Goffman in *The Presentation of Self in Everyday Life* (1956b); and, as he makes clear, it goes beyond an actor seeking to manipulate others' interpretations in order to serve her or his own interests – we also sometimes communicate what we are doing so as to avoid misunderstanding and/or to pre-empt insult or injury to others. But Garfinkel's claim is more fundamental than this: it is that the design of actions so as to make them identifiable is a feature of *all* social interaction; and that, given indexicality and reflexivity, social phenomena only come to be what they are through the processes in which these displays are ratified, challenged, etc., in the course of subsequent social interaction.

However, this seems to get things the wrong way round. To repeat a point from the previous section: the intelligibility of actions surely stems, in large part, from the fact that we know what sorts of goal people may be pursuing, especially given that in most situations we already know something about who they are and what role they are playing, and we know what kind of specific actions may be necessary to pursue various goals, as well as what goals particular types of action are typically aimed at. Similarly, we know that specific forms of action are common in particular sorts of situation, and we have knowledge of a range of

16 In some of his early writings Garfinkel suggests that the notion of an individual mind is as problematic, from the point of view of rigorous analysis, as the notion of a group mind: see Garfinkel 1948/2005: 195–6. It is not clear whether there is a third option between these two, though there have been attempts to produce this on the basis of systems theory; see, for instance, Buckley 1967.

17 On the different senses that can be given to the word 'accountability' and 'account', and an indication of some of the voluminous literature, see Robinson 2016.

standard types of situation and roles associated with them. This knowledge takes the form of what Schutz referred to as 'typifications', and he made clear the central role that these play in social life.[18] What people appear to be doing, much of the time, is what we would expect them to do in the circumstances, and what we do in response is frequently a matter of habit; even though it may involve some adaptation to circumstances (see Dewey 1922: Part 1).

In other words, generally speaking, other people's behaviour can be fitted into an expected pattern, and we assume that this pattern holds *until further notice* – only if something untoward occurs will we reassess the situation. Similarly, a great deal of our own behaviour follows established, institutionalised routines, and relates to goals that we have as persons or as performers of particular roles; and, generally speaking, we assume that others will recognise what we are doing and why, and will align their actions with it, in one way or another. As I have suggested, not much *active* 'work' is usually involved, even though we are not simply 'dopes': we keep track of what is happening and may adapt or change our behaviour accordingly, but for the most part even this will be done within the established frame by which our and (we assume) others' behaviour is guided (Goffman 1974).

So, we expect, rightly, that much of the time others will recognise what we are doing without our needing specifically to design actions to communicate this. Indeed, it is striking that this capacity is by no means entirely dependent upon our having a shared language: visiting a society where people use a language which we do not know, much of the time we will not be *completely* baffled by what they do – because their actions reflect the usual needs, preoccupations, and activities of human beings – even though there will, of course, be aspects of what is happening that we do not understand, and to which we do not know how to respond. So, it is only on some occasions that people specifically attend to the design of actions so as to try to ensure that there is no misunderstanding; and, as Goffman (1969) pointed out in his discussion of strategic interaction, sometimes the aim is precisely to create or sustain misunderstanding. So, in these respects, Garfinkel's concept of accountability seems to mis-describe the nature

18 Sacks (1974) provides a specific elaboration of these in his discussion of membership categorisation devices and category-bound activities. His discussion highlights that there are resources that people carry with them to situations, rather than these being constituted anew on each occasion. Indeed, he explicitly appeals to the reader's knowledge of some of the rules he is discussing (p. 229). Hester and Eglin (1997: 13–22) argue that Sacks was ambiguous on this issue and seek to formulate MCDs as occasioned phenomena, but it is hard to see how this would be viable: they claim that the fact that such devices 'are made and found relevant by members across a variety of social occasions speaks only to their relevance to members, not to any cultural pre-programming' (p. 19). The circularity, and appeal to an extreme contrast, here signals that the problem is unresolved, I suggest.

of social action. In effect, what is involved here is the reduction of all action to communication.[19]

The problem of 'ethnomethods'

The final issue I want to examine, in this section relating to ontological assumptions, concerns the status of the 'methods' that ethnomethodology claims to identify. Actually, some ambivalence seems to have arisen towards these on Garfinkel's part, as noted earlier. This may be reflected in the fact that various phrases are used as apparent synonyms: 'constitutive rules' (Garfinkel 1963), 'interpretive rules' (Garfinkel 1967a: 273), 'members' procedures' (Garfinkel 1967a: 1). In his early work he assumed that social phenomena, while being uniquely constituted on particular occasions, are generated by *methods* that are trans-contextual or 'invariant' in character. While, in some respects, these methods parallel the *essences* that, according to Husserl, enable the identification within our experience of phenomena as phenomena of particular types, for Garfinkel they played the double role of allowing people to make sense of social phenomena as what they are *and* at the same time enabling them to display their own understandings and intentions through their actions, thereby collectively generating orderly, institutionalised patterns of behaviour.[20]

Zimmerman and Pollner (1970: 95) provide an excellent summary of this subtle position. They write that

> Accordingly, from the point of view of the analyst, the features of the setting as they are known and attended to by members are unique to the particular setting in which they are made observable. Any feature of a setting – its perceived regularity, purposiveness, typicality – is conceived as the accomplishment of the work done in and on the occasion of that feature's recognition. *The practices through which a feature is displayed and detected, however, are assumed to display invariant properties across settings whose substantive features they make observable. It is to the discovery of these practices and their invariant properties that inquiry is to be addressed.* (emphasis added)[21]

19 Interestingly, the difference between a concern with pursuing goals and displaying what one is doing is highlighted by a common criticism of modern bureaucratic forms of account- ability, in the non-ethnomethodological sense of that term. Critics argue that people subject to modern accountability regimes become more concerned with meeting the accounting criteria than with doing their jobs. Garfinkel's conception of accountability seems to obliterate any such distinction.

20 For a discussion of 'sense-making practices' and other members of this 'family' of concepts, specifically in the context of Cicourel's work, but with more general implications, see Heap 1976.

21 One source of this concern with invariant features may be Kaufmann's (1944: 8–9 and *passim*) discussion of the nature of science, where he refers to the idea of invariants. Gurwitsch (1964) was also concerned with identifying invariant features within perception.

And we can find a similar claim on the part of Sacks et al. (1974: 699), who refer to the turn-taking organisation they identify as 'context-free but capable of extraordinary context-sensitivity' (emphasis added).

However, there have long been serious questions raised about the character of these methods (see, for instance, Heap, 1980; Atkinson 1988: 454). Furthermore, there is a difference between the sort of methods to which Garfinkel refers and what Sacks and some other early ethnomethodologists apparently had in mind. This emerged in discussions at the Purdue Symposium. In his own presentation Garfinkel identifies 'etcetera', 'unless', 'let it pass', 'wait and see', 'pretense of agreement', 'sanctioned vagueness', and 'monster-barring' (see Hill and Crittenden 1968: 225) as some of the practical devices, or *ad hoc* strategies, whereby people deal with difficulties in making sense of rules and situations. By contrast, Sacks and Sudnow make explicit their concern with identifying what we might call micro-rules that order people's behaviour, for example in how they identify others in talk, or in how they negotiate going through doors one after another. Here what is involved is a 'machinery' or an 'apparatus'. Sacks (1984: 26) writes: 'Thus it is not any particular conversation, as an object, that we are primarily interested in. Our aim is to get into a position to transform … our sense of "what happened," from a matter of a particular interaction done by particular people, to a matter of interactions as products of a machinery' (see also Sacks 1992b: 169). And, at the Purdue Symposium, Sudnow declared that the aim is to try to build an apparatus that will 'reproduce a particular piece of behavior' (Hill and Crittenden 1968: 68). As this makes clear, the aim is a formal analysis of the kind that was pursued in much subsequent conversation analysis. Sudnow (Hill and Crittenden 1968: 51) describes 'the programmatic task of ethnomethodology' as 'to take whatever the member does and deal with it in describably formal ways'.[22] These two conceptions of the nature of ethnomethods are strikingly at odds with one another, I suggest.

Another important issue concerns the epistemic status of the methods that enable sense to be made of actions and situations. Writing about conversation analysis, Coulter (1983b) claims that at least some of them, such as rules about the sequencing of 'adjacency pairs', are synthetic *a priori* in character. He notes that no amount of evidence of unanswered questions could reasonably persuade us that answers do not follow questions, or that they are tied instead to some other kind of speech act. Rather than treating cases that do not display this structure as counter-evidence, we treat them either as snubs or as the product of incompetence or misunderstanding on the part of participants.

22 What this entailed is illustrated by Sacks 1972a. One source of this conception of method may be Chomsky's generative grammar; see Schegloff 1992b: xxxvi; Zimmerman 1978: 9. For a brief characterisation of this difference between Garfinkel and Sacks, in the context of an argument challenging some claims about how their orientations diverged, see Lynch 2017: 11. See also Phillips' (1978) instructive discussion of different meanings of 'practice' and 'method' in the work of Garfinkel.

However, as I noted earlier, the existence of *a priori* synthetic truths has been a controversial matter ever since Kant formulated the distinctions between *a priori* and *a posteriori*, and between analytic and synthetic, knowledge.[23] Furthermore, Coulter's position has some important implications for the practice of conversation analysis. As he makes clear, it runs against the notion of proof employed by Sacks, Schegloff, and Jefferson (1974), which implicitly treats sequential structures in conversation as *a posteriori* in epistemological terms, appealing to the evidence of participants' understandings displayed in the data and/or to the capacity of an analysis to explain all of the data (Schegloff, 1968).[24] Indeed, in a later article, Schegloff specifically contrasts CA with approaches that rely on *a priori* knowledge (Schegloff, 1997). At the very least, Coulter's argument implies that close analysis of empirical materials may not be *essential* in order to discover sequential structures. More significantly, it follows from this that these sequential structures are normative in character. As a result, insofar as it is primarily concerned with these *a priori* sequential structures, CA (and therefore ethnomethodology) is not an empirical science. It is perhaps closer in character to a form of philosophy.

As I noted earlier, Wilson (2003, 2012) has argued that in his later work Garfinkel abandoned the idea that *anything* can transcend particular occasions, even methods. Indeed, this is one of the reasons for the split that took place between ethnomethodology and much conversation analysis (see Lynch 1993, 2000c, 2016a, 2016b; Lynch and Bogen 1994; Bogen 1999; Watson 2008). Part of the motivation for this shift may have been that the idea of context-transcendence raises the problem ethnomethodologists had already identified with cultural rules and norms: even methods cannot be self-applying, and therefore we cannot provide standard, literal descriptions of them in action.[25]

The effect of abandoning the notion of context-transcendent methods is the adoption of an even more radical form of ontological occasionalism than that presented by Zimmerman and Pollner (1970), whereby it is assumed that *nothing* exists independently of being continually constituted on particular occasions, so that there is no recognisable stability in character across those occasions (other than a sense of enduring stability that may, or may not, be constituted on any particular one). Thus Moerman (1992: 21) quotes Pollner (1979: 249) to the effect that 'We see, hear, and understand [social] phenomena to be "continuously created and recreated through … situated praxis"'. Along the same lines, Liberman (2008: 252) writes that 'Parties may collaborate in making a phenomenon evident to each other, but there is no phenomenon that abides with a status that is independent of those collaborative practices.' Moreover, as I

23 For a useful discussion of these distinctions, see Bennett 1966.
24 For a discussion of the 'next turn proof', see Clayman and Gill (2012).
25 Clayman and Maynard's (1995: 17) response to this criticism is to suggest that 'the locus of order is the situated work of the interactants themselves', but the result of this is that it is unclear what role the concept of 'methods' now plays.

noted, ethnomethodologists sometimes argue that it is the practices, not people, that are the agent here; indeed, the implication may even be that people have no existence independently of the practices in which they engage (Rawls 2002: 55). What seems to be implied by this is that the lifeworld is a collective subject or system that constitutes itself continually on particular occasions through the participation of its members, where the character of membership is itself part of what is ongoingly, and differentially, constituted; a very distinctive ontology.[26]

As ethnomethodologists often explicitly recognise, their accounts are sharply at odds with how the world is experienced in the natural attitude, what Pollner (1987) refers to as the world of 'mundane reason'. In terms of that attitude we tend to assume that most objects exist independently of our perceptions and actions, and that many of them operate independently of most other people's perceptions and actions as well – that they are simply there in the world. Furthermore, we are concerned with why they have the features they do, why particular events relating to them occur, and what their consequences are. We also treat ourselves and others as having intentions, goals, motives, beliefs, feelings, etc., and assume that ascriptions of these can be true or false. We are concerned with whether we or others are pursuing goals effectively, and what the consequences of actions have been and will be, and so on. It is necessary to ask: what are the grounds for adopting an ontology that is at odds with this common-sense viewpoint? Furthermore, why should we adopt *ethnomethodology*'s radical alternative rather than, say, that of one or another version of absolute idealism, historical or neurobiological materialism, Whitehead's metaphysics, actor network theory (Latour 2005), or, say, Harman's post-Heideggerian object-centred philosophy (Harman 2009; Latour et al. 2011)?[27]

Furthermore, if context-transcendent methods do not exist, the accounts ethnomethodology generates can themselves only be glosses on how sense was made on particular occasions – in other words, they have the same epistemic status as ethnomethodology assigns to conventional sociological accounts, and to the accounts that lay people provide in the course of everyday life. The critical edge of ethnomethodology in relation to mainstream social science seems to have been lost here. And, as a result, it is unclear what grounds there could be for our adopting its radical perspective.

26 This emerges particularly clearly from some expositions of ethnomethodology. See, for example, Hester and Francis 2001: Intro.

27 There has been little discussion by ethnomethodologists as to why the assumptions built into such alternatives are less convincing than those of ethnomethodology, with the exception of positions labelled as 'cognitivist'. Lynch (2000b) is relatively unusual in mentioning alternatives such as actor network theory, but he simply dismisses them as 'diseases of the intellect', appealing to the authority of Wittgenstein and Winch. My point is that if assumptions are adopted in social research that are radically discrepant with those of the natural attitude, there is a responsibility to provide a sustained justification for them.

This leads me, finally, to the question of what the *product* of ethnomethodological work is intended to be. If the goal is not the production of knowledge of the universal, though context-sensitive, methods through which social life, or at least orderly social interaction, is constituted (with examples used solely for evidence and illustration), then the intended product can only be explications or elucidations of particular events or activities (Sharrock and Anderson 1986: 82–3). But this raises a question about the *point* of this form of analysis. Why would such explications be of interest and value to audiences? In discussing the purpose of conversation analysis, Schegloff (1997; see also Moerman 1988: ch. 1) draws a parallel with literary criticism, but the reason why readers are interested in literary criticism is because it deals with works of literature that are taken to illuminate life or to have intrinsic aesthetic value. It is far from clear that the same is true of the mundane patterns of action that are the focus of ethnomethodological enquiry. Rather, for the most part, any interest in these usually lies in the extent to which they represent general patterns of action and the reasons why these occur.[28]

Literal description versus reliance upon unexplicated resources

On the basis of the ontological arguments I discussed in the previous section, ethnomethodologists often conclude that conventional social science not only does not rigorously analyse social phenomena but cannot do so. These arguments also underpin the alternative approach that ethnomethodologists recommend, which they claim *can* meet the demands of rigour (Sharrock and Anderson 1986). But there are clearly epistemological assumptions being made here about the nature of rigorous inquiry. There appear to be two of these, though they are closely related: that it must *not* rely upon unexplicated resources; and that it must produce literal descriptions.[29]

Ethnomethodologists have argued that conventional social science is defective – in other words, its claim to scientific status fails – because it trades on common-sense knowledge without explicating it; it confounds topic and resource. Thus, Zimmerman and Pollner (1970: 81) write that 'sociological inquiry is addressed to phenomena recognized and described in common-sense ways (by reliance on the properties of natural language), while at the same time such common-sense recognitions and descriptions are pressed into service as fundamentally unquestioned resources for analysing the phenomena thus made available for study'. As a result, and specifically because of the indexical and reflexive character of common-sense knowledge, such inquiry is incapable of producing literal descriptions: it can only

---

28 I have discussed the value of the products of ethnomethodological work in Chapter 3.

29 These two features are central, for instance, to Sacks' (1963) critique of social science, and to that of Cicourel (1964: ch. 1 and *passim*).

provide glosses. Furthermore, the meanings of these accounts are themselves necessarily indexical and reflexively determined – they have the same character as the accounts that ordinary actors provide.

Both of these assumptions are open to cogent challenge. Why must rigorous inquiry avoid *all* reliance upon unexplicated resources? Indeed, could this ever be achieved? Cartesian rationalism was concerned with finding grounds for inference whose validity is simply evident, thereby avoiding reliance on any presuppositions; and this also appears to have been the goal of Husserl's phenomenology. However, much epistemological discussion has shown that no such starting point is available: epistemological foundationalism of this kind, like that which treats sense data as premises for logically deriving scientific conclusions, has been rejected.[30] Furthermore, it has been argued that, instead of seeking apodictic certainty based upon inference from a presuppositionless starting point, in practice successful natural scientific inquiry adopts the more modestly sceptical strategy of trying to avoid reliance on assumptions that are open to reasonable doubt.[31]

But perhaps the argument here is more specific in character: that social science cannot be rigorous if it relies as a resource upon what it is investigating as a topic? Yet, in fact, most social scientists are not concerned with investigating how people find social actions intelligible, or with how (wittingly or unwittingly) they design their actions to be so – ethnomethodologists have criticised them precisely for their failure to attend to these matters. Given this, conventional social scientists do not conflate topic and resource in this specific sense: they rely upon common-sense understandings and practices, and not usually in an entirely uncritical fashion, *in order to investigate other topics*. It is ethnomethodology that takes this topic as its focus, and so in these terms the problem is its own: it can claim rigour only if it can itself avoid reliance on common-sense knowledge and practices. Later I will suggest that it cannot do this, but I will put that issue on one side for the moment and turn to ethnomethodology's second epistemological assumption: the idea that rigorous inquiry requires literal description.

Ethnomethodologists criticise conventional social scientists for failing to live up to the demand for literal description that is built into the model of science to which, it is claimed, they adhere (see Wilson 1970b; Heap 1980; see also Sacks 1963). Such description requires stabilising the meaning of terms through specifying the necessary and sufficient conditions of their application (Wilson 1970a; Wieder 1974: 217). Yet, while it is true that some social scientists in the 1950s and 1960s were committed to such a model, it is far from clear that most are today. Moreover, in effect, ethnomethodologists themselves take over a similar

30 For very different accounts that both take this line see Williams 2001; Haack 2009.
31 This is, for example, a central theme of pragmatist philosophy, and especially of the writings of Peirce, who was also a working scientist for much of his career. It is also characteristic of much modern philosophy of science; see, for instance, Haack 2007.

ideal for their own work: as already noted, it is precisely on the grounds that they can *display* the constitution of social meanings that they claim their mode of inquiry is more rigorous than conventional social science. Commitment to this revised conception of literal description is evidenced by claims that ethnomethodological analysis 'makes observable' or 'inspectable' the constitutive practices that generate social phenomena. For example, Lynch (2000c: 525) insists that analysis is 'a matter of exhibiting and explicating the procedures that composed a vast array of recognisable discursive objects'. Similarly, Button et al. (2015: 36) write that the task is 'to make visible how the orderliness of a setting is achieved *by those who are party to it*'. In line with some other ethnomethodologists, and following Garfinkel (1967a: 78), these authors contrast such literal description of practices with the 'documentary method of interpretation', whereby indicators are used to try to establish the existence of underlying theoretically defined entities (latent functions, social contradictions, etc.) that social scientists claim are in operation (Button et al. 2015: 78–80).[32]

At face value, the notion of 'making visible' implies that what is required is not really a description at all but involves 'showing', and there are understandable reasons for giving this impression. After all, *any* description, even of common-sense practices, surely depends upon processes of making sense that are analogous to the documentary method. It would also necessarily rely upon the use of natural language; and in doing so deploy indexical expressions, in Garfinkel's sense of that term. In short, all descriptions are 'glosses'. In this context, the contrast between literal description and the documentary method of interpretation collapses, since the former is an unrealisable ideal.

There is a deeper problem as well. Button et al. (2015: 80) write that 'The achievement of "constructive analysis" is to make out that what essentially only exists in theory is a real feature of the world.' However, if members also use the documentary method, the implication is that they too are continually 'constructing' a fictional 'reality'.[33] Along similar lines, Zimmerman and Pollner declare that social scientists, but also everyday actors, rely on 'an implicit and fundamental *faith* that the referents of investigation are possessed of a determinate structure, which may be exposed by the judicious selection and use of a method' (p. 82; emphasis added). Against this, it is important to emphasise that use of the documentary method does not amount simply to a matter of faith: as noted earlier, it can be applied in ways that provide evidence to check and modify the understanding

---

32 Sharrock and Anderson (1982: 121) appear to deny any commitment of ethnomethodology to the goal of literal description: they describe the term as 'opaque', and they are certainly right that it is problematic. However, it is hard to see what else the commitment to rendering practices visible or inspectable could mean.

33 This is what Mehan and Wood (1975: ch. 8) referred to as 'the reflexivity of reflexivity'.

that is being developed. In other words, it need not involve vicious circularity, even though it cannot produce literal descriptions, in the sense of descriptions that simply re-present the phenomena being described 'in their own terms', or apodictic knowledge of any other kind.

The upshot of my argument here is that the rationale for ethnomethodology is vitiated because the kinds of rigorous inquiry that it proposes, and against which it judges conventional social science negatively, are impossible. Not surprisingly, then, in practice it too relies in practice upon common-sense knowledge and the forms of reasoning characteristic of it (Pollner 1987: 148). Anderson and Sharrock (1984: 109 and *passim*) have shown that the work of Schegloff depends upon this, and Turner (1970: 177) and ten Have (2002b, 2004: ch. 3) have also acknowledged that this is true of conversation analysis.[34] Ten Have writes:

> So the problem for ethnomethodology is how common sense practices and common sense knowledge can lose their status as an unexamined 'resource', in order to be a 'topic' for analysis. Formulated in this way, it is a double-faced problem: on the one hand a problem of minimising the unexamined use of common sense, and on the other that of maximising its examinability. This double-sided problem seems to be in principle unsolvable, one is bound to lose either the resource or the topic. So what one has to do is to find practical solutions, which are unavoidably compromises. (ten Have 2002b: para. 18)

So, ethnomethodology itself cannot avoid the 'problem' it has identified – the alleged incompatibility between rigorous inquiry and study of the social world (see Dennis 2003: 167 and *passim*). And, as I pointed out earlier, because of its distinctive focus, it is 'guilty' of conflating topic and resource in a way that other kinds of social science are not. Moreover, even an argument to the effect that ethnomethodology is more rigorous than conventional social science because it explicates more of the common-sense resources on which it relies is not sustainable, because it has not been, and probably cannot be, shown that these resources are finite and therefore could ever be fully explicated. More fundamentally, there is the question, raised earlier, of why it would be necessary to achieve this in order for an analysis to be sufficiently rigorous. For these reasons, it remains unclear why more explication is better than less. What is required, surely, is *sufficient* explication: these are the terms in which any argument about this matter must be framed.

Aside from the problem of grasping phenomena in an unmediated fashion, ethnomethodology's modified ideal of literal description also requires that it is possible to communicate what has been observed to an audience in a way that preserves this intact, or reconstitutes it as it was. There have been at least a couple of strategies adopted by ethnomethodologists for dealing with this problem.

34 Cicourel 1973: 123 acknowledges the point for ethnomethodology more generally.

The first is characteristic of, but not limited to, conversation analysis. Sacks proposed that, for any analysis to be rigorous, the data must be available to readers so that they can assess the validity of the analysis for themselves. Does this solve the problem?

There is much to be said for the provision of data in research reports; and, indeed, this is more common on the part of qualitative researchers today than it was in the past, even if to a large extent it takes the form of 'exampling': providing brief extracts from the data that are intended to support the analytic points being made. What Sacks had in mind was more extensive and demanding than this; and, generally speaking, articles reporting conversation analytic studies *do* provide more data overall, and pay closer and more sustained attention to it, than is the case with much other qualitative work; though this is less true of some other kinds of ethnomethodological investigation.

However, we must ask whether this enables the production of literal descriptions, in the sense of 'exhibiting' the processes involved; indeed, whether the use and handling of data is *fundamentally* different in conversation analysis than it is in other kinds of qualitative inquiry.[35] There are problems even as regards the extent of the data provided. Two questions must be addressed here: how much of the data that were used for the analysis is provided to readers; and how does this body of data relate to the universe to which the conclusions generated by the analysis are intended to apply, assuming that the aim is not simply to explicate what was happening in a particular conversation or set of conversations? In some cases conversation analysts may provide the whole of the data that they have analysed, as for example with Sacks' (1992a: 236–42) discussion of 'The baby cried. The mommy picked it up', or Dorothy Smith's (1978) analysis of the story 'K is mentally ill'. But in most cases this is not done: what are presented in reports are brief extracts from a larger body of data that was used as a resource in the analysis. And, as I noted, we must also ask how far these extracts represent all the relevant variation in the phenomena being analysed. In their analysis of a particular article by Schegloff (1979), Anderson and Sharrock (1984: 110) write: 'Although Schegloff bases his analysis upon the 450 items which are contained in his corpus, he does not cite all of them in his paper. Furthermore, the 450 items comprise just a miniscule proportion of the possible corpus of materials

35 Anderson and Sharrock's (1984) analysis of the work of Schegloff suggests that there is little difference: both involve the development of general categories through selective attention, and the organisation of data in terms of these, with examples then provided for the different categories, both for illustration and as evidence. Indeed, these authors appeal to much the same notion of 'double-fitting' that Williams (1988) used in his discussion of Goffman's methods. Watson (1992, 1999) has criticised Goffman's use of this analytic and presentational strategy.

that the analysis is intended to apply to.'[36] Some examples of conversation analysis attempt to cover the domain they are addressing by providing a range of instances, varying in what are taken to be significant ways; but many do not.

A second area of problems concerns how far readers are provided with all of the *contextual* data that was available to the participants (see Psathas 1995). In the case of telephone conversations this may be achievable, since an audio recording and transcript will capture most of what participants heard, and there would have been no shared visual data. Much the same applies in analysing online textual communication. However, the situation is quite different with other kinds of conversational data, where participants have visual and olfactory access to one another, as well as aural contact. This is no doubt one reason why some conversation analysts, along with some of those carrying out workplace studies, have used video recordings. This certainly increases the analyst's access to visual data, and to a degree also the reader's; though we should not assume that a video recording can provide all that was available to participants in the conversation, and it may also provide access to some things that were not accessible to them (to do with angle of vision, sensitivity of microphones, replay facility, etc.).

A further issue relates to the fact that, generally speaking, readers are provided with extracts from *transcripts* rather than access to the electronic recordings themselves; though provision of the latter is becoming increasingly possible in online digital environments. The problem is that, however detailed transcripts are, they will not represent all that is recorded. Moreover, it is important to remember that what they provide is a representation: transcriptions do not simply 'make visible' what is on the recording in an unmediated sense, what is involved is more like translation (Hammersley 2010a). And this is true whether the transcription is based on an audio or a video recording. Furthermore, as Atkinson (1988: 454) points out, no transcription used by conversation analysts is 'a literal

36 They go on to comment that 'we raise the data's representativeness ... not in order to fault its base but to investigate how its base is secured as a practical, analytic (i.e., methodological) matter', in other words how Schegloff 'manages to bring off the analytic representativeness of his data'. However, they do not establish that he has achieved this. In conversation analysis the evidence of practical achievement of some action is found in the subsequent responses of other participants, effectively displaying that what had been done was an invitation, an apology, etc. However, it is not clear what the equivalent would be in this case, and the authors do not examine responses to Schegloff's article. As noted earlier, Coulter (1983b: 370) has in any case raised questions about this form of 'proof'. There is a further problem. Even in conversation there may be disputes about what has been done – for example whether or not an apology has actually been provided. The conversation analyst would respond to these by examining how the dispute is managed, but this leaves unresolved the question of whether an apology has actually been made or not. Yet, in the case of Schegloff's work, whether the 'data's representativeness' has actually been established is the critical issue.

description, but depends on the reader's reception of the ethnomethodological text'. And we should note that reading Jeffersonian transcripts requires a very distinctive reader competence.

Finally, there is the issue of what we might call broader context. With some of the data used in conversation analysis, notably recordings of helpline conversations, there is little of this: since the participants are usually strangers and know little about one another.[37] By contrast, many ordinary conversations are episodes in shared lives, and the participants engage in them in light of past encounters and perhaps also projected futures. Yet much of this background will not be available to the analyst, and certainly not to readers; whereas it can simply be taken for granted by participants, it does not need to be even alluded to for much of the time. Of course, one can adopt a study policy which ignores this background on principle – treating people in Schutz's terms as if they were contemporaries rather than consociates; but this is surely a distortion of the situation being studied, since important aspects of the context available to the participants are not being accessed and/or presented to readers.[38]

In my view this problem of background context is unavoidable, but we should not assume that it will always seriously undermine the analyses carried out, or readers' assessments of those analyses. This is precisely because uncertainty of meaning is a matter of degree. Nevertheless, the fact that this problem is not fully resolvable is fatal to any claim that by providing extracts from transcripts of electronic recordings, or even the recordings themselves, it is possible to 'make visible' how the meanings of the actions recorded were constituted by participants.[39]

37 Even here there will be assumptions about the organisation the callers are contacting, on one side, and about the sort of people that make contact with it, on the other.

38 Much of what we all 'know' does not need to be mentioned unless the situation is disrupted. Garfinkel's rationale for breaching experiments was precisely on these grounds. Even if we accept that relevant context is only what is 'displayed', in the sense of explicitly referred to or in some other way acknowledged, it is important to recognise that relevant contextual features may have been displayed earlier in the material from which the extract examined has been selected, or on a previous occasion.

39 One way of avoiding this problem would be to argue that the analysis focuses not on what was happening in the situation to which the data relate but rather on what sense the analyst-as-member makes of those data. Several points can be made about this. First, it is not clear how making sense of electronic recordings relates to sense-making 'live' in the course of social interaction: can we assume that it is 'essentially' the same? Secondly, there is a problem of potential interference between member understanding and analytic concerns, given that the same person is producing both the data (the understanding to be analysed) and the analysis. Finally, we should note that this approach is much closer to phenomenology in character – focusing on individual sense-making – than to Garfinkel's characterisation of ethnomethodology as an empirical enterprise studying how social events organise themselves.

We could, of course, argue that what is involved here is also a matter of degree, and that conversation analysis is superior in this respect to most qualitative analysis. I believe this is true, not just because of the amount of data provided, and the manner in which it is presented and treated, but also because of the focus of analysis: for instance, turn-taking features are probably not as context-dependent as the meanings of the *contents* of informants' accounts on which most sociologists rely, or their interpretations of what they observe. But, even if this is true, the question must be addressed: what is the threshold above which descriptions are close enough to being 'literal'; and how should we decide where to draw that line?[40]

There has been a second strategy adopted by ethnomethodologists for dealing with this problem of communication; one that is at odds with that adopted by conversation analysts.[41] Writing about Garfinkel's later position, Wilson (2003: 489) reports: 'accounts of EM investigations cannot be understood as ordinary reports to be read and reflected on. Instead, they must be engaged as tutorial instructions that are actively followed (the "praxeologization of descriptions")'. On this interpretation of the implications of ethnomethodology, 'there can, then, be no "presentation of evidence" as that might ordinarily be understood' (p. 492). The only solution to the problem of communicating findings is to produce research reports that instruct readers in how to carry out actions that enable them to experience the phenomena to which the study relates and how these phenomena were generated (see for example Livingston 1987; Bjelić and Lynch 1992; Bjelić 1995; Lynch and Jordan 1995).[42] Along these lines, Bjelić (1995: 206) argues that instructions can become literal descriptions.

Yet any instructions are themselves indexical, they are not self-applying. Moreover, while they can enable us to see, for example, the effects of a prism on light or why Pythagoras' theorem is correct, this does not give us *direct* access to the methods by which scientific demonstrations and mathematical proofs are achieved; at best, what it does is enable us to carry out particular demonstrations and proofs ourselves. The two are not the same: to use a standard example, I can ride a bicycle without having any scientific understanding of the forces operating on me as I do so, or how I adapt to and use them. Perhaps what is involved here is a denial that the aim of social research is to produce propositional knowledge? But, if so, this is an even more radical re-specification of its goal than

40 This is another formulation of the question of what level of methodological caution must be adopted in social research: see Hammersley 2008: ch. 5.
41 However, Lynch (2000c) identifies a rationale for this in the early work of Sacks. There may also be a source in the work of Schwartz 1971 (see Mehan and Wood 1975: 155–8).
42 See Rawls' (2006: 5) report that Garfinkel did not want his work to be 'merely read', believing that understanding would only occur through readers actually doing the activities listed as 'tutorial problems'.

is usually suggested: it turns social science into a quite different activity, no longer research but a kind of skills training. As Wilson (2003: 493) writes:

> It appears that … we must view EM as an experiential practice, the purpose of which is to bring one to encounter directly and unmediatedly the lived orderli-nesses of concrete situations. What one takes away from such an encounter is not information about the phenomena that can be passed on to others for their independent use but just the remembrance of one's own experience of it and, perhaps, advice to others who might want to experience it for themselves. (p. 492)

In relation to this, Lynch (1999: 217) remarks that 'Garfinkel's teaching amounted to an apprenticeship system', but that it was unclear what practice this was an apprenticeship in: the students were 'trained not taught' but 'it was not always clear what they were being trained to do or say' (p. 217). And while it required learning other practices, it was not clear that there was anything over and above this. Lynch comments that 'the students were left to wonder (and many of them did wonder) if there was a common practice they were being trained to master' (p. 218).

Fortunately, as I indicated earlier, there is no need to make literal description a requirement of rigorous inquiry. What are required are descriptions whose accuracy and precision are sufficient for the purposes of the investigation. That there are many difficulties involved in producing adequate descriptions, and that much social science fails to do this, may well be true. But to set up literal description, however defined, as the ideal effectively makes rigorous inquiry of any kind impossible, at least of social phenomena.

Conclusion

In this chapter I began by arguing that while ethnomethodologists typically deny that theirs is a theoretical enterprise, and while there are respects in which this is true, they nevertheless rely upon some presuppositions about the nature of the social world and how it can be understood; in fact, ones that are very distinctive. Moreover, whether it is claimed that these have been discovered, that they are true *a priori*, or are merely working assumptions, they serve as regulative principles that guide ethnomethodological work. And, as I have tried to show, some of them are open to serious question.

I sought to spell out these presuppositions as clearly as possible, distinguishing between *axiological* assumptions about the purposes of inquiry; *ontological* assump-tions about the indexicality and reflexivity of the meanings of actions, as well as about the accountable character of actions; and *epistemological* assumptions regarding the nature of rigorous investigation. I suggested that there is reasonable doubt about the validity of the ontological assumptions: about the major role assigned to indexicality and reflexivity, and about whether actions, for the most part, need to be *designed* to display their meaning. While meanings are context-sensitive, they are also to a large extent determined by background knowledge of various kinds, including that relating to the meaning of words and grammar, and the situations in which various linguistic forms are used. This is why, most of the time, there is not great uncertainty about who is doing what and why. This highlights a problem with the ethnomethodological argument that indexicality of meaning is dealt with through *work*: often little work seems to be involved or required, and this is always a matter of degree. There are also questions about who or what does this work, given ethnomethodologists' downplaying of the role of individual actors in favour of the constitutive capacities of practices or 'local orders' of interaction. In addition, I noted the ambivalence surrounding the notion of 'methods' and the problems associated with this concept, which was in many ways the linchpin of early ethnomethodological analysis.

In examining the epistemological assumptions to which ethnomethodologists seem to appeal, I argued that it is not clear why analysis must avoid reliance upon unexplicated resources if it is to be rigorous, suggesting that this implies a kind of epistemological foundationalism that has rightly come to be rejected by most philosophers. And there are good reasons to believe that it is impossible to avoid such reliance, and that this is as true of ethnomethodology as of any other enterprise. Moreover, in terms of conflating topic and resource, this may be more of a problem for ethnomethodology than it is for conventional sociology. What is required for scientific analysis is not avoidance of all reliance upon common-sense knowledge but rather to avoid assumptions that are open to reasonable doubt (Rescher 1978).

There are also questions to be asked about the other epistemological assumption on which ethnomethodologists appear to rely: that rigorous analysis must produce literal descriptions. One formulation of this task, that to which ethnomethodologists appeal in order to justify their own work, is to 'make visible' the practices involved in constituting social phenomena as what they are. This requires, first of all, that the analyst can gain direct access to the phenomena to be described, but I suggested that this is to ignore the fact that we inevitably rely on something like the documentary method of interpretation in making sense of any object. Neither phenomenologists nor ethnomethodologists can escape this. The implication of this seems to be that what is produced will always be 'glosses' rather than literal descriptions. There is also the problem that, even if phenomena could be accessed directly, it is unclear how what is gained through this could be communicated to others without mediation. I examined attempts to do this in the form of seeking to provide readers with the data on which analyses were based, or of asking them to carry out the activities being described. I argued that neither of these strategies is successful in solving the problem; and that, in effect, the second abandons the activity of social research for a form of pedagogy.

My overall conclusion is that while the presuppositions of ethnomethodology seem to have been fruitful in generating illuminating lines of investigation, especially in the field of conversation analysis, many of them do not withstand close scrutiny. Their radical character involves exaggeration, and they are subject to serious internal problems. In particular, they cannot provide the basis for a sound critique of conventional social science, nor for the proposal that only ethnomethodology can offer a rigorous form of social inquiry.

5 The influence of ethnomethodology on qualitative research methods

As I indicated in earlier chapters, ethnomethodology arose, in large part, from Garfinkel's concern with some fundamental methodological problems facing social science. It should not be surprising, then, that one of the fields where his work has had the greatest impact has been that of research methodology. Yet, Garfinkel himself has written very little that could be classified as falling under this heading.

In the 1960s and 1970s, many sociologists – and researchers in other areas – had their first contact with ethnomethodology through reading Aaron Cicourel's (1964) book *Method and Measurement in Sociology*. This appeared three years before Garfinkel's *Studies in Ethnomethodology*, and, while he had published some articles prior to this, Garfinkel's work – and the distinctive approach it presented – were not widely known. Moreover, even after the appearance of *Studies*, Cicourel's book continued to have considerable influence in the field of methodology.[1] As its title implies, *Method and Measurement* was intended very much as a contribution to that area, and its impact was particularly significant amongst qualitative research-ers. It was widely regarded as offering a fundamental challenge to the then dominant quantitative approaches in Anglo-American sociology; and, along with Cicourel's empirical work, and other developments, it stimulated detailed qualitative investigation of processes of social interaction, and encouraged a reflective, rather than procedural, approach to research method. Its impact was much greater than that of later ethnomethodological critiques of conventional social research.

However, *Method and Measurement* is not the only channel through which ethnomethodology has had an influence on the field of research methodology. Somewhat later, conversation analysis (CA) played an important role, for instance in shaping the arguments underpinning much of the large body of discourse and narrative analysis that emerged in the 1980s, as well as influencing ethnographic

---

1 The term 'ethnomethodology' was not used in Cicourel's book (and apparently Garfinkel did not use it in his teaching before 1964: see Wieder et al. 2010: n. 6), but Garfinkel's work is discussed in detail by Cicourel and shaped the whole approach. Indeed, the book began as a collaboration between the two authors, but this fell through and, in the end, Garfinkel refused Cicourel permission to quote from his published and unpublished materials: see Cicourel 1964: iv–v and Cicourel 2016.

and other kinds of qualitative work. Moreover, here the challenge was not so much to quantitative work but to older-established forms of qualitative inquiry. In this chapter I want to outline and assess these two routes by which ethnomethodology has affected social scientists' thinking about their practice.

Cicourel and social research methodology

Cicourel was amongst the earliest of those sociologists influenced by Garfinkel who went on to produce significant work in his own right. He has had a distinguished career, engaging in research in several fields, but throughout there has been a central concern with developing theoretical understanding of the communicational processes that underpin the very possibility of social science. The programme for this was laid out in *Method and Measurement* (Cicourel 1964), and I will focus primarily on that book here, albeit with occasional references to his other work. I will examine how he interpreted and used resources from Garfinkel, how these were blended with more mainstream methodological ideas, and the implications he derived for social research practice (see also the discussion in Chapter 1).

Prior to the appearance of *Method and Measurement*, Cicourel had published a very influential paper, with John Kitsuse (1963), entitled 'A note on the use of official statistics', and it is worth briefly examining this. They started from some fundamental problems concerning the relationship between official statistics and the phenomena these are taken to represent in the field of crime and deviance. The problems had been outlined in Merton's (1956: 32) caution against assuming that official statistics are a sound basis for testing sociological theories about factors generating deviant behaviour. Merton argued not simply that there may be substantial error in such statistics, which could obscure causal relationships or generate spurious ones, but also that the categories employed will rarely correspond to those of sociological analysis, or be causally homogeneous. In response to these problems, Kitsuse and Cicourel propose a radical change in the focus of the sociology of deviance, away from the social factors causing behaviour defined as deviant and on to the *rate-producing processes* that generate official statistics about crime and deviance, including the operation of the courts and the police. In the course of making this argument they acknowledge Garfinkel for supplying the concept of 'rate-producing processes'.[2]

2 Kitsuse and Cicourel's argument here is in line with the 'societal reaction' approach to the study of deviance that Kitsuse (1962) had already proposed, which is closely related to what came to be called 'labelling theory' (see, for instance, Becker 1963). Holstein (2009: 52) has described this as a 'radically sociological definition of deviance'. Note, though, that Kitsuse and Cicourel specifically denied that they were implying that factors producing deviance 'have no factual basis or theoretical importance' (p. 139). Later, Kitsuse extended this approach to the study of social problems more generally, in association with Spector

This radical critique of the use of official statistics came to be widely regarded as undercutting conventional forms of sociological research that rely upon this type of data (see Douglas 1967). Moreover, while *Method and Measurement* broadened the criticism to include all other sources of data, as I noted earlier its main message was usually taken to be a challenge to the forms of quantitative research that were dominant at the time. This reading was no doubt encouraged by the term 'measurement' in the book's title and by the opening chapter, headed 'Mathematics and Measurement', in which Cicourel suggested that the assumptions built into the quantitative scales used by sociologists are frequently at odds with the nature of the phenomena they study. He argued that researchers tend to rely on what he called 'measurement-by-fiat', simply assuming a correspondence between concept and measure, instead of investigating their relationship. In this respect, he implied, much quantitative research fails to live up to its scientific ideals.

However, his book addressed a methodological problem that potentially applies to all sociological research: the gap between the meaning of concepts at the level of knowledge claims and conclusions, on the one hand, and the data that are employed, on the other. Thus, in Chapter 2, entitled 'Theory and Method in Field Research', and in the chapter that follows on interviews, Cicourel indicates that this problem has major implications for qualitative as well as for quantitative research. His central concerns in these chapters are the reactive effects of researchers on the phenomena being studied, and their analytic reliance upon common-sense practices and assumptions. Above all, he emphasises the fact that they must operate in the same conceptual terms as the people being studied, if the latter's actions are to be understood, but must simultaneously adopt the very different, 'theoretical', perspective required in doing scientific research.

Cicourel argues that, for the most part, these problems are glossed over, with sociologists adopting over-simplified or inaccurate models of social action, both substantively and methodologically. Drawing on the work of Garfinkel, he notes that, in fact, the process by which people assign meaning to features of their environments is highly contingent: it arises out of patterns of social interaction taking place in particular places at particular times, the outcomes of which are not predetermined. He suggests that what is required to increase the rigour of sociological research is to develop a more adequate *theory* of those activities; in

(Spector and Kitsuse 1977; Weinberg 2009), with the focus being on how issues come to be defined as problems (see Holstein and Miller 1993). This line of argument closely parallels Cicourel's methodological arguments, and has an affinity with ethnomethodology, though it is generally labelled 'social constructionist'. Kitsuse was a colleague of Garfinkel's in the sociology department at the University of California, Los Angeles. In a later discussion of crime and deviance that drew heavily on ethnomethodology, Hester and Eglin (1992) criticise Kitsuse and Cicourel for retaining 'elements of causal theorizing, common-sense "realism" and variable analysis' (p. 13).

particular, to identify the invariant features of the processes by which people assign meanings to objects and events; in other words, the 'methods' they use for this. He argues that this would provide a sounder foundation on which conventional kinds of sociological research could be carried out, both quantitative and qualitative.

Cicourel insists that, in methodological terms, much quantitative research places implicit reliance upon a crude, behaviourist model of social interaction. This assumes that by standardising the stimuli presented to people – for instance by asking them questions worded in exactly the same way, in exactly the same order – any differences in response will reflect genuine differences in people's characteristics, rather than being an artefact of the research process. Yet it is clear that this assumption does not match the complex character of the understandings built into the processes of social interaction that are involved in data collection. By its very nature qualitative research tends to pay more attention to these processes, and does not adopt this crude behaviourist model. Nevertheless, Cicourel argues that, generally speaking, it does not set out explicitly to develop theoretical understanding of communicational processes, nor even give much reflexive attention to the implications of how the data were generated for the conclusions that can be drawn from it.

Some of the methodological issues that Cicourel addressed in *Method and Measurement* had already been noted by earlier writers, for instance in the long-running debates within US sociology in the 1930s and 1940s about the relative merits of 'case study' and 'statistical' methods, and over analytic induction (see Hammersley 1989a: ch. 4). But they had typically been treated as open to technical solutions: for example via the development of better measurement scales, more rigorous procedures for eliciting data, better interviewing technique, and so on. Cicourel's view was that the problems are more fundamental than such a response implies, that basic theoretical and empirical work is essential so as to provide a foundation for making social research strategies and theories more effective in methodological terms.[3]

Cicourel also argues that simplistic assumptions about the nature of social interaction are frequently operative at the level of theory as well. He points out that it tends to be assumed that people's behaviour is caused in a manner similar to the effects of physical forces on objects, for instance that it is controlled by cultural norms whose application is automatic and unproblematic. Yet, once again, this is clearly at odds with the nature of social processes, as we find them in everyday experience, or at least what we discover if we pay close observational attention to them.

3 There is a parallel here with Willer and Willer's (1973) criticisms (from a very different perspective) of the 'systematic empiricism' characteristic of much sociological research. See also Hindess' (1973) discussion from yet a third, radical perspective.

Cicourel went on to explore these issues in studies concerned with juvenile delinquency (Cicourel 1968), fertility decisions (Cicourel 1974), and school achievement (Cicourel et al. 1974). For instance, he argues that demographers effectively assume that fertility decisions are made at a single point in time and are subject simultaneously to the effect of various causal factors that can be weighted according to their contribution to the outcome. And they collect their data principally through fixed-choice questionnaires. Thus, in both theoretical and methodological terms, they neglect the complex contexts and processes of social interaction out of which the 'decisions' they are studying emerge, and without attention to which these cannot be understood. Running alongside this is Cicourel's emphasis on the problems of interpretation and inference involved in analysing responses to questionnaire items or interview questions about fertility decisions, or about anything else, in which the scope for misunderstanding is considerable, and where what people say tends to be forced into one or another category constructed by the researcher, rather than explored for the meanings that it carries. Again, these processes have been neglected, he argues, and yet they have major implications for the validity of research findings.

Cicourel (1973) went on to explain patterns of social order in terms of cognitive competencies. So, whereas Garfinkel sought to break with all models of an actor engaging in action governed by intentions, motives, commitment to values and norms, attitudes, etc., Cicourel tried to ground the understanding of social phenomena in the psychological capabilities of actors, and especially those of a cognitive character. In doing so, at the same time, he challenged the accounts offered of such capabilities by cognitive psychology, proposing a 'cognitive sociology' instead. He also questioned the explanations put forward by structuralist linguists, notably Chomsky, albeit taking over some features of this work. Like Chomsky he saw these capabilities as not simply a matter of compliance with rules but rather as involving a more creative process in which intelligible patterns of action are generated in particular situations.

Quantitative researchers largely ignored Cicourel's arguments, though subsequently there has been methodological criticism of conventional measurement practices along somewhat similar lines (see, for instance, Michell 1999, 2007; Gorard 2010). And some commentators have also questioned the kind of 'variable analysis' characteristic of much quantitative work (see Abbott 2001; Byrne and Ragin 2009). By contrast, as I noted earlier, *Method and Measurement* was very influential on qualitative researchers. For them, it served to challenge the legitimacy of the methodological ideas associated with quantitative method that were dominant at the time. The book also encouraged a growing tendency for many qualitative researchers to investigate the details of patterns of social interaction, as against adopting the more molar approaches that had previously been common in describing social action: a predominant emphasis came to be on what has come to be referred to as 'micro-ethnography' (Garcez 1997).

Another important effect of Cicourel's work on qualitative research was that it stimulated an emphasis on reflexivity, in a sense of the term different from that used by Garfinkel: referring to a need to pay close attention to how data are produced, the assumptions on which researchers operate, and the effects of these. Initially this was seen as a means of assessing, and thereby providing a basis for improving, the likely validity of findings. It allowed for the identification and discounting of any biases, by contrast with the belief that use of 'objective' and standardised procedures could eliminate these. However, later, rather against the spirit of Cicourel's work, the idea of reflexivity often came to be associated with rejection of the assumption that findings can be valid or invalid, in favour of the view that studies simply provide different perspectives on the world that must be regarded as true in their own terms, and judged by means of other criteria (political, ethical, or aesthetic).[4]

Cicourel's approach in *Method and Measurement* involves interesting differences from those of Garfinkel and other ethnomethodologists. On the one hand, it is clearly at odds with the stance of ethnomethodological indifference, where mainstream sociology is treated as having the same status as other activities carried out by 'members', so that it must be treated as successfully establishing the validity of its findings in and through the practices it already employs. In these latter terms, there could be no evaluation of those practices by ethnomethodologists, any more than there can be of other types of member activity: the task would simply be to explicate 'how the work is done'. This is a stance frequently recommended by Garfinkel, and there are some examples of ethnomethodological analyses of sociological practices along these lines. On the other hand, when ethnomethodologists have evaluated mainstream sociology (for example, Zimmerman and Pollner 1970; Hutchinson et al. 2008), their attitude has usually been much more strongly critical than is Cicourel's. He does not deny the value of conventional sociology, nor does he recommend that its focus be re-specified (Button 1991). Rather, as we have seen, he believes that ethnomethodological work can provide a more solid foundation for it, thereby guiding its improvement.[5]

Evaluating Cicourel's critique and its impact

The methodological problems that Cicourel identified are significant ones. It is commonplace to find measurements employed whose construct validity is open

4 On different meanings of the term 'reflexivity' see Lynch (2000a), who rejects all of them apart from that given to the term by Garfinkel: the reciprocal process whereby actions and contexts mutually define one another.

5 It seems likely that some of the difference in orientation stems from the fact that Cicourel's arguments reflect Garfinkel's early thinking, which the latter was moving beyond even at the time of their aborted collaboration.

to serious question, whether this relates to what happens in an experimentally controlled situation as against 'in the wild', or the relationship between the answers that people give to questionnaire items and the attitudinal and/or behavioural variables these are taken to measure. Moreover, Cicourel was certainly correct to note that similar problems arise in the case of qualitative research. Items of data are frequently cited simply to illustrate points being made by the analyst (what is often referred to as 'exampling') whose reliability and support for the theoretical claims they are meant to underpin is questionable. Furthermore, qualitative researchers frequently make claims that imply relatively simple and direct causal processes, without subjecting these to systematic investigation (see Foster et al. 1996; Cooper et al. 2012: ch. 3).

What is less clear is that these problems stem from either the reliance placed by social researchers on common-sense knowledge and reasoning, or the lack of an adequate theory of communicative processes on which they could draw. Like some other ethnomethodologists, Cicourel seems to assume that if scientific inquiry is to be rigorous it must place no unexplicated reliance on common-sense. But this is to take over a key assumption from a positivistic account of science that is now largely discredited; indeed, one that had already been mostly abandoned within philosophy even by the time that Cicourel wrote his book. And any attempt to avoid reliance on common-sense knowledge and practices seems likely to be futile.[6]

Furthermore, while Cicourel is right that overly simplistic models of people's behaviour need to be amended in light of what we know and can learn about the basic processes of social interaction and communication, it is not desirable, even if it were possible, in carrying out sociological research to rely on assumptions that take *full* account of the complexity of social interaction and communication (Hammersley 2008: ch. 2). It seems likely that employing simplifying models is essential if research is to be viable. Given this, we need to think about how and why particular simplifications cause problems, and how to develop ways of dealing with these, as well as trying to get a clearer sense of for which purposes particular models are of value.

Cicourel's argument is also problematic from an ethnomethodological point of view. The idea that there could be a *theory* of communicative processes that would remedy indexicality, and thereby allow social research to produce 'literal measurement' of social phenomena, is sharply at odds with Garfinkel's views, at least in his work from the publication of *Studies in Ethnomethodology* onwards. Indeed, Garfinkel increasingly moved away even from the idea that it is possible

---

6 To be fair to Cicourel, Schutz's work, on which he relied heavily, seems to put forward a notion of social science that is quite close to the positivist model (see Chapter 1). He presents science as one of 'multiple realities' in which human beings participate, and one in which the researcher acts in a highly formalised manner, disengaged from the world.

to identify invariant methods that generate the contingent meanings to be found in processes of social interaction (Wilson 2003), an idea that is central to Cicourel's position.

So, while Cicourel identifies genuine problems, it is less clear that these are correctly diagnosed, and that his proposed solution to them is effective. Indeed, his approach is regarded as inadequate, and indeed misdirected, by many ethnomethodologists. Nevertheless, in my view, his work's reinforcement of a trend towards micro-ethnography was beneficial in many key respects. Less so was the conclusion, drawn in some quarters, that this is the only legitimate, or the only rigorous, form of research, thereby ruling out as illegitimate modes of qualitative research that were once standard, for example in the tradition of the Chicago School or the community studies movement.

The way that Cicourel's book encouraged increased reflexivity was also positive in important respects, countering a widespread (and continuing) tendency largely to take for granted the processes by which data are produced and analysed. Closer attention to the ways in which data are generated in order to detect potential sources of error is wise, and Cicourel's recommendation that methods be combined – the use of questionnaires, for example, being accompanied by ethnographic observation – is worth serious consideration. It represents an early version of the idea of 'mixing methods'. That said, I suspect that few qualitative or mixed methods researchers would regard his substantive research studies as models to be followed, and probably with good reason since they tend to get bogged down in the complexities of the data and their generation. Finally, it is worth noting that Cicourel can hardly be blamed for the excesses of those who came to treat reflexivity as part of an argument against the very idea that research can represent social phenomena that exist, and possess characteristics, independently of the accounts of researchers (for an early example, see Denzin 1997).

The methodological influence of conversation analysis

Conversation analysis is probably the strand of ethnomethodology that has had the biggest impact on qualitative research methodology. A key aspect of this has been its role in the emergence of various kinds of discourse analysis over the second half of the twentieth century. Some of these – notably those deriving from linguistics (Levinson 1983; Johnstone 2008) and those coming out of psychology (Potter and Wetherell 1987; Edwards and Potter 2009) – have been strongly influenced by conversation analysis and thereby indirectly by ethnomethodology. Equally important, conversation analysis, like the work of Cicourel, reinforced the shift within ethnography towards a more micro-focus. It also provided tools by which the micro-analysis of behaviour could be pursued. In addition, in discourse analysis, ethnography, and other kinds of qualitative research there was an increasing concern with how social phenomena are constructed through discourse, and this derived to some extent from ethnomethodology's focus on the constitution of social phenomena; though there were other influences pushing in this broad direction as well, notably various kinds of French structuralism and poststructuralism.

These developments challenged traditional forms of qualitative research in several, quite specific, ways. Up to the early 1970s a great deal of it relied on fieldnotes as data. However, with cheap and portable audio-recorders becoming available towards the end of that period, these increasingly came to be used alongside, or instead of, writing fieldnotes.[7] Later still, camcorders or video cameras also began to be employed by some qualitative researchers, and these too offered advantages, in particular the possibility of replaying recordings of sequences of social interaction audiovisually and thereby analysing them in detail. While fieldnotes continued to be used as a supplement to electronic recordings in many studies, they came to be treated by some qualitative researchers as inadequate as a main form of data. All these trends were strongly reinforced by the influence of conversation analysis.[8]

There was also increased criticism of the widespread reliance of qualitative researchers on interview data. It came to be argued by many discourse analysts (see, for instance, Potter and Hepburn 2005), and by some influential ethnographers (Silverman 1993b; Atkinson and Silverman 1997; Atkinson 2015), that because such data are necessarily co-constructed, and rely on discursive conventions, they cannot be treated as a means of identifying the attitudes, beliefs, perspectives, etc., of informants, or as a reliable source of information about the world, in the way that they had been previously (see Hammersley 2008: ch. 5, 2017b). This 'radical critique' of interviews (Murphy et al. 1998: 120–3) led some commentators effectively to rule out the use of such data, while others argued that it can only be analysed for the discursive practices it reveals; in other words that the research interview should be treated as a site in which social phenomena are discursively constituted. In effect, this critique denied that what is said in interviews can be treated either as relating to a world lying beyond it or as telling us anything about the speakers. At most it can allow us to document the discourses that are in circulation in some context and how these formulate the world in particular ways.[9]

---

7 It is worth noting that Sacks started out by using fieldnotes, and then turned to audio recordings and transcripts when he discovered that calls to a suicide prevention centre had been recorded (Schegloff 1992b: xvii).

8 For a discussion of the methodological implications of conversation analysis for ethnography, see Silverman 1998: ch. 4.

9 See, for example, Edley and Wetherell's (1997; Wetherell and Edley 1999) analysis of discourses around masculinity.

Underpinning this critique is a set of methodological commitments that derive in significant respects from ethnomethodology. These reject two common types of inference from interview data commonly deployed by social scientists:

1. The attribution to actors, or categories of actor, of distinctive, substantive psychosocial features – ones that are relatively stable across time and/or social context – as a basis for explaining what they say and do, not just within the interview but also beyond. These features could be attitudes, perspectives, role expectations, beliefs, values, etc.
2. Treating what people say about the social world as a source of information about it. A great deal of social science had used, and continues to use, interview accounts as sources of what we might call witness information.

Rejection of the first kind of inference stemmed from ethnomethodology's resistance to treating attitudes, beliefs, norms, values, etc., as *governing* people's behaviour rather than as resources that people use in context-sensitive ways (see Wieder 1974). As a result, what people do is not seen as relying on anything specific about *them* as actors: what they do is what any 'member' could or would do. Even more obviously, relying on informants' accounts of the world trades on their exercise of members' methods in making sense of this world, with the result that those methods remain unexplicated.

In the same way that Cicourel's advocacy of reflexive attention to how data are generated and analysed came to be turned by many qualitative researchers into a rejection of the very idea that claims about the world are true or false independent of the perspective from which they were produced, so too many proponents of discourse and narrative analysis exceeded the stated commitments of ethnomethodology in a constructionist direction. It frequently came to be denied that there is any reality beyond accounts. In other words, the natural attitude, which relies on both of the forms of inference outlined above, was not simply suspended for the purposes of analysis, but was treated as presenting a fictional or false picture of the social world.[10] By contrast, most ethnomethodologists would insist that they are not denying that people's accounts make reference to the world nor that their behaviour can be understood as the product of attitudes, beliefs, etc. – after all, everyone makes both of these assumptions routinely in everyday life. Their point, instead, is that people's behaviour cannot be *explained in a scientific fashion* by appeal to such attributes. Similarly, they insist that a concern with how facts are constituted does not imply that there are no facts disclosed in research interviews, only that there is no *rigorous* way to establish the validity of these.

10 See, for example, Wetherell and Potter's (1992) analysis of racist discourse in New Zealand.

Evaluating the influence of conversation analysis

As with the impact of *Method and Measurement*, there have certainly been benefits from the effects of conversation analysis on methodological thinking and practice, in all three of the areas mentioned above. Compared with sole reliance upon fieldnotes, the use of electronic recordings increases the accuracy of the data, and provides more comprehensive coverage of what was said and done in the situation observed. In addition, the influence of conversation analysis led to more attention being given to the processes by which data are produced, particularly transcription of recordings. Also beneficial has been the drawing of attention to the extent to which interview data are co-constructed, and to the fact that accounts provided by informants are created through reliance upon discursive conventions and strategies of various kinds. Many qualitative researchers had tended to treat (indeed, continue to treat) interview data as if they were direct indications of attitudes or perspectives that could then be used to explain the behaviour of the people studied, with insufficient attention given to how the interview data were generated, and to the processes of inference involved, with a view to checking the validity of interpretations. Finally, also of value is the way that conversation analysis has encouraged detailed analysis of patterns of social interaction, and led to more caution about moving straight to explanation, whether in terms of micro or macro factors.

At the same time, there has been a tendency in some influential quarters for these moves to be taken to excess. One cause of this has been the influence of the constructionism which was partly encouraged by ethnomethodology. As I noted, fieldnotes have come to be regarded by many qualitative researchers as simply inadequate as a source of data (see Tessier 2012), the major traditional uses of interviews have been rejected by some discourse analysts and ethnographers (Hammersley and Gomm 2008), and micro-analysis has been treated as *defining* rigorous investigation (Douglas 1970; Moerman 1988: 1).[11]

Fieldnotes are sometimes dismissed as data, on the grounds that they are necessarily highly selective, and are filtered through the preconceptions and preferences of the researcher. Or it is argued that, rather than representing what has been observed, they provide only one construction of what happened where other versions would be equally legitimate. There is some truth in this, but an effort is usually made in writing fieldnotes to keep the description as concrete as possible, thereby minimising the assumptions built into it (see Emerson et al. 2011). Conversely, it is important to recognise that fieldnotes can include information

11 Interestingly, some ethnomethodological work, coming under the heading of what I referred to in Chapter 3 as 'mundane ethnography', shows little reluctance to employ fieldnotes and interview data, and does not confine itself to the detailed analysis of sequences of actions. See, for example, Anderson et al. 1989; Rouncefield and Tolmie 2011.

about the physical setting in which interaction is taking place, and about non-verbal behaviour, that will not be available from audio recordings. Indeed, even video recording cannot provide a complete picture of what is going on, especially where only one camera is used. And the use of video cameras increases the likely level of reactivity and may tend to reduce the mobility, and perhaps the capacity for observation, of the researcher. We should also note that listening to audiotapes or watching video recordings does not give direct access to social phenomena: in both cases the data are technologically mediated in significant ways. Similarly, as I noted in the previous chapter, the process of transcription is, in an important sense, one of construction. It does not simply re-present 'what actually happened' (see Hammersley 2010a).

A similarly mixed judgement can be reached about the influence of conversation analysis on attitudes towards the use of interview data. Here, too, the arguments have been overplayed (Hammersley and Gomm 2008; Hammersley 2015a, 2017b). The fact that interview accounts are co-constructed, and use discursive strategies, does not mean that they are false or fictional. This would only follow if a true account had to be the literal expression of a direct impression made by the world upon consciousness. And there is no good reason for adopting this definition of 'truth' (which would, in any case, render knowledge impossible). Similarly, while interviews certainly involve reactivity, as Cicourel pointed out the same is also usually true of observation: where people know that they are being researched they are likely to adapt their behaviour in some respects as a result; indeed, even where observation is covert, their behaviour may be affected by the personal characteristics of the researcher. Furthermore, the risk of reactivity is present even in most of the data on which conversation analysts rely. So what is involved here is a dimension, not a dichotomy; and judgements must be made about the level of threat involved to the validity of the particular conclusions reached.[12]

Finally, the same mixed results have arisen from conversation analysis's encouragement of a shift towards more micro-forms of analysis. Despite the benefits, there has been a tendency for this form of analysis to be treated as the only legitimate one. There are a couple of aspects to this. First, a focus on behaviour, and the meanings made publicly available through it, has been privileged, whereas research aimed at exploring the *substance* of people's experiences, feelings, beliefs, etc., has been dismissed as 'romantic' (Silverman 1989; Atkinson and Silverman 1997), or as involving spurious reference to mental entities (Coulter 1989: ch. 5). However, in my view these arguments are excessive (see Hammersley and Gomm 2008: 96). The second aspect relates to the micro-focus itself: there has been an unfortunate tendency to treat more molar or macro accounts of actions as necessarily lacking in rigour, simply because they do not specify the details of

12 For discussion of some of the issues raised here, see Speer 2002a; 2002b; ten have 2002a; Lynch 2002; Potter 2002; Speer and Hutchby 2003; Hammersley 2003.

exactly how the actions were carried out. Here there is a reliance on a notion of literal description that, I have suggested, cannot be defended (see Chapter 4).

Over and above these specific effects, in general terms the influence of eth-nomethodology and conversation analysis has reinforced an increasing tendency towards adopting a form of sceptical constructionism, albeit rarely with full consist-ency, according to which accounts simply construct competing versions of the world, so that no 'objective' account is possible. While ethnomethodologists and conversation analysts often reject such constructionism, there is a key ambiguity in their position relevant to this: if social phenomena (families, schools, tax authorities, governments, etc.) are constituted in and through processes of social interaction that are necessarily indexical and reflexive, this is at odds with the way in which, within the natural attitude, we treat such phenomena as entities in the world whose behaviour is shaped by various factors and that have effects on us. The implication drawn by some constructionists – that the natural attitude is a form of false consciousness – seems to follow from this, despite ethnomethodologists' denials.[13]

Conclusion

In this chapter I have been concerned with some of the methodological implications that have been drawn from ethnomethodology, and their impact. I began by examining Cicourel's book *Method and Measurement in Sociology*. I noted how he envisaged the possibility of developing a theory of communicational processes that would serve as a foundation on which conventional social research could be carried out more rigorously. I argued that he does not provide a convincing case that this is possible or necessary, but that his work had positive (though also some negative) consequences. It contributed to undermining the dominance of quantitative method in many quarters, as well as encouraging valuable develop-ments among qualitative researchers at the time: towards a more micro-focus, and an emphasis on the need for reflexivity. However, there was also a tendency for a micro-focus on the details of social interaction to be taken as a requirement in all qualitative research, and for sensible reflexive attention to the processes of data production and analysis to become obsessive or radically constructionist.

Cicourel's approach, not least in recommending ethnographic investigation as a useful complement to other methods, contrasts interestingly with later eth-nomethodological criticism of much qualitative inquiry (see Hammersley 2019c). This tended to argue that conventional forms of ethnographic work – in anthropol-ogy, sociology, and applied areas – fail to meet the necessary standard of rigour. Thus, in their article 'Taking Professor Gluckman seriously', Anderson and Lee

13 Pollner (1987) has explored these implications from within ethnomethodology.

(1986) discuss their own research projects in light of the tradition of anthropological participant observation research represented by Max Gluckman. They recount how their attempts to employ a conventional ethnographic approach foundered on problems that they came to regard as inherent in such work. The core problem they identify is that it necessarily relies upon common-sense resources without explicating these, and thereby cannot achieve the scientific rigour that it claims. As a result, they conclude that the focus of investigation must be shifted on to the processes by which social phenomena are constituted in the course of practical activities. Furthermore, by contrast with Cicourel, they do not see studying this topic as a necessary preliminary to more conventional ethnographic work, but rather as representing a very different and more rigorous enterprise. They conclude, in Maynard's (1998: 344) memorable phrase, that we are faced here with 'trains that are going in different directions'. Generally speaking, though, Cicourel's position seems to have been more influential outside of ethnomethodology than these more fundamental critiques.[14]

In the second half of the chapter I examined the influence of conversation analysis on methodological thinking. I argued that while it had some beneficial effects there were also damaging ones. These involved the tendency for fieldnotes to be completely disqualified as a major source of data, for rejection of the traditional uses of interview material, and for a privileging of the micro-analysis of behaviour. More generally, like Cicourel's work, CA encouraged a spurious form of constructionism. And I argued that this stemmed in part from a significant ambiguity within ethnomethodology, one which remains unresolved.

14 For a discussion of ethnomethodological criticism of ethnography along somewhat different lines from mine here, see Pollner and Emerson 2011.

Conclusion

Some fifty or so years since its emergence, ethnomethodology has survived as an approach, within and outside of sociology, despite its marginal position and in contrast to the disappearance of many other approaches over that period. And it has been developed in diverse directions. Aside from Garfinkel's own studies, these have included: Cicourel's (1973) 'cognitive sociology'; the conversation analysis of Sacks, Schegloff, Jefferson, and others; early ethnographic studies (Bittner 1967a, 1967b; Sudnow 1967; Zimmerman 1970a, 1970b; Wieder 1974); Blum and McHugh's notion of 'Analysis' (see McHugh et al. 1974; Raffel and Sandywell 2016); Pollner's (1974, 1975, 1987) work on mundane reason and reality disjunctures; various kinds of 'workplace studies' (Garfinkel 1986; Anderson et al. 1989; Travers 1997, 1999, 2007); as well as self-description of individual experience, relating to such diverse matters as playing jazz piano (Sudnow 1978) and the experience of disability (Robillard 1999). While ethnomethodology no longer attracts the level of broad attention within the discipline that it did in the 1970s, its influence has spread quite widely, either stimulating work that calls itself ethnomethodological, across many fields, or shaping approaches named in other ways. My purpose in this book has been to evaluate the arguments that underpin it, along with some of their sources, and its relationship to more conventional forms of sociology and of social science generally.

In this final chapter, I will begin by formulating what I take to be the main principles to which ethnomethodologists appeal, and some of their implications, and then go on to assess these. Before doing so, however, I should perhaps address the question of whether ethnomethodology is an enterprise that can be characterised in terms of commitment to a set of principles, and indeed whether it can be treated as a *single* enterprise. These two issues are linked, in that, arguably, it is precisely appeal to shared principles that provides any intellectual movement with coherence. At the same time, most such movements display some internal differences in orientation, as well as disputes; and this is certainly true of ethnomethodology, as I outlined in the Introduction (see also Mehan and Wood 1975; Maynard and Clayman 1991; Psathas 1995; Lynch 2016a, 2016b; Heritage 2018). But I suggest that these differences and disagreements can, to a large extent, be made sense of in terms of variation in the priority given to key commitments, and diverging interpretations of them.[1]

The principles that I identify as guiding ethnomethodology are: a commitment to rigour, of a particular kind; an insistence that action meanings are indexical and reflexive; the idea that the world we experience is socially constituted; a belief that the analytic task is to 'capture the phenomena'; the adoption of an appreciative stance towards the social; a commitment to naturalism, of a certain kind; and the appeal to a form of foundationalism.

Rigour

The ethnomethodological commitment to rigorous analysis seems originally to have come from recognition of the continuing failings of social science to meet its own proclaimed standards. Anderson et al. (1985b: ix–x) capture the dissatisfaction as follows:

> Though many, and plausible, reasons are offered … the fact of the matter is that sociology falls far short of its advertising, and opens itself to mockery from the more well-established disciplines, dissatisfaction among its students, and a more or less constant need for self-apology. … Its arguments fail to come to firm conclusions, its inquiries do not close off avenues of dispute, its studies do not fit together in neatly cumulative ways, and it has no fundamentals to speak of.[2]

Given this dissatisfaction, it is perhaps not surprising that the concept of rigour is one of the key principles to which ethnomethodology appeals; and that conventional sociology is accused of being 'speculative' (Randall and Sharrock 2011: 7) for its lack of rigour.

In more specific terms, in the case of the largely quantitative research that was dominant in US sociology during the 1950s and 1960s, ethnomethodologists argued that it did not produce literal descriptions of social phenomena, as claimed, but relied instead upon measurement-by-fiat, drawing implicitly on the common-sense knowledge that it criticised and sought to replace (see, for instance, Cicourel 1964; Wilson 1970b; Zimmerman and Pollner 1970). There was a parallel critique of much qualitative research as purportedly concerned with producing thick

---

1 There is a deeper objection to the sort of approach I have adopted here: that I discuss ethnomethodological principles as if they stood above, or at least outside of, ethnomethodological work. Instead, it may be argued that ethnomethodology is, and can only be, what is constituted as such in and through the processes of social interaction engaged in by ethnomethodologists. This argument represents a fundamental impasse for *any* dialogue between ethnomethodologists and others. However, it is not one that is adhered to in most ethnomethodological commentary on ethnomethodology.

2 However, they also note that these features 'typify more disciplines, including scientific ones, than one might imagine' (p. x). For a similar indictment, see Liberman 2008: 254–5.

descriptions of social interaction, but as actually offering relatively abstract or generalised theoretical accounts that simply recycle the concepts and knowledge of the people studied, while also being strongly shaped by the assumptions and behaviour of the researcher. For instance, Button et al. (2015: 12) suggest that: 'descriptions generated through the analytic apparatus of contemporary ethnography provide generalised accounts of social life that are of an order, despite the disciplinary rhetoric, that anyone can provide: the man in the street, the tourist, the journalist, anyone whomsoever'.

Indeed, one of the key features of ethnomethodology, unlike many of the other 'alternative' approaches of the 1960s and 1970s, is that it offered an approach that claimed to be more rigorous, albeit in significantly different terms from mainstream sociology.[3] Here, rigour amounts to the production of *descriptions* that *exhibit* the orderly character of social actions, this goal replacing the concern of most conventional social science with producing explanations and theories. This also prompts a sharp break with the predominant commitment of social science to addressing issues of immediate lay interest, in favour of understanding the character of social phenomena *in themselves*, as orderly phenomena. So, the task is careful, detailed description of how mundane patterns of social interaction, and the phenomena they entail, are produced. One model here, appealed to by Sacks, is 'primitive natural sciences', such as nineteenth-century biology (see Lynch and Bogen 1994). Another is the phenomenological commitment to describing phenomena *as they appear within our experience* (Sharrock and Anderson 1991; Anderson and Sharrock 2018: ch. 1). For ethnomethodology, this requires suspending prior assumptions – those deriving from common-sense knowledge and from social theories – and focusing on what is 'visible' or 'inspectable' in mundane social interaction. This emphasis on observability is most obvious in the case of conversation analysis, but it is also present in other kinds of ethnomethodological work. For instance, in their ethnographic study of entrepreneurship, Anderson et al. (1989: 13) state that 'visibility in the materials' is their guiding principle.

Meaning is indexical and reflexive

Another central assumption of ethnomethodology, this time an ontological rather than epistemological one, is that the meanings of actions are context-dependent. Furthermore, they are constituted over time through prospective and retrospective processes. Thus, the means by which any action is made sense of involves reciprocally identifying relevant features of its context; a hermeneutic circle is involved (Heritage 1984: 83; Watson 1997: 55). Garfinkel drew here on Mannheim's (1952) account of the documentary method of interpretation. What seems to be implied is that meanings, and indeed social settings themselves, are gestalt-contextures that are

3 Bittner (1973: 115) describes ethnomethodology as 'extraordinarily rigorous'.

self-constitutive, much in the manner suggested by Gurwitsch's (1964) discussion of processes of perception.[4]

It is argued that conventional social science, as well as linguistics and psychology, assume that the meanings of actions are simply given via some abstract formal procedure. Garfinkel developed ethnomethodology in large part in response to the theorising of Parsons, which he treats as also making this assumption. While Parsons recognised that social order necessarily relies upon there being a shared symbol system, he assumed that this system operates in such a way as to *fix* the meanings of actions and situations consensually and immediately (rather than these emerging over time through *work* on the part of participants). In effect, he believed that these meanings can be read off via a semantic code, and are specifiable on this basis by the analyst. Garfinkel questioned this assumption, pointing to the fact that 'the same' utterance can have different meanings depending upon the context in which it is produced.

So, an important corollary of indexicality and reflexivity is that rules are not self-applying but are used as resources in making sense of, or deciding on, actions: work is involved in their 'application'. This is because the implications of a rule vary according to the situation, and at the same time any situation must be made sense of in terms of the rules. On this basis it is argued that analysts must pay attention to how rules are applied, and more broadly to how activities are actually done, rather than treating the rules themselves as accurate descriptions of action. Furthermore, it is claimed that the fact that rules are used in contextually sensitive ways means that, if an analysis is to be rigorous, it cannot treat them as causal factors generating the action concerned, in the way that Parsons and many other sociologists do.

The socially constituted character of the world

This is the principle that social phenomena (perhaps all phenomena) are what they are solely by virtue of the way they are constituted through processes of social interaction – in which actors effectively display what they are doing and recognise what others are doing, contexting these in the process – what Garfinkel refers to as 'accountability'. So, for instance, human actions are not to be regarded

4 Wilson (1970a: 700–1) relates Mannheim's documentary method of interpretation to the 'way that the "part" and "whole" mutually determine each other in gestalt phenomena', referring to Gurwitsch (1964). And in his discussion of this method, Mannheim himself acknowledges the influence of Husserl. Elsewhere, Gurwitsch (1964: 432) writes that 'Unless certain appearances and presentations are intersubjectively organized in a determinate specific form, the object in question either does not exist at all or not as an object of a certain particular kind. In this sense the object may be said to derive its existence and the meaning of its existence from intersubjectively concatenated and interlocking experiences, and we may speak of the "intersubjective constitution" of the world: that is, of the world as originating in intersubjectively interlinked experiences.'

as the products of private, individual intentions: their character is generated entirely through social interaction in particular settings on particular occasions. Ethnomethodologists argue that the meanings of social actions and other objects must be publicly displayed, and therefore accessible to members, if coordinated processes of social interaction are to occur; which they evidently do.

Moreover, it is claimed that it is precisely this feature of human social interaction that makes rigorous analysis of it possible. If, instead, the meanings of actions were to lie in private intentions, or other hidden factors, it would be impossible to document how they were generated, in a rigorous fashion. Indeed, the argument is that if *anything* in the social world can be investigated rigorously it is the processes through which the meanings that actions have for participants are produced, since these are necessarily made publicly available in the course of coordinating social interaction.[5]

Garfinkel later added a qualification to this, recognising that what is publicly recognisable varies even within a single society; so that, for example, what is going on in a physics laboratory will only be recognisable to those who are party to the activities concerned, or those who have acquired the necessary understanding elsewhere. He argued that in such circumstances distinctive forms of 'unique adequacy' are required; in other words, the analyst must have or acquire the specialist knowledge and skill involved, at least to some degree.

Capturing the phenomena

A fourth commitment is a concern with documenting *haecceity*, the 'just-thisness' of things (see Sharrock and Anderson 1986: 23, 82–3; Lynch 2018). For example, Lynch (1999: 225, 1985) describes the aim in his research on neuroscientists as being to 'recover the specificity of laboratory work'. Meanwhile, in the context of conversation analysis, Schegloff (2005) emphasises the need to respect the 'integrity' of the phenomena. Here, once again, the parallel with phenomenology is illuminating, in that there is an assumption that if one suspends the natural attitude it is possible to document *in their own terms* the processes by which social phenomena are constituted, as orderly and meaningful. In other words, they can be rendered observable and reportable without use of the documentary method. The possibility of describing phenomena in their own terms was at the heart of phenomenology's opposition to neo-Kantian philosophy at the beginning of the twentieth century (see Chapter 4). For the latter, any scientific or philosophical investigation necessarily constructs the phenomena it investigates, whereas Husserl

---

5 Here there is, of course, a sharp distinction between what phenomenology and ethnomethodology treat as open to rigorous investigation. Indeed, in some respects the two could not be more strongly opposed, in that ethnomethodology rejects phenomenology's focus on individual consciousness.

insisted that it is possible to describe things as they appear in experience in an unmediated fashion. Ethnomethodology makes a parallel claim about social life.

An appreciative stance

Another key ethnomethodological idea is that conventional social science evinces a lack of respect for the concerns, interests, and rationality of lay people, and for the complex varieties of knowledge and skill involved in their activities. Thus, not only do social scientists treat their own preoccupations and preconceptions as more important, but the beliefs and activities of ordinary people are often explained away as the product of factors of which they are allegedly unaware, or about which they are mistaken; for example, their views are treated as 'ideological'. In other words, ethnomethodologists complain about what they see as the ironic stance adopted by conventional social science towards common-sense understandings of the world: in this context, irony is the converse of appreciation (see Watson 1998).

Appreciation here does not mean admiring or applauding the activities being studied and the people involved, even less promoting their interests or acting as an advocate. Rather, it means adopting the principle of charity, a stance in which prejudicial prior assumptions about those activities and people – about what is being done and why, and especially evaluative judgements about this – are suspended so that a serious effort is made to understand and describe people's perspectives or actions.

In line with this commitment to appreciation, in his early work Garfinkel resisted the tendency to judge ordinary patterns of action as irrational, or non-rational, by comparison with scientific rationality. He insisted that they are rational in their own practical terms, and that the task is to understand their logic. A rather different example of the appreciative stance is provided by Sudnow (1967: 138–9), when he challenges Durkheim's (1915: 397) claim that people mourn because group pressures force them to do so, suggesting that Durkheim here is 'debunking bereaved persons and eliminating the possibility of "genuine grief"'. While commitment to an appreciative stance is not restricted to ethnomethodology (see Matza 1969), it is nevertheless central to it; and in a particularly strong form, since the whole task of analysis is portrayed as explicating participant understandings as these are displayed in the process of social interaction.

Naturalism[6]

This is a commitment, once again not unique to ethnomethodology, to examine social activities *as they normally happen* 'in the wild', rather than as they occur in

6 For a discussion of the very different ways in which this term has been used, see Matza 1969: ch. 1.

artificial research settings such as experiments or in other situations that have been highly structured by social researchers, for instance via questionnaires and interview questions. This commitment is motivated by a concern to minimise the effects of researchers' preconceptions and actions on what is being studied. It is clearly related to the other commitments I have listed: the aim is to describe the processes by which social phenomena are produced in their own terms, rather than as filtered through prior assumptions or procedures.

This emphasis on naturalism is particularly obvious in the case of conversation analysis, where there is an insistence on the use of data from 'naturally occurring talk-in-interaction'. But it is also clear in the ethnographic work that many ethnomethodologists have done. An apparent exception to naturalism is Garfinkel's use of 'breaching experiments', but we should note that not only did these lack the usual trappings of psychological experiments – control groups, random allocation, matching, etc. – but also they were frequently carried out in 'natural' situations, and sometimes by participants in those situations (his students).

Foundationalism[7]

This is the idea that unless and until we have rigorous descriptions of the processes by which social phenomena are produced on particular occasions, the more abstract and general claims made by conventional social science can be no more than speculative. One version of this is what Knorr-Cetina (1981: 22) has referred to as 'methodological situationism': 'the principle which demands that descriptively adequate accounts of large-scale social phenomena be grounded in statements about actual social behaviour in concrete situations'. Cicourel's work has been strongly guided by this concern, being aimed at providing a new foundation for social science (see Chapter 5).

Along similar lines, Anderson et al. (1989: 12) suggest that 'progress towards the goal of explanation can only be achieved (if at all)' on the basis of careful 'descriptions of *naturally occurring social activities*' (emphasis in original). However, these authors' evident lack of confidence about whether rigorous explanatory social theory can ever be achieved is shared by most ethnomethodologists: indeed, many would reject that very possibility, insisting that the goal of social science must be re-specified as wholly concerned with description (Sharrock and Watson 1988; Button 1991). But, even here, there is a sense in which a form of foundationalism still operates, since it would be insisted that the processes of social interaction that ethnomethodology is concerned with describing serve as the basis on which both lay people and conventional social scientists generate

7 This is also a term that has been used in a variety of ways, often with negative connotations. I outline the specific sense intended here, with no evaluation implied.

the accounts they give of the world. Thus, in a more recent discussion, Anderson and Sharrock (2018: 189) argue that: 'ethnomethodology concerns itself with the primordial social facts on which Sociology's research depends'. In this sense it serves as a 'first sociology', in much the same manner that Husserl proposed phenomenology as a 'first philosophy'. Anderson and Sharrock claim that ethnomethodology 'discloses what Sociology presupposes'. Another form that foundationalism has taken, this time in relation to conversation analysis, is treating the turn-taking system characteristic of conversation as the basis for other forms of talk (see Sacks et al. 1974: 730–1; Drew and Heritage 1992). A more philosophical version can be found in Coulter's (1979) treatment of ordinary language competence as underpinning more technical or esoteric forms of discourse, including those of science.[8]

The principles I have outlined above are routinely appealed to by ethnomethodologists; even if, as I noted, there is variation in the emphasis given to each of them, and sometimes in what their implications are taken to be. Moreover, while a few of these principles are shared with other approaches within social science, most are distinctive; and I have argued that, collectively, they mark ethnomethodology off sharply from competing approaches. Indeed, it should be clear that – despite denials, notably on the part of Garfinkel – they imply a fundamental challenge to conventional social science. This amounts, above all, to a *methodological* challenge: the implication is that, in all of its varieties, it lacks the intellectual authority it claims; that what it produces is not scientific (Hutchinson et al. 2008), or is no better than bar talk (Button et al. 2015: 137). Meanwhile, the implication is that ethnomethodology involves a radically different focus, and mode of inquiry, one that can *legitimately* claim a high degree of rigour.

In this book, I have argued that, while they have been fruitful, these radical principles generate serious problems. These concern both ethnomethodology's relationship to conventional social science and the alternative form(s) of investigation proposed.

The relationship to sociology

As just noted, ethnomethodology demands not just a re-specification of sociology's whole manner of proceeding but also a shift in its focus. But, as indicated in Chapter 4, there are questions about some of the assumptions motivating this re-specification.

8 These last two arguments have been subjected to criticism from within ethnomethodology: see Bjelić and Lynch 1992: 54; Hester and Francis 2001 on the first, and McHoul 1982: ch. 1–2 on the second.

Conclusion

What counts as rigour?

The standard of rigour against which ethnomethodology judges existing social science requires literal descriptions or measurements to be produced: in other words, the substantive terms employed must have fully explicit and contextually invariable meanings, these being fixed through the identification of necessary and sufficient conditions for their application (see Wilson 1970b: 71–4; Wieder 1974: 217). However, while it is clear that social science has generally failed to produce literal descriptions of this kind, most social scientists have not in fact adopted that goal. Furthermore, there are grounds for believing that it is unachievable: work in the history and sociology of science, including some by ethnomethodologists (for instance, Lynch 1985), has suggested that it is not even achieved in natural science. More importantly, the need for it in the human sciences has long been questioned (see, for instance, Dray 1957 and Taylor 1964). It has been argued that more pragmatic standards are appropriate, with the expectation that these will vary somewhat across the sciences (Kaplan 1964). Of course, it remains an open question whether conventional social science can even meet a more relaxed, but appropriate, standard of this kind.[9]

So, I am not denying that there is a problem concerning description and measurement in the social sciences: there is often insufficient conceptual clarity, and frequently a gap between the meanings of concepts and the indicators or evidence used to 'operationalise' them. However, to formulate this gap in terms of a failure to achieve literal description is misleading. What is required, instead, is a level of clarity and stability of meaning needed for the purposes of producing knowledge in the field concerned. And what this entails is a pragmatic matter, not something that can be determined by theoretical or philosophical fiat. Nor is it clear that conventional social science is bound to fail in these terms.

Closely associated with the goal of literal description, indeed a presumed prerequisite for it, is the requirement that scientific analysis must not conflate topic and resource. That social science also fails to meet this requirement is one of the major criticisms made by ethnomethodologists. However, the more pragmatic sort of standard I am suggesting would not preclude reliance on common-sense

---

9 Ethnomethodological critics of conventional social science also apply a very demanding conception of *explanation*. For example, Pollner (1991: 371) argues that 'If … the application of a rule requires judgments that cannot themselves be specified by rule, then normative explanations are insufficient explanations of social order.' Again, it seems that what is required is the specification of necessary and sufficient conditions, this time identifying causal factors. While there have certainly been social scientists who have advocated this explanatory standard, few have sought to achieve it in practice, and there are good reasons to doubt that it is required (Hammersley 2014: chs 1, 2).

knowledge and skills, only reliance upon assumptions whose validity is open to reasonable doubt (Hammersley 2011).[10]

What are the implications of indexicality?

In Chapter 4 I argued that ethnomethodologists' claims about the context-dependent nature of action meaning are exaggerated. It is true that, in the case of linguistic utterances, meaning cannot be read off *solely* from knowledge of the meaning of words (for example, as specified in a dictionary) plus the rules of grammar; that it is context-sensitive. However, most of the time, this does not result in our being puzzled or wrong about what people are saying and doing and why; nor does it imply that background knowledge of a linguistic kind, and of other sorts (including, for instance, about what types of utterance and meaning are common in what types of situation), does not play a major role in reducing the likelihood of puzzlement or error.

Ethnomethodologists acknowledge that there is not ubiquitous puzzlement, but they put this down to the 'work' involved in making sense of actions *in situ*.[11] However, if, in fact, much of the time meanings are largely determined by background knowledge then, in most cases, little work 'on the spot' will be necessary. Moreover, as already suggested, there is no reason why social scientists themselves cannot rely on their ability to recognise action meanings in much the same manner, and drawing on the same resources, as anyone else; subject to these being questioned where there is reasonable doubt about the assumptions and conclusions involved. While such reliance would be ruled out by the very sharp distinction between scientific and practical rationality proposed by Schutz (1943), and initially adopted by Garfinkel (1962), as I have argued this is associated with an excessive standard of rigour.[12]

Does conventional sociology 'miss', or 'ignore', the 'just-thisness' of the phenomena it studies?

In his later writings Garfinkel announced a programme of 'studies of work', concerned with the 'distinctive organizations of competent practice that make

10 Moreover, as I indicated in Chapter 4, it seems that conventional social science is less guilty of such a conflation of topic and resource than ethnomethodology itself, given that social scientists do not usually focus on common-sense knowledge and skills as a topic, even if these are necessarily implicated in what they study.

11 Note that, in acknowledging this, ethnomethodologists are effectively conceding that the problem of double contingency is rarely an actual problem. Indeed, Garfinkel's early breaching experiments show how difficult it is to generate meaningless situations.

12 For an excellent discussion of some of the complexities surrounding the investigation of meanings, albeit one that retains the idea of complete determination of meaning as a standard by which to judge such investigation, see Wootton 1975: chs 1–3.

up the *performance* of particular arts, sciences, and technical professions, as well as more ubiquitous activities in a given society' (Lynch 2018: 6). Garfinkel argued that conventional sociology had 'missed' or 'ignored' the 'just-thisness' of the phenomena it studies, so that for instance the sociology of work neglected to describe the actual forms of work with which it is concerned, focusing instead on their political, economic, and social aspects. As Lynch points out, for Garfinkel this '"missing what" is nothing other than the practices themselves, as coordinated embodied performances, identical with, carried out through, and constitutive of socially organised activities'. This criticism is clearly closely related to the ethnomethodological commitment to 'capturing the phenomenon'.

How cogent is this criticism? There can be no doubt that conventional sociology covers the phenomena Garfinkel is referring to here only partially at best, and superficially compared with the kinds of account that have been provided by ethnomethodologists (see Garfinkel 1986). But the question is: why is it necessary to document social practices in such detail? Indeed, how should we decide how much detail is required? Moreover, there is considerable variation across ethnomethodological studies of work in what they provide.

The key point is that conventional sociology, generally speaking, has no commitment to 'capture the phenomenon'. Indeed, Garfinkel and other ethnomethodologists criticised Parsons precisely for adopting an analytic stance that denied the possibility of this. But they did not establish that this stance is unacceptable; their argument was that it is unnecessary because order can be found 'in the phenomena'. And we can ask whether 'capturing the phenomenon' is ever possible, and whether attempting to achieve this is desirable. It seems to me that whatever investigation we carry out will be framed by some specific set of questions that have relevances built into them. This is as true of ethnomethodological inquiries as of any others.

Does the ethnomethodological critique also apply to common-sense knowledge?

A final problem with the ethnomethodological critique of social science is that, on one reading, it would also apply to much lay knowledge. If ethnomethodologists argue that social science is defective because it seeks *general* knowledge about the social world, this being at odds with the indexical and locally constituted meanings of actions, then the same charge would apply to a great deal of what passes for 'common-sense' knowledge or lay reasoning. A glance at any newspaper, for example, would reveal general as well as specific knowledge claims. Similarly, in everyday talk, generalisations are routinely made about people, groups, organisations, countries, etc. Also, social actions, events and institutions are frequently treated as causal agents and products. Must we regard such lay thinking, along with conventional social science, as defective by contrast with the rigour of ethnomethodological investigation (Dennis 2003: 164 and *passim*)? This sometimes seems to be implied. For instance, writing about the work of Wieder and Pratt (1990), Liberman (2008) suggests that the common belief that ethnic identity is given by descent is a myth, insisting that such identity is constituted by members through processes of social interaction.[13]

Of course, it can be argued that common-sense generalisations are produced on particular occasions for particular purposes and audiences, and in that sense are nevertheless locally organised and context-sensitive. But the same is true of sociological generalisations: sociologists' accounts are generated within society just as much as those of anyone else. What seems to be at issue here is rejection of a view of language-use as producing representations of the world (see Button and Sharrock 1993: 8; Lynch 1993: 38). But, while it is true that all accounts are performative or praxiological – in the broad sense that they are produced in, and attuned to, particular situations, and are designed to serve particular purposes and to address particular audiences, etc. – this does not alter the fact that they put forward, and/or presuppose, factual claims about the world. So, while social scientists' accounts are situated or occasioned, and relate to actions and events that are themselves situated or occasioned, this no more counts against their claim to representational knowledge than it does against that of lay people.

So there is a dilemma, I suggest: in criticising conventional social science ethnomethodologists may also be criticising common-sense accounts, and this is at odds with some of their commitments. In the face of this, there appear to be two options. One is to make a distinction *within* common-sense: between what we might call constitutive and idle talk, with the latter treated as spurious or dogmatic.[14] Yet, for ethnomethodology, *all* talk surely belongs within processes of social interaction that constitute phenomena as what they are, with no time out? How could ethnomethodology justify the judgement that some of this talk is idle? Certainly, Garfinkel and Sacks (1970) seem to treat all of it, including formulations or glosses, as grist for the ethnomethodological mill.

13 See also Liberman's (2017: 7) reference to 'the dogmatism of the natural attitude', quoting Fink. Pollner (1987) also verges on this position, though it is rejected by some other ethnomethodologists; see, for instance, Bogen 1990; Button and Sharrock 1993. It seems to me that no one can ever fully escape from adopting the natural attitude, nor would there be benefit in achieving this. Rather, we must recognise the complex topography within it, patterned by the ways in which various activities suspend some parts of the natural attitude for particular purposes. This is true, for instance, of natural and social science, as well as of philosophy.

14 For attempts to do this, see Lynch's (1985: 15) distinction between scientists' 'talk about science' and their 'talk in science', and Coulter's (1999: 166) and Button et al.'s (2015: 10) similar, more general, distinction. See also Sharrock's (2001: 250) distinction between 'upper-case' and 'lower-case' theorising. There may be a parallel here with Wittgenstein's (1972: para. 241, p. 88e) contrast between 'agreement in opinions' and 'agreement in form of life', and with his notion that in much philosophy 'language goes on holiday' (para. 38, p. 19e).

The other option would be to argue that there is nothing wrong with sociological *practice*, that what is at fault is simply the discipline's claim to be a science. But, even if this could be accepted, and the ethnomethodological critique often seems to impugn sociologists' practice as well as their formulations of what they are up to, we should note that social scientists are by no means alone in claiming the intellectual authority to produce knowledge about social phenomena (various other occupations do this in relation to particular domains – doctors, social workers, and the police – as too do official inquiries of various kinds). So these others must be subject to the same criticism.

Aside from this, to be consistent, ethnomethodologists must surely argue that scientificity is itself constituted locally on particular occasions: this seems to be the upshot of ethnomethodological accounts of natural science. And, if this is true, on what grounds could it be argued that social science fails to be scientific? Not only do social scientists treat their work in this way but, despite its relatively low status, it is nevertheless sometimes granted considerable intellectual authority in the public sphere.[15]

There are, then, some genuine questions about the force of the ethnomethodological critique of social science. The same is also true of the rationale for the kind of alternative work that ethnomethodologists propose and practise.

Questions about ethnomethodological investigation

Is ethnomethodology vulnerable to its own critique?

A first point here is that it seems clear that ethnomethodology cannot avoid *itself* being subject to one of the main criticisms it makes of conventional social science: that it treats common-sense knowledge as both topic and resource. Certainly, some ethnomethodologists have explicitly acknowledged that their work necessarily relies upon common-sense knowledge and skills (Turner 1970: 177; Coulter 1979: 23; Pollner 1987: 148; ten Have 2002b). Indeed, if it did not do this it would be unable to detect the phenomena that it sets out to investigate. But their suggestion is that conflation of topic and resource is minimised, if not avoided, because a two-step process is involved; the second step, the analysis, explicates the common-sense knowledge that was involved in the first. However, this would only be true if what were involved were not empirical sociological study of the world but rather explication of the analyst's own competence as a member in 'reading' that world. Yet ethnomethodology is typically presented as

15 Some might say too much, see Hammersley 2015b. Sharrock and Button (1991: 148–9) insist that sociologists have no authority in society, but their grounds for this lie in their own normative account of the necessary limits of social science knowledge, rather than this being an empirical claim.

a form of empirical, rather than phenomenological, investigation; and this prevents the two stages being separated. In the case of conversation analysis, for instance, common-sense knowledge and skills are involved not only in the initial phase of, say, identifying a sequence as one of question and answer but also in observing how participants orient to the utterances concerned: common-sense knowledge and skills are implicated throughout the process of ethnomethodological analysis, for instance even in the 'next-turn-proof procedure'.

It is also worth saying that while ethnomethodology proposes that rigorous social inquiry must be concerned with description not explanation, it is far from clear that this is true of conversation analysis. It sets out to explain what leads to what, and why: that questions lead to answers because human social interaction is guided at many points by this adjacency-pair apparatus. This concern with causal analysis is confirmed by conversation analysts' reliance on the logic of 'next turn proof' and on deviant case analysis. And the same is true of some other sorts of ethnomethodological work. For instance, in an article that discusses a study of air traffic controllers, Sharrock and Randall (2004: 191) deny that ethnomethodology involves causal analysis but then go on to describe how the work of controllers is affected by a variety of factors, and how it has certain consequences – relying on such words as 'engendered', 'prevented', 'attunement', and 'effected'.[16]

The problems of literal description

A second point concerns the claim that what is involved in ethnomethodological work is simply the 'exhibiting' of meanings and the methods that constitute them. Here a form of literal description is being claimed (Sacks 1963: 2), albeit a different one from that used as a standard to judge conventional social science. But, as I indicated in Chapter 4, this notion of simply displaying meanings is unconvincing. For one thing, such display relies upon the use of natural language, which ethnomethodologists argue is necessarily constitutive in character.

As with phenomenology, what seems to be required is a suspension of the natural attitude, as well as of the theoretical concerns of science. The assumption is that once this has been done it is possible to gain direct acquaintance with constitutive processes and to describe them *in their own terms*. However, it is far from clear that this is possible. After all, phenomenology portrays perception and cognition as necessarily constitutive. And ethnomethodology presents everyday forms of understanding as relying on the documentary method. In both cases,

---

16 Of course, there is an issue here about what the terms 'causal' and 'explanation' mean (see Hammersley 2014: chs 1, 2). While this issue is not addressed by Sharrock and Randall, at one point they dismiss 'mechanistic causation' (p. 194), which suggests they may accept that some other sort of causation is operating.

the obvious question that arises is: how can phenomenological or ethnomethodological analysis avoid having a constitutive character itself?[17]

Furthermore, ethnomethodological analysis not only requires grasping meanings and their methods of constitution – which I have suggested cannot be simply a matter of 'observing' or 'seeing things in their own terms' – but also conveying the nature of these meanings and methods to some audience *without further mediation*. And I argued that neither of the two solutions to this problem proposed by ethnomethodologists is effective in this respect: conversation analysts' efforts to provide readers with the data, so as to enable them to check the analysis; and the proposal that ethnomethodological research reports serve as instructions that allow readers to re-create the phenomena being studied.

As already noted, one argument might be that ethnomethodologists simply 're-present' what members do, in and through their own analyses as member/analysts: this amounting to a form of self-exemplification. But even if ethnomethodology were to be redirected in this fashion, we must recognise that the orientation of the analyst differs sharply from that of ordinary members, in two key respects. First, it focuses on how meanings are constituted, whereas most of the time participants do not. Second, it adopts a non-evaluative orientation towards those meanings, when members engage in evaluation much of the time. But, in any case, conversation analysts point to the dangers of relying upon 'intuition' as against *analysis of empirical data* (see, for instance, Atkinson and Heritage 1984: 3–4); whereas, of course, ordinary participants necessarily rely solely on such 'intuition'. Of relevance here is Jefferson's (1989) 'reprimand' (Button and Sharrock 2016: 614) of Pomerantz (1989) for suggesting that the findings of ethnomethodology could be translated into those of common-sense. Also open to question is whether, even if meanings themselves could be exhibited in the manner claimed, this would also be true of the methods by which they were produced. It sometimes seems to be implied that the two are identical, but logically they cannot be.

All of this throws doubt on the idea that ethnomethodological investigation can involve simply attending to the 'observable' character of members' practices of meaning constitution, and then 'exhibiting' this to readers or auditors. And, if this is not possible, then the claim to superior rigour that ethnomethodologists make, as against social science's failure to be rigorous, is greatly weakened. Indeed, ethnomethodological work is faced with many of the same sorts of methodological problem as conventional social science.

---

17 Pollner (1991) celebrates the recognition that ethnomethodology must itself constitute its phenomena as 'radical reflexivity'. This is also central to the 'Analysis' of Blum and McHugh.

Are there context-transcending methods?

The concept of methods is central to most understandings of ethnomethodology. But it is by no means clear to what the term refers. Indeed, there appears to be a conflict between the sorts of method that Garfinkel identified in his early work and what Sacks and some other ethnomethodologists aimed to describe. The central example for Garfinkel was the documentary method of interpretation, along with various strategies – such as etcetera, let it pass, etc. – employed to cope with the fact that rules are not self-applying. However, conversation analysts and some other ethnomethodologists have been concerned instead with identifying an 'apparatus' or 'machinery' that would generate the phenomena they are investigating (Hill and Crittenden 1968: 68, 81; Sacks 1974: 218, 1984: 26). Here, for example, is Sacks (1992b: 169): 'Our aim is to get into a position to transform, in what I figure is almost a literal, physical sense, our view of [a given bit of talk] as some interaction that could be treated as the thing we're studying, to interactions being spewed out by machinery, the *machinery* being what we're trying to find' (emphasis added). As Schegloff (1992b: xxi) indicates, one model here for Sacks seems to have been the sort of syntactic apparatus developed by Chomsky in order to distinguish grammatical from ungrammatical sentences.[18]

It has been suggested that Garfinkel moved away from the idea of context-transcendent methods in his later work, as he had earlier from the idea that meanings are constituted through reliance on shared, prior background knowledge (Wilson 2003, 2012). Garfinkel seems increasingly to have treated the production of intelligible social order as taking place without reliance upon prior standing resources of any kind on the part of participants. In other words, he came to see both what is known and what is meant, on any particular occasion, as reflexively constituted entirely within that occasion. This move has provoked some criticism of conversation analysis. Thus, Lynch (2000c: 517) has complained that much work in that field is concerned with the development of 'abstract models' designed 'to account for general features of conversational organization'. He contrasts this with what he takes to be implied by its 'ethnomethodological foundations', suggesting as an alternative the 'explicative style of conversation analysis exemplified by many of Harvey Sacks' lectures, in which he explicates singular instances of activity'. This indicates a fundamental ambiguity in the work of Sacks, and perhaps in the early writings of Garfinkel too.[19] There seems to be

18 Interestingly, this second conception of method is also to be found in the article jointly authored by Garfinkel and Sacks (1970: 355–8), which is usually attributed primarily to Garfinkel (but see Lynch 2017). The claim that ethnomethodology can produce general knowledge precisely relies on the idea that it is able to identify apparatuses or machinery (see Benson and Hughes 1991: 130–1).

19 As regards Sacks, see Watson 2008. As Sharrock (2000) points out, the primitive sciences, to which Sacks appeals as a model, were not concerned with explicating particular situated processes but with developing general accounts.

uncertainty, then, both about whether or not the aim is to document general methods, and (if so) about the nature of these methods.

Moreover, while abandoning the attempt to identify general methods avoids the problems associated with conceptualising them, it does so at great cost, rendering ethnomethodology an entirely idiographic enterprise. The implication seems to be that analysis can only provide descriptions of, say, how particular conversations progressed (rather than that they are governed by a turn-taking system), or of how particular queues formed (rather than a general account of how queues form).[20] Yet, unlike historical work, which is necessarily idiographic but focuses on events, trends, etc., of general significance, to a large extent ethnomethodology focuses on matters that most people most of the time would regard as of little importance *in themselves*.

Problems surrounding agency and accountability

As I noted earlier, ethnomethodologists wish to claim that any understanding of actions is produced by 'work' carried out *in situ*, rather than being predetermined by a semantic code: they insist that understanding is an 'achievement' or 'accomplishment'. They also argue that, in acting, people display what they are doing, and why, in a manner that is intelligible ('accountable') to other members, so that here too work is involved. However, as I argued in Chapter 4, while, sometimes, active indication of intent or purpose is required, as in the establishment of formal contracts ('I hereby promise …'), much of the time we do not need to engage in active display because, by drawing on their background knowledge, other people can immediately recognise what is being done, and to some extent why, sufficient for their purposes. Indeed, there are often constraints on spelling out what we are doing, identified by Grice (1975), and some of these relate to the sorts of concern about 'face' that are at the centre of Goffman's work.[21] Equally important, and also documented in the latter's work, people sometimes engage in *strategic* interaction, where what they present themselves as doing is not what they are actually doing (Goffman 1969). While in the course of this they rely on the same processes of communication as on other occasions, a clear difference is involved.

Aside from this, there is a question about exactly who or what carries out the work involved in constituting meanings. It might be assumed that this is done by the human participants, but ethnomethodologists have frequently denied that the achievement of social order relies upon the cognitive capacities of actors, for instance in the manner implied by Cicourel (1973), this often being dismissed

20 Having said this, Garfinkel and Livingston's (2003) discussion of queues is patently general in reference.

21 Not all of them do, as Bittner (1977) makes clear.

as 'cognitivism' or 'mentalism' (Coulter 1983a, 1989, 2008; Watson and Coulter 2008; Leudar and Costall 2009).[22] Indeed, it is suggested that social settings must be regarded as self-organising: as orchestrating the actions of participants within them (Garfinkel 1967a: 33–4). For instance, in seeking to explain the preferences surrounding the delivery of bad news, Schegloff (1988b) appeals to the notion of a 'servo-mechanism' that governs people's behaviour. But here we seem to be back to a view of people as cultural dopes (Atkinson 1988: 449), acting out roles that are defined for them by social settings. Furthermore, the notion of agency involved here needs explication and defence if it is to steer clear of assuming the existence of a collective subject of some kind.[23]

Closely related is the refusal of ethnomethodologists to assign intentions and motives to participants, insisting that the focus should be on how these are ascribed in the process of social interaction (see Bruce and Wallis 1983, 1985; Sharrock and Watson 1984). This results in a sharp difference in character between ethnomethodological and common-sense accounts, which routinely assign intentions and motives to people, often treating these as grounds for blame or praise, and necessarily involving the ascription of causes and effects. An illustration of the attempt to sustain this distinction is conversation analysts' discussions of preference structures, where they usually insist that '"preferred" and "dispreferred," ... refer to sequential properties of turn and sequence construction, not participant desires or motivations' (Schegloff 1988b: 445). The implication is that preference structures are institutionalised, and therefore 'cohort-independent'. This is surely true, but people must still be motivated to comply with them, as well as to breach them. Indeed, the sequential structures on which conversation analysts focus would not occur without intentions and motives on the part of participants.[24] There is a parallel here with Simmel's distinction between social forms and their contents.

Also relevant is ethnomethodologists' insistence that the only relevant context for any piece of social interaction is what is displayed in that interaction, and their

---

22 To some extent this is in line with Husserl's critique of psychologism, on which see Kusch 1995; though, of course, ethnomethodologists deny Husserl's assumption of an independent realm of ideal objects, insisting that these are immanent in sociality, more in line with Durkheim. They also deny Husserl's claimed access to subjective processes. For an assessment of ethnomethodological critiques of cognitivism, see Hammersley 2018b.

23 It seems close to the problematic notion of 'functioning-accomplishing subjects' that Husserl (1970: para. 54, pp. 182–3) employs. It is also worth noting that Goffman has adopted a similar strategy of de-centring the actor, in his emphasis on 'moments and their men', rather than 'men and their moments' (Goffman 1967: 3). One clarification of what is involved here is, perhaps, that institutionalised technologies motivate the behaviour of those who use them. This may represent a link to actor network theory.

24 Interest in these can, perhaps, be suspended for the purposes of analysis, but their existence independently of publicly available accounting practices cannot reasonably be denied. Nor is it clear why, once an excessive concept of rigour has been abandoned, motives should not be open to scientific investigation.

criticism of social science for 'importing' external contextual matters.[25] Thus, Button and Sharrock (2016: 615) argue that

> The warrant for the social science attribution of omni-relevant identities to people as grounds for understanding what they do resides in the particular social theory being articulated. However, Garfinkel, Sacks and Schegloff break with traditional constructive-analytic social science; the radicalness of their pioneering work resided in placing the warrant for invoking the identity of the doer as relevant for their doings in the actual doings themselves. That is, the warrant for invoking the gender identity of a person resides not on all-encompassing social theory of gender or gender relationships, in the fact that the person is, for example, a man, but that it is possible to see in what he does, that in how he does what he does, his identity as a man rather than, for example, a teacher, is relevant.

Yet, it must be noted that, as participants in everyday conversations, we frequently explain one another's behaviour in such omni-relevant terms, and do so *without drawing on social science theory*. And while we do this in local, context-dependent ways, so do social scientists in their research, unavoidably. This reinforces the point I made earlier about how the criticisms that ethnomethodologists make of conventional social science seem to extend to common-sense reasoning as well; and that a more pragmatic conception of social science may avoid the problems that ethnomethodology identifies here.

The cost of adopting an ethnomethodological approach

Ethnomethodology effectively excludes from rigorous investigation most of what conventional social science studies. This is not a problem if ethnomethodology is a separate discipline, but it certainly is if it is pitched as a replacement for sociology, or for social science generally. One source of this switch in focus is the restricted notion of meaning that stems from ethnomethodology's preoccupation with accountability and sequential activity (Atkinson 1988: 447–52). For ethnomethodologists, the meaning of an object (an action, a person, etc.) is simply what it is publicly treated as being in the course of some stretch of social interaction. So the focus is on, say, whether an utterance was treated as a comment, a complaint, or a request; whether a sequence of action in a laboratory was a rigorous test or 'just going through the motions' (as this is established by the scientists concerned); whether a human body just brought to a hospital is dead or alive (as determined by the doctors); whether an action is an offence against 'the convict code' (as judged by inmates); and so on. Yet most participants in

25 For a challenge to this from within conversation analysis, see Moerman 1988. For discussion of his work, see Hopper 1990/91. This has also been an issue in relation to research on 'institutional talk' and in debates about the relationship between conversation analysis and 'studies of work': see Psathas 1995.

social interaction would recognise, I suggest, that the meanings involved in it go beyond such classificatory matters, and that much meaning (for the parties to it, as well as for others) is not evidenced in this fashion – this including, often, how people feel about the situations they face, or about the actions in which they have engaged, their more remote goals, their motives for engaging in particular actions, the cultural significance of actions and institutions, etc. While such matters are *sometimes* openly displayed in talk, a great deal of the time they are not, and certainly not at the time. In this respect, ethnomethodological studies no more capture 'the feel and ambience that some activities might have for the ordinary persons involved in them' (Sharrock and Anderson 1986: 15) than does much conventional sociology.

The narrowness of focus involved here is illustrated if we make a contrast with the picture of human social life presented in many novels and short stories (including Garfinkel's own 'Color Trouble', 1940), or even in academic stories such as the following:

> At the conference 'Orders of Ordinary Action' in 2001 … Kenneth Liberman asked me if he could borrow a pen and commented 'it's a nice pen, I like the way it writes' to which I responded that he should keep it (I too had got it for free, not that I said so!). He then asked me if I was a Buddhist, to which I responded that I was not. I later reflected on his unusual question and thought that it was to do with present-giving in Buddhism, but after reviewing two of his books on or using Tibetan philosophical discourse as empirical data I now think that Kenneth Liberman was 'alluding' to something else. Having read his work I now realize that the members' knowledge I didn't have at the time was that of the Buddhist concep-tion of the essential emptiness of things and, as a consequence, the impossibility of any real 'ownership' of them. The reason for my recounting this is to attempt to illustrate that I did not need to have knowledge of Buddhism (or of his, as then, unpublished writings), nor he have knowledge of the cost or otherwise of the pen, for us to produce the emergent order that was our conversation. That is not to say that that emergent order would not have produced a different conversa-tion had we been more 'compatible' members. (Jenkings 2009: 775–6)

To take a grimmer example, there were many more meanings surrounding the phone calls Sacks (1967) studied in which people declared that they had 'no one to turn to' than those he focused on, illuminating as his analysis is. In light of this restricted conception of meaning, it must be said that ethnomethodologists' claim to capture the perspective of participants has a hollow ring to it for many other researchers who are committed to understanding the meanings involved in human social life, whether symbolic interactionists or exponents of interpretive phenom-enological analysis, say.

The reason for this restriction on what counts as 'meaning' is, in part, an instrumental one, deriving from the quite specific focus of ethnomethodological inquiry on how those meanings are produced that are required for social actions to be coordinated. From this point of view, any meanings that are not publicly displayed in the course of the relevant piece of social interaction are simply irrelevant, since (it is assumed) they can have played no role in bringing about the coordination displayed in that interaction.[26] Even if, in these instrumental terms, such a severe restriction on what counts as meaning is reasonable, the argument is often pushed beyond this, for example in attacks on 'cognitivism', to imply that there are no meanings other than those exhibited publicly (what might be referred to as 'ontological behaviourism'); or that, if there are, they can play no role in social inquiry ('methodological behaviourism').[27] But these claims are implausible, their cogency has certainly not been established effectively. As I suggested in Chapter 4, very strong reasons would be required to persuade us to abandon virtually all of the component assumptions of the natural attitude in favour of the alternative ontology that ethnomethodologists seem to propose.

The value of ethnomethodological work

A closely related issue, addressed in Chapter 3, is the question of the value of ethnomethodological research. I suspect that, to a considerable extent, for its practitioners the appeal lies in what is felt to be the intrinsic interest of the empirical field opened up, and the illumination of this it provides. Complex and delicate order is found in apparently trivial and largely taken-for-granted forms of action. Early on, for instance, there were studies of how people navigate to avoid one another in walking down the street (Ryave and Schenkein 1974) and how they frame verbal directions to suit the person to whom these are being given (Schegloff 1972). Moreover, the topics addressed have typically been ones that are open to relatively direct investigation, in a way that many of those studied by conventional social science are not. As Sharrock (2000: 537) remarks in relation to conversation analysis: 'Highly unusual in sociology, [it] became capable of setting problems that could be solved.'

At the same time, as Lynch (1999: 221) notes, there has been a problem in convincing other sociologists 'that the questions and topics ethnomethodologists take up are worthy of attention' (see also Sharrock and Anderson 1986: 64–5). Part of the reason for this is that, as I pointed out in the Introduction, these questions and topics do not fit well with the typical 'news values' of social science, even if they are a better fit with those of some other disciplines, such as linguistics and psychology. Moreover, I suspect that this problem extends more widely than just

26 In Schutz's terms, this involves treating actors as 'contemporaries' rather than 'consociates'.

27 See Anderson et al.'s (1985b: 153–4) discussion of methodological behaviourism in the work of Goffman.

fellow sociologists. After all, most of the topics addressed by ethnomethodologists would be a long way down any conventional ranking of public significance, if they were on that list at all. Conventional social science has typically addressed much more obviously significant issues, and yet its findings have frequently been challenged as offering nothing new and/or as putting forward patently fallacious or ideological interpretations. Ethnomethodology offers a counter to the second of these charges, but makes things worse as regards the first.

Indeed, in *general* terms, ethnomethodology reduces all topics to the single one of how social order is accomplished, in the specific senses of the intelligibility and coordination of action. And this issue is not one that is usually of central concern for most sociologists, even less for lay people, so that often the effect of ethnomethodological re-specification is to downgrade the likely significance of any findings. An example is Wieder's study of a 'halfway house' for those coming out of prison, where the original focus of the research – on why such institutions are less successful than anticipated – shifted to a concern with how the 'convict code' is invoked by inmates and others in rendering actions intelligible (see Wieder 1974: 10). The first of these topics is likely to be regarded as of much greater public significance than the second; and, while the two are related, I am not convinced that Wieder adds much to our understanding of that connection, despite the great virtues of his study.[28]

Moreover, in Chapter 3 I argued that, while conversation analysis has generated a valuable body of academic knowledge, and some 'studies of work' (along with some conversation analysis) has had *practical* value, in both cases ethnomethodology seems largely to have played the role of catalyst, at most, rather than active ingredient. Indeed, the cumulative development of knowledge in conversation analysis, facilitated by its narrow focus on sequential analysis, appears actually to be at odds with ethnomethodological principles (Pollner 1991; Bjelić and Lynch 1992: 54; Lynch 1993, 2000c; Lynch and Bogen 1994; Livingston 1987; Watson 2008). If this is the case, it seems that the only worthwhile product from ethnomethodology is a general caution about the complex relationship between rules and practices.

In one of very few attempts to address this issue of value, Lynch (1999) argues that ethnomethodology can make two contributions. First, it can offer reminders to participants about how they do their work; and, second, it can serve as therapy to counter the effects of the sort of theorising characteristic of conventional

---

28 A positive spin could perhaps be put on this. For instance, Pollner (2012b: 27) has suggested that 'One reading of [Garfinkel's] more recent work is that its product is "nothing" in the sense that it explicitly deconstructs itself ... The "nothing" is of the Zen/T.S. Eliot kind where one is returned to the point from which one started with a sense of awe or appreciation.' However, this justification is unlikely to have broad appeal.

social science.[29] He writes that 'for as long as theorists continue to captivate their readers with grand theories which purport to describe and critique what the rest of us do in our daily lives, there will be a gap in the literature for ethnomethodologists to address and dissolve' (p. 229). However, neither of these types of contribution is likely to be widely valued, it seems to me. For example, I doubt that the scientists Lynch (1985) studied needed 'reminders of how they go about their work' (Lynch 1999: 228). Reminders must be tailored to a need: we do not need reminding about most of what we do. Yet ethnomethodological investigations do not seem to have this focused character. Moreover, the therapy argument depends upon a diagnosis of cultural ills that is by no means widely accepted; and its character has only been hinted at by ethnomethodologists, not spelt out and justified.[30]

A potentially more effective justification for ethnomethodology is foundationalist in character. For example, Sharrock and Anderson (1986: 66) comment that 'If the big problems of sociology are to be solved it may be that the way to them is to be found by starting a good way off, with problems on a much smaller scale which can be tackled and carried through to solution.' Along the same lines, it has been argued that it is worth studying the organisation of talk-in-interaction because virtually all human social life relies upon it. However, it needs to be shown that such foundational analysis is required in order to pursue conventional sociological inquiry effectively. Furthermore, as I noted, this kind of foundationalism is rarely presented unequivocally, and seems to be at odds with some other ethnomethodological principles, notably its radical ontology.[31] Moreover, to the extent that ethnomethodology is an idiographic enterprise concerned solely with explicating particular instances of sense-making, it cannot offer any kind of foundation.

The value of what ethnomethodology produces is an important issue. As I have suggested, there is a lack of clarity about the terms in which this should be assessed. Making a contribution to practical activities, building a body of academic knowledge, and serving as therapy, are very different enterprises, involving

29 This also seems to be more or less the position taken by Sharrock and Randall (2004) in their discussion of the value of ethnomethodological work for system design. Interestingly, much earlier Schwartz (1971) had proposed ethnomethodology as a cure for paranoia (see the discussion in Mehan and Wood 1975: 157–8).

30 An example of the hinted-at cultural critique is Bogen (1990: 410): 'It is not only philosophers who have inherited the burdens of transcendental knowledge; the mundane world is saturated with the paradoxes of reason and their accompanying existential anxieties.'

31 Other parts of Sharrock and Anderson's (1986) discussion seem to confirm this, where they insist that ethnomethodology involves a re-specification of the focus of sociological work. See also Button 1991.

potentially conflicting requirements. Today, all academic work is required to be 'accountable' in the sense of showing its 'value for money', a different meaning of the word from Garfinkel's; and, in practical terms at least, this demand cannot be ignored. More fundamentally, justification for academic work – while by no means necessarily formulated in instrumental or direct terms – is a key requirement of researcher integrity (Macfarlane 2009). In my view, this is an issue that has not been addressed very effectively in the case of ethnomethodology, though the same is true of much other work in social science. Of course, it is extremely difficult to assess the likely value of different types of investigation, and great caution should therefore be exercised in any negative judgements. Nevertheless, the issue is unavoidable.[32]

Antinomies

By way of highlighting the problems I have discussed, there are a series of antinomies that seem to be *intrinsic* to ethnomethodology, leading to a tendency to oscillate between opposing positions:

1. Is its orientation towards conventional social science one of critique or of 'indifference'? The dilemma here is that if its attitude is critique then some of the criticisms it makes of social science (for instance, regarding the ascription of psychological characteristics, such as motives, and of causal relations) also apply to much common-sense reasoning and knowledge, thereby breaching the commitment to appreciation. Indeed, this attitude entails an 'ironicising' approach towards both these forms of reasoning and knowledge.

    If, on the other hand, the attitude is indifference, then social science is legitimate, and ethnomethodologists should make no criticisms of it; it is, in Garfinkel's terms, simply 'incommensurate' with their orientation. But if ethnomethodology is not to reform or replace conventional social science, why is it necessary (see Dennis 2003)?

2. Do ethnomethodologists employ a rigorous form of inquiry that relies upon distinctive methods, or do they simply observe and exhibit members' accounting practices? If the first position is adopted, they must address many of the standard methodological problems that social scientists face. The need for this is reflected, for instance, in conversation analysts' emphasis on electronic recording and a technical form of transcription as a preliminary to any analysis, their focus on detailed micro-analysis of social interaction, and their appeal to 'next turn proof' and to deviant case analysis (Schegloff 1968).[33]

32 Schegloff 2005 links the notion of researcher integrity to respecting the integrity of the phenomenon. In effect, he reduces the one to the other. But this is to neglect other important aspects of researcher integrity, including that mentioned here.
33 For a useful discussion of evidence in conversation analysis, see Wootton 1988.

On the other side, some ethnomethodologists renounce any claim to a distinctive method, proposing to rely instead on a suspension of the natural attitude so as to reveal the phenomena in which they are interested, simply employing members' methods in doing so (Lynch 1993). However, this appeal to revelation is implausible, as I showed in Chapter 4: whatever methods are used by ethnomethodologists must surely be treated as *constituting* the phenomena investigated, rather than as merely representing them, given that this is a feature of all account-giving. Furthermore, ethnomethodologists clearly have a very different orientation from most members, since they focus on what the latter routinely take for granted. We might also ask what reason there is to believe that members' methods can serve this distinctive function. At the same time if, in the course of social interaction, members necessarily display to one another the methods they use to make sense of, and produce, actions, what distinctive role is left for ethnomethodologists to perform?

3. Is the task of ethnomethodology to document empirical patterns that the analyst observes and records, or is it to explicate the analyst-as-member's competence in being able to make sense of social actions? The first position makes unexplicated reliance upon common-sense knowledge and reasoning unavoidable, and tends to lead back into the kind of work characteristic of standard disciplines, and the methodological problems associated with this.[34]

However, the second position amounts to a phenomenological form of inquiry, in which the analyst is claiming a capacity to explicate her or his own thinking or practices. This would seem to be at odds with what ethnomethodologists do in most of their work, and with their empirical sociological orientation, as well as amounting to a form of cognitivism.[35]

---

34 Witness, for instance, recent moves within conversation analysis that not only introduce quantitative measures but also employ a framework concerned with weighing the relative causal contributions of different factors: see, for instance, Clayman et al. 2006; Heritage et al. 2007; Stivers 2007; Stivers and Majid 2007. There has also been a parallel development concerned with using experimental methods, see Kendrick 2017 (I am grateful to Rod Watson for drawing my attention to this).

35 There is another alternative to viewing ethnomethodological work as empirical social science, which has influenced some ethnomethodologists: the conceptual analysis characteristic of ordinary language philosophy. However, there are questions about the compatibility of this with ethnomethodology and conversation analysis. For example, some of the arguments deployed by Coulter (1999) against discursive psychology could also apply to conversation analysis. This is illustrated when Coulter says that 'people can, and do, misuse words on occasion, and may even do so in ways which are not locally corrected nor challenged by participant interlocutors' (p. 171). Central here too is the question of whether what is to be discovered is an empirical or *a priori* matter, from which flow different answers to the question of how to investigate it.

4. Do the meanings that are generated in the process of social interaction create reality, or are there external constraints operating on what meanings can be generated on particular occasions? Pollner (1978, 1987, 1991) has elaborated the first position, drawing out the constructionist implications of the radical concepts of indexicality and reflexivity. However, this interpretation of ethnomethodology seems to be at odds with that of others, for example Bogen (1990) and Button and Sharrock (1993).

There are undoubtedly problems with the constructionist interpretation, in that, logically, it must treat ethnomethodology as constructing its own reality (see, for instance, Mehan and Wood 1975). Moreover, it seems to conflate the issue of how meanings are constituted with that of what exists. At the same time, there are serious difficulties with the non-constructionist interpretation, notably about whether it is sustainable given ethnomethodology's commitments (see Hammersley 2019b). For example, while Button and Sharrock (1993) insist that the meanings generated in processes of social interaction are not arbitrary, they do not provide much indication of what the source of constraint is, and it is not clear how ethnomethodological inquiry could document this.[36]

5. Are there context-transcendent methods or is ethnomethodology an idiographic approach? Initially, Garfinkel and early ethnomethodologists gave the impression that while all accounts are occasioned there are context-transcendent methods that structure the production of actions, and that these are the focus of analysis. This was built into the work of Cicourel and that of many conversation analysts. It is what grounds claims to the effect that ethnomethodological work provides a more 'generative' form of knowledge than conventional social science (see Watson and Sharrock 1991).

However, there is some ambiguity about the character of these methods – the documentary method of interpretation, etcetera, let it pass, etc., or an 'apparatus' or 'machinery'?; as well as uncertainty about how the former generate agreement in understanding and how the latter could avoid the problem Garfinkel identified with norms and their application. Perhaps because of these issues, in his later work Garfinkel seems to have moved away from any notion of context-transcendent methods. But this carries the implication that

36 Ethnomethodologists can document how people constitute phenomena as constraints, but that is not the same thing. Drawing on Wittgenstein, Button and Sharrock (1993: 13) appeal to 'natural reactions', which they regard as reflecting 'our sensible activities', but these are treated as simply given (rather than, for example, as the product of evolutionary and/or other processes), and it is not clear whether they are held to cover all of the external constraints involved.

that ethnomethodology is an entirely idiographic enterprise, and its purposes and value would be hard to justify in these terms.[37]

6. Is the task of ethnomethodology to provide textual descriptions of how social phenomena are constituted as what they are, or is it to instruct readers in how to go about constituting those phenomena for themselves?[38] If description is taken as the task then, as Pollner (1987) indicates, radical indexicality and reflexivity would seem to imply that what is described is constituted in ethnomethodological terms, rather than simply exhibited.

But even if the task of ethnomethodology is to instruct readers, the instructions it provides are themselves necessarily indexical and reflexive. Moreover, if the task is instruction, then social science seems to have been abandoned for pedagogy, as I pointed out in Chapter 4.

7. Do utterances and actions require interpretation for people to grasp their meaning, or is their meaning understood and displayed in a more direct way? In *Studies*, Garfinkel (1967a: 40, 78) seems to adopt the first position, hence his suggestion that people rely upon the documentary method of interpretation, so that 'work' is involved in making sense of what is happening. However, in his later writings he appears to move away from this, and some ethnomethodologists have denied that understanding people's actions involves interpretation, often appealing to the writings of Wittgenstein (Coulter 1989: ch. 3) or Austin (Hutchinson et al. 2008: 14–15) in support of this. However, this appears to move back to an emphasis upon the causal role of socialisation that is analogous in some respects to Parsons' approach. There are complex and difficult issues involved here, and it is by no means obvious that ethnomethodology has resolved them (see Phillips 1978; but also Heritage 1978).

8. Finally, there is the problem of agency: is it individual people who carry out the work involved in constituting phenomena as what they are, or are settings self-organising, this involving the mutual constitution of actions and their contexts on each and every occasion? The first position seems necessarily to involve the attribution of cognitive, and perhaps other, capabilities and dispositions to

---

37 ten Have (2004: 174) suggests that the tension between the focus on the individual case and the search for 'generalities' is inherent in ethnomethodology, and treats it as productive. In my view it represents a serious lack of clarity about the purpose of the enterprise, one which damages its practice in ways that I have outlined.

38 A striking illustration of the latter is, perhaps, the 'Sudnow Method' for learning to play jazz piano: see http://www.sudnow.com/, derived from Sudnow's (1978) earlier ethnomethodological account of this process. Another illustration could be Atkinson's books on speech-making, deriving from his ethnomethodological study of political speeches: Atkinson 1984, 2004, 2008.

people, thereby being open to the charge of cognitivism. The second raises challenging questions about the nature of the agency involved, and also appears to reduce people to 'dopes', an accusation that Garfinkel (1967b: 68) had directed at conventional sociology.

Closely related to this is the issue of what the term 'member' means for ethnomethodologists. 'Membership' is defined in terms of competence, so that a member is someone who has the competence to be able to make sense of what is going on in a particular situation and to act appropriately in it. There is a question here, though, about who decides what comprises membership and who is a competent member. Garfinkel (1967b: 57, 76) initially defined 'membership' in Parsons' terms as 'collectivity membership' or role incumbency, and here what constitutes membership and who is a member seem to be determined by the analyst. However, subsequently ethnomethodologists have typically argued that the nature of membership, and who is and is not a member, are determined by members in and through their interactions with one another (see, for instance, Anderson and Lee 1986). But there is circularity here. And, if 'membershipping', inclusionary or exclusionary, is an interactional process, what legitimate analytic role it can play?

It seems to me that these antinomies are difficult to resolve without a major re-evaluation of ethnomethodological principles. They explain, in part, why ethnomethodology has generated severe internal conflict and debate, and considerable diversity in practice.

Coda

As I have emphasised, ethnomethodology is of value in raising important questions about the validity of much social science (see Chapter 3). There is certainly a tendency for sociologists to treat the ideas or practices of the people studied as either proto-scientific or ideological, and therefore as in need of replacement by social scientific knowledge. In other words, they often seem to take it for granted that their own conclusions are superior to those of lay people simply as a result of being the product of research, while lay people's views are treated as defective because subject to the play of interests and ideological misconceptions. Yet, any such general conclusion is false, not least because social science is itself subject to the effects of interests and ideology.[39]

A second issue that ethnomethodology highlights is the question of how the concepts and perspectives of participants are to be incorporated into social

---

39 For illustration, see Hammersley 2014: ch. 6.

science explanations. The role of these in generating actions must surely be recognised – but how are they to be conceptualised scientifically, given their complex and dynamic character?[40] This is closely related to the problem of how to accommodate the fact that actors do not simply conform to or reject norms and values, but employ them flexibly in context-sensitive ways. Similarly, they do not merely follow their interests or abide by their preferences; but, rather, determine what those interests or preferences are in the course of pursuing them (see Wieder 1974: 212–14). Can social scientists ignore these complexities in order to use norms, values, or interests as causal factors, or solve the problem by acknowledging that they are relying upon simplifying models? Schutz offered one possible solution to this by building on Weber's methodological writings about ideal types, but is this successful? This cannot be a foregone conclusion (see Wilson 2005), nor is the solution he proposed generally adopted within social science (Hammersley 2014).

Ethnomethodology also shows why social scientists need to be more modest in their claims to knowledge than they often are. The charge that what they produce draws in unexplicated ways on what is taken to be 'common-sense', some of which is open to reasonable doubt, and that their findings are therefore *sometimes* little different from lay views in epistemic status, is surely true. And it raises questions about what ontological and epistemological assumptions can be relied upon.

In positive terms, the studies ethnomethodology has produced – whether ethnographies, conversation analytic investigations, or of other kinds – have often generated important forms of knowledge about previously neglected topics. While I have raised questions about the value of some of this work, it cannot be denied that many of these studies have made a significant contribution to the social science literature, as well as to other areas, notably linguistics and psychology.

At the same time, as I have emphasised in this conclusion, there are serious problems with the rationale for ethnomethodology. These stem in large part from its commitment to a radical stance that questions the foundations of social enquiry, and that effectively puts itself forward as a replacement science. As I have indicated, in effect this amounts to questioning the natural attitude itself, and yet we can hardly avoid relying on this to a considerable degree: even ethnomethodologists must do so. A more pragmatic conception of inquiry is required: 'radical' should not be treated as a synonym for 'good', in the epistemological any more than in the political realm. As I have noted, there would need to be very strong reasons for us to abandon all of the fundamental assumptions about the social world on which we rely in everyday life, in favour of the kind

---

40 Much the same problem arises within symbolic interactionism: see Hammersley 1989b, 2010b.

of radical alternative ontology proposed by ethnomethodology. And I do not believe this case has been made cogently.

Also misguided, it seems to me, is to adopt a radical *methodological* stance, according to which the knowledge that science produces must meet fundamentally different standards from those guiding lay social investigations. That there will be a difference in standards, attuned to the particular purposes of social research, is true enough. I suggest that this difference amounts to a greater concern than is usual in most (but not all) lay inquiries with the clarification of concepts, with the development and refinement of explanatory ideas, and with checking the validity of descriptions and explanations. However, neither a radical positivist conception of science, modelled on physics, of the kind that ethnomethodologists use to fault sociological research, nor the very different version of rigorous enquiry adopted by ethnomethodology itself, modelled on phenomenology, seem viable as a basis for social science.

It is also unfortunate that the radical ontological and methodological stance adopted by ethnomethodology encourages sharply dismissive attitudes on both sides of whatever line is drawn around it. This threatens the possibility of fruitful dialogue and of progress in resolving the serious problems that social science faces. Of course the issues involved are deep and challenging ones. As Sharrock and Randall (2004: 189) note:

> there is nothing akin to 'knock out' criticism in the social sciences, and the fact that some people have what they think are profound and fatal objections to a position does not prevent other people from continuing to – in many cases, actually – believe in the position that is supposedly discredited. Indeed, the situation is pretty much that every position continues in the face of the fact that a substantial part of the social studies public regards that same position as seriously, if not fatally, flawed. Issues typically get resolved only to the satisfaction of the already converted.

However, while the issues are certainly very difficult, I do not believe that we should, or can, be satisfied with the situation that Sharrock and Randall describe.

Understandably, in the face of fundamental disagreement there can be impatience with opposing views. Button (1991: xi) suggests that within sociology 'there persists an obstinate, at times almost wilfully malicious misunderstanding' of ethnomethodology. Yet, while it is true that misunderstanding is rife, Button's statement seriously underestimates the difficulties in comprehending, and above all grasping the point of, what he himself labels a call for 'a radicalising re-specification of sociological method' (p. xi). And, in fact, he goes on to indicate why ethnomethodology is so difficult to understand for other sociologists. I suggest that his views both point to and exemplify the fact that it is easy to resort to oversimplification, to reduce others' arguments to stereotypes, and thereby to fail to engage with what may be pertinent. No neutrality is possible in this situation, but engagement directed at comprehending why those on each side hold the views they do is essential.[41]

Of course, it could be argued that there is actually no prospect at all of resolving the differences between ethnomethodologists and other social scientists, because these derive from fundamental commitments that are (in effect) matters of 'faith' and are therefore irreconcilable. As I noted in the Introduction, Bergner (1981) put forward an argument along these lines, many years ago, suggesting that social science is condemned to generating a plurality of incommensurable approaches. In this book I have assumed that this *not* the case: that while the issues that divide approaches within social science may be fundamental ones, there is some scope for resolving them if they are patiently explored. As I pointed out, despite acknowledging the rampant pluralism in their field, most social scientists believe that their own approach is the correct one: in other words, at most they are pluralists by convenience rather than by commitment. Needless to say, many of them, perhaps especially ethnomethodologists, want to get on with their own distinctive work, rather than engaging in what they may see as programmatic discussion or pointless debate. But, as Max Weber (see Bruun and Whimster 2012: xiv–xv) grudgingly acknowledged in turning to methodological issues, sometimes attention to these is necessary. And I suggest that the present state of social science, with its lamentable array of competing 'approaches', makes it especially so today. Felix Kaufmann (1944; Cohen and Helling 2014), whose work significantly influenced Garfinkel in his early career, very much followed in Weber's footsteps in seeking to clarify, and resolve, the issues facing social science at the beginning of the twentieth century. More than half a century later, this book has been written in the same spirit – though it is chastening to recognise that many of the problems remain the same.

---

41 An admirable case for just such an approach is provided by Anderson et al. 1985b: 146–7 and *passim*.

References

Abbott, A. (2001) *Chaos of Disciplines*, Chicago, University of Chicago Press.

Abercrombie, N. (1974) 'Sociological indexicality', *Journal for the Theory of Social Behaviour*, 4:1, pp. 89–95.

Alpert, H. (1938) 'Operational Definitions in Sociology', *American Sociological Review*, 3:6, pp. 855–61.

Anderson, D. (1978) 'Some organizational features in the local production of a plausible text', *Philosophy of the Social Sciences*, 8:11, pp. 113–35.

Anderson, I. G. and Lee, J. R. E. (1986) 'Taking Professor Gluckman seriously: the case of participant observation', in Frankenberg, R. (ed.) *Custom and Conflict in British Society*, Manchester, Manchester University Press. Also available at: https://zenodo.org/record/31701#.Wko67d9l-70 (accessed 4 Jan. 2018).

Anderson, R. J. (2016) 'Critique, complacency, cumulativity and comparators: Notes on "radical ethnomethodology"'. Available at: http://radicalethno.org/documents/anderson.pdf (accessed 4 Jan. 2018).

Anderson, R. J., Hughes, J. A., and Sharrock, W. W. (1985a) 'The relationship between ethnomethodology and phenomenology', *Journal of the British Society for Phenomenology*, 16:3, pp. 221–35.

Anderson, R. J., Hughes, J. A., and Sharrock, W. W. (1985b) *The Sociology Game*, London, Longman.

Anderson, R. J., Hughes, J. A., and Sharrock, W. W. (1989) *Working for Profit: The social organisation of calculation in an entrepreneurial firm*, Aldershot, Avebury.

Anderson, R. and Sharrock, W. (1984) 'Analytic work: aspects of the organisation of conversational data', *Journal for the Theory of Social Behaviour*, 14:1, pp. 103–24.

Anderson, R. and Sharrock, W. (2018) *Action at a Distance: The practicalities of management*, London, Routledge.

Antaki, C. (ed.) (2011) *Applied Conversation Analysis*, Basingstoke, Palgrave Macmillan.

Argyle, M. (1969) *Social Interaction*, London, Methuen.

Aron, R. (1969) *Main Currents of Sociological Thought*, Vol. 1, Harmondsworth, Penguin.

Asch, S. E. (1951) 'The effects of group pressure in the modification and situation of judgements', in Guetzkow, H. (ed.) *Groups, Leadership and Men*, Pittsburgh, PA, Carnegie Press.

Asch, S. E. (1955) 'Opinions and social pressures', *Scientific American*, 193, pp. 31–5.

Ashmore, M. (1989) *The Reflexive Thesis*, Chicago, University of Chicago Press.

Atkinson, J. M. and Heritage, J. (eds) (1984) *Structures of Social Action*, Cambridge, Cambridge University Press.

References

Atkinson, M. (1984) *Our Masters' Voices: The language and body language of politics*, London, Methuen.

Atkinson, M. (2004) *Lend Me Your Ears: All you need to know about speech-making and presentations*, London, Vermilion.

Atkinson, M. (2008) *Speech-Making and Presentation Made Easy*, London Vermilion.

Atkinson, P. (1988) 'Ethnomethodology: a critical review', *Annual Review of Sociology*, 14, pp. 441–65.

Atkinson, P. (1989) 'Goffman's poetics', *Human Studies*, 12, pp. 59–76.

Atkinson, P. (2015) *For Ethnography*, London, Sage.

Atkinson, P. and Silverman, D. (1997) 'Kundera's immortality: the interview society and the invention of the self', *Qualitative Inquiry*, 3, pp. 304–25.

Axelrod, C. D. (1977) 'Towards an appreciation of Simmel's fragmentary style', *Sociological Quarterly*, 18:2, pp. 185–96.

Backhaus, G. (1998) 'Georg Simmel as an eidetic social scientist', *Sociological Theory*, 16:3, pp. 260–81.

Bar-Hillel, Y. (1954) 'Indexical expressions', *Mind*, 63, pp. 359–79.

Barber, M. (2004) *The Participating Citizen: A biography of Alfred Schutz*, Albany, State University of New York Press.

Barnes, B. (1974) *Scientific Knowledge and Sociological Theory*, London, Routledge and Kegan Paul.

Beattie, G. (1983) *Talk: An analysis of speech and non-verbal behaviour in conversation*, Milton Keynes, Open University Press.

Becker, H. S. (1960) 'Notes on the concept of commitment', *American Journal of Sociology*, 66:1, pp. 32–40.

Becker, H. S. (1963) *Outsiders*, New York, Free Press.

Becker, H. S. (2003) 'Continuity and change in Howard S. Becker's work: an interview with Howard S. Becker (by Ken Plummer)', *Sociological Perspectives*, 46:1, pp. 21–39.

Beiser, F. (2014) *The Genesis of Neo-Kantianism*, Oxford, Oxford University Press.

Bell, D. (1976) *The Cultural Contradictions of Capitalism*, New York: Basic Books.

Bennett, J. (1966) *Kant's Analytic*, Cambridge, Cambridge University Press.

Benson, D. (1974) 'A critical note. A revolution in sociology?', *Sociology*, 8, pp. 125–9.

Benson, D. and Hughes, J. (1983) *The Perspective of Ethnomethodology*, London, Longman.

Benson, D. and Hughes, J. (1991) 'Method: evidence and inference', in Button, G. (ed.) *Ethnomethodology and the Human Sciences*, Cambridge, Cambridge University Press.

Berger, P. and Luckmann, T. (1966) *The Social Construction of Reality: A Treatise in the Sociology of Knowledge*, Garden City, NY, Doubleday.

Bergner, J. (1981) *The Origin of Formalism in Social Science*, Chicago, Chicago University Press.

Bird, A. (2001) *Thomas Kuhn*, London, Routledge.

Birdwhistell, R. (1970) *Kinesics and Context*, Philadelphia, University of Pennsylvania Press.

Bittner, E. (1963) 'Radicalism and the organization of radical movements', *American Sociological Review*, 28:6, pp. 928–40.

Bittner, E. (1967a) 'The police on skid-row: a study of peace keeping', *American Sociological Review*, 32:5, pp. 699–715.

References

Bittner, E. (1967b) 'Police discretion in emergency apprehension of mentally ill persons', *Social Problems*, 14:3, pp. 278–92.

Bittner, E. (1973) 'Objectivity and realism in sociology', in Psathas, G. (ed.) *Phenomenological Sociology*, New York, Wiley.

Bittner, E. (1977) 'Must we say what we mean?', in Ostwald, P. F. (ed.) *Communication and Social Interaction*, London: Grune and Stratton, pp. 83–97.

Bjelić, D. (1995) 'An ethnomethodological clarification of Husserl's concepts of "regressive inquiry" and "Galilean physics" by means of discovering praxioms', *Human Studies*, 18, pp. 189–225.

Bjelić, D. and Lynch, M. (1992) 'The work of a (scientific) demonstration: respecifying Newton's and Goethe's theories of prismatic color', in Watson, G. and Seiler, R. (eds) *Text in Context*, Newbury Park, CA, Sage.

Blau, P. (1969) 'Sociological analysis: current trends and personal practice', *Sociological Inquiry*, 39, pp. 119–30.

Bleicher, J. (2007) 'From Kant to Goethe: Georg Simmel on the way to *Leben*', *Theory, Culture and Society*, 24:6, pp. 139–58.

Blomberg, J. and Karasti, H. (2013) 'Reflections on 25 years of ethnography in CSCW', *Computer Supported Cooperative Work*, 22, pp. 373–423.

Bloor, D. (1976) *Knowledge and Social Imagery*, London, Routledge and Kegan Paul.

Blum, A. and McHugh, P. (1971) 'The social ascription of motives', *American Sociological Review*, 36:1, pp. 98–109.

Blumer, H. (1969) *Symbolic Interactionism*, Englewood Cliffs, NJ, Prentice-Hall.

Bogen, D. (1990) 'Beyond the "limits" of *Mundane Reason*', *Human Studies*, 13:4, pp. 405–16.

Bogen, D. (1999) *Order Without Rules: Critical theory and the logic of conversation*, Albany, NY, SUNY Press.

Braun, D. (2017) 'Indexicals', in Edward N. Zalta (ed.) *The Stanford Encyclopedia of Philosophy* (Summer), Available at: https://plato.stanford.edu/archives/sum2017/entries/indexicals (accessed 16 Dec. 2017).

Bruce, S. and Wallis, R. (1983) 'Rescuing motives', *British Journal of Sociology*, 34, pp. 61–71.

Bruce, S. and Wallis, R. (1985) '"Rescuing motives" rescued: a reply to Sharrock and Watson', *British Journal of Sociology*, 36, pp. 467–70.

Bruun, H. and Whimster, S. (2012) 'Introduction', in Bruun, H. and Whimster, S. (eds) *Max Weber: Collected Methodological Writings*, London, Routledge.

Buckley, W. (1967) *Sociology and Modern System Theory*, Englewood Cliffs, NJ, Prentice-Hall.

Bulmer, M. (1984) *The Chicago School of Sociology*, Chicago, University of Chicago Press.

Burke, K. (1935) *Permanence and Change: An anatomy of purpose*, New York, New Republic.

Burns, T. (1992) *Erving Goffman*, London, Routledge.

Burr, V. (2015) *Social Constructionism*, 3rd edn, London, Routledge.

Button, G. (ed.) (1991) *Ethnomethodology and the Human Sciences*, Cambridge, Cambridge University Press.

Button, G. (ed.) (1993) *Technology in Working Order: Studies of Work, Interaction and Technology*, London, Routledge.

References

Button, G. (2012) 'What does "work" mean in "ethnomethodological studies of work"?', *Design Studies*, 33:6, pp. 673–84.

Button, G., Crabtree, A., Rouncefield, A. and Tolmie, P. (2015) *Deconstructing Ethnography: Toward a methodology for ubiquitous computing and interactive system design*, Cham, Springer.

Button, G. and Sharrock, W. (1993) 'A disagreement over agreement and consensus in constructionist sociology', *Journal for the Theory of Social Behaviour*, 23:1, pp. 1–25.

Button, G. and Sharrock, W. (1995) 'The mundane work of writing and reading computer programs', in ten Have, P. and Psathas, G. (eds) *Situated Order: Studies in the social organization of talk and embodied activities*. Lanham, MD: University Press of America.

Button, G. and Sharrock, W. (2016) 'In support of conversation analysis' radical agenda', *Discourse Studies*, 18:5, pp. 610–20.

Byrne, D. and Ragin, C. (eds) (2009) *The Sage Handbook of Case-Based Methods*, London, Sage.

Camic, C. (1987) 'The making of a method: a historical reinterpretation of the early Parsons', *American Sociological Review*, 52:4, pp. 421–39.

Camic, C. (1991) 'Introduction', in Camic, C. (ed.) *Talcott Parsons: The early essays*, Chicago, University of Chicago Press.

Carey, J. (1975) *Sociology and Public Affairs: The Chicago School*, Beverly Hills, CA, Sage.

Cassirer, E. (1953) *Substance and Function*. English translation, New York, Dover. (First published in German in 1923.)

Chapoulie, J. (1996) 'Everett Hughes and the Chicago tradition', *Sociological Theory*, 14:1, pp. 3–29.

Chriss, J. (1993) 'Looking back on Goffman: the excavation continues', *Human Studies*, 16:4, pp. 469–83.

Cicourel, A. V. (1964) *Method and Measurement in Sociology*, New York, Free Press.

Cicourel, A. V. (1968) *The Social Organization of Juvenile Justice*, New York, Wiley.

Cicourel, A. V. (1973) *Cognitive Sociology*, Harmondsworth, Penguin.

Cicourel, A. V. (1974) *Theory and Method in a Study of Argentine Fertility*, New York, Wiley.

Cicourel, A. V. (2016) 'Response to Smith and Atkinson', *International Journal of Social Research Methodology*, 19:1, pp. 111–20.

Cicourel, A. V., Jennings, K., Jennings, S., Leiter, K., MacKay, R., Mehan, H., and Roth, D. (1974) *Language Use and School Performance*, New York, Academic Press.

Cicourel, A. V. and Kitsuse, J. I. (1963) *The Educational Decision Makers*, Indianapolis, IN, Bobbs-Merrill.

Clayman, S., Elliott, M., Heritage, J., and McDonald, L. (2006) 'Historical trends in questioning presidents 1953–2000', *Presidential Studies Quarterly*, 36, pp. 561–83.

Clayman, S. and Gill, V. (2012) 'Conversation analysis', in Gee, J. and Handford, M. (eds) *The Routledge Handbook of Discourse Analysis*, London, Routledge, pp. 120–34.

Clayman, S. and Maynard, D. (1995) 'Ethnomethodology and conversation analysis', in P. ten Have and G. Psathas (eds) *Situated Order: Studies in the social organization of talk and embodied activities*, Lanham, MD: University Press of America.

Cohen, R. S. and Helling, I. K. (eds) (2014) *Felix Kaufmann's Theory and Method in the Social Sciences*, Boston Studies in the Philosophy and History of Science, Cham, Switzerland, Springer.

References

Coleman, J. (1968) 'Reviewed work: *Studies in Ethnomethodology*, by Harold Garfinkel', *American Sociological Review*, 33:1, pp. 126–30.

Collins, R. (1975) *Conflict Sociology*, New York, Academic Press.

Coombs, C. (1953) 'Theory and methods of social measurement', in Festinger, L. and Katz, D. (eds) *Research Methods in the Behavioral Sciences*, New York, Dryden Press.

Cooper, B., Glaesser, J., and Hammersley, M. (2012) *Challenging the Qualitative–Quantitative Divide*, London, Continuum/Bloomsbury.

Coser, L. (1956) *The Functions of Social Conflict*, Glencoe IL, Free Press.

Coser, L. (1958) 'Georg Simmel's style of work: a contribution to the sociology of a sociologist', *American Journal of Sociology*, 63, pp. 635–41. (Reprinted in Frisby, D. (ed.) (1994) *Georg Simmel: Critical assessments*, 4 vols, London, Routledge, Vol. 2.)

Coser, L. (1975) 'Presidential address: two methods in search of substance', *American Sociological Review*, 40:6, pp. 691–700.

Coser, L. (1976) 'Reply to my critics', *American Sociologist*, 11, pp. 33–8.

Coser, L. (1979) 'A dialogue of the deaf', *Contemporary Sociology*, 8, pp. 680–2.

Coulter, J. (1979) *The Social Construction of Mind*, London, Macmillan.

Coulter, J. (1983a) *Rethinking Cognitive Theory*, London, Macmillan.

Coulter, J. (1983b) 'Contingent and a priori structures in sequential analysis', *Human Studies*, 6, pp. 361–76.

Coulter, J. (1989) *Mind in Action*, Atlantic Highlands, NJ, Humanities Press International.

Coulter, J. (1991) 'Logic: ethnomethodology and the logic of language', in Button, G. (ed.) *Ethnomethodology and the Human Sciences*, Cambridge, Cambridge University Press.

Coulter, J. (1999) 'Discourse and mind', *Human Studies*, 22, pp. 163–81.

Coulter, J. (2008) 'Twenty-five theses against cognitivism', *Theory, Culture and Society*, 25:2, pp. 19–32.

Crespo, R. (1997) 'Max Weber and Ludwig von Mises, and the methodology of the social sciences', in Koslowski, P. (ed.) *Methodology of the Social Sciences, Ethics, and Economics in the Newer Historical School*, Berlin, Springer.

Czyzewski, M. (1994) 'Reflexivity of actors versus reflexivity of accounts', *Theory, Culture and Society*, 11, pp. 161–8.

Davies, M. (1995) *Childhood Sexual Abuse and the Construction of Identity: Healing Sylvia*, London, Taylor and Francis.

Davis, M. (1973) 'Georg Simmel and the aesthetics of social reality', *Social Forces*, 51:3, pp. 320–9. (Reprinted in Frisby, D. (ed.) (1994) *Georg Simmel: Critical assessments*, 4 vols, London, Routledge, Vol. 2.)

Dawe, A. (1970) 'The two sociologies', *The British Journal of Sociology*, 21:2, pp. 207–18.

Demerath, N. and Peterson, R. (eds) (1967) *System, Change, and Conflict*, New York, Free Press.

de Mille, R. (1990) 'Ethnomethodallegory', in de Mille, R. (ed.) *The Don Juan Papers*, Belmont, CA, Wadsworth.

Dennis, A. (2003) 'Skepticist philosophy as ethnomethodology', *Philosophy of the Social Sciences*, 33, pp. 151–73.

Dennis, A. (2004) 'Lynch on Schutz and science: postanalytic ethnomethodology reconsidered', *Theory and Science*, 5, 1. Available at: http://theoryandscience.icaap.org/content/vol5.1/dennis.html (accessed 4 Jan. 2018).

References

Dennis, A. (2011) 'Symbolic interactionism and ethnomethodology', *Symbolic Interaction*, 34:3, pp. 349–56.

Dennis, A., Philburn, R., and Smith, G. (2013) *Sociologies of Interaction*, Cambridge, Polity Press.

Denzin, N. (1969) 'Symbolic interactionism and ethnomethodology: a proposed synthesis', *American Sociological Review*, 34:6, pp. 922–34.

Denzin, N. (1989) 'Sociology and the spirit of sixty-eight', *British Journal of Sociology*, 40:3, 418–41.

Denzin, N. (1997) *Interpretive Ethnography*, Thousand Oaks, CA, Sage.

Dewey, J. (1922) *Human Nature and Conduct*, New York, Henry Holt.

Dewey, J. (1938) *Logic: the theory of inquiry*, New York, Henry Holt.

Doubt, K. (1989) 'Garfinkel before ethnomethodology', *American Sociologist*, 20:3, pp. 252–62.

Douglas, J. D. (1967) *The Social Meanings of Suicide*, Princeton, NJ, Princeton University Press.

Douglas, J. D. (1970) 'Understanding everyday life', in Douglas, J. D. (ed.) *Understanding Everyday Life*, Chicago, Aldine.

Dray, W. (1957) *Laws and Explanation in History*, Oxford, Oxford University Press.

Drew, P. and Heritage, J. (eds) (1992) *Talk at Work: Interaction in institutional settings*, Cambridge, Cambridge University Press.

Dunne, J. (1997) *Back to the Rough Ground: Practical judgment and the lure of technique*, Notre Dame, IN, University of Notre Dame Press.

Durkheim, É. (1894) *Les Règles de la méthode sociologique*, Paris, Payot.

Durkheim, É. (1902) 'Simmel, Georg, *Philosophie des Geldes*', *Année Sociologique*, 5, pp. 140–5. (English translation: Baehr, P. (1979) *Social Research*, 46:2, pp. 321–8.)

Durkheim, É. (1915) *The Elementary Forms of Religious Life*, London, Allen and Unwin.

Durkheim, É. (1933) *The Division of Labour in Society*, New York, Free Press. (First published in French in 1893.)

Durkheim, É. (1938) *The Rules of Sociological Method*, Chicago, University of Chicago Press.

Durkheim, É. (1979) 'Review of Georg Simmel *Philosophie des Geldes*', *Social Research*, 46, pp. 321–8. (First published in French in 1895.)

Ebeling, R. (1999) 'Human action, ideal types, and the market process: Alfred Schutz and the Austrian economists', in Embree, L. (ed.) *Schutzian Social Science*, Dordrecht, Kluwer.

Eberle, T. (2010) 'The phenomenological life-world analysis and the methodology of the social sciences', *Human Studies*, 33:2/3, pp. 123–39.

Eberle, T. (2012) 'Phenomenological life-world analysis and ethnomethodology's program', *Human Studies*, 35, pp. 279–304.

Edley, N. and Wetherell, M. (1997) 'Jockeying for position: the construction of masculine identities', *Discourse and Society*, 8, pp. 203–17.

Edwards, D. and Potter, J. (2009) *Discursive Psychology*, London, Sage.

Eglin, R. (1986) 'Introduction to a hermeneutics of the occult: alchemy', in Garfinkel, H. (ed.) *Ethnomethodological Studies of Work*, London, Routledge.

References

Embree, L. (1972) 'Biographical sketch of Aron Gurwitsch', in Gurwitsch, A. and Embree, L. (eds) *Life-World and Consciousness*, Evanston, IL, Northwestern University Press. Available at: https://web.archive.org/web/20120204102358/http://www.gurwitsch.net/bio.htm (accessed 4 Jan. 2018).

Emerson, R., Fretz, R., and Shaw, L. (2011) *Writing Ethnographic Fieldnotes*, Chicago, University of Chicago Press.

Farber, M. (1943) *The Foundations of Phenomenology*, Cambridge, MA, Harvard University Press.

Fine, G. A. (1993) 'The sad demise, mysterious disappearance, and glorious triumph of symbolic interactionism', *Annual Review of Sociology*, 19, pp. 61–87.

Fitzgerald, R. and Housley, R. (eds) (2015) *Advances in Membership Categorisation Analysis*, London, Sage.

Flynn, P. (1991) *The Ethnomethodological Movement: Sociosemiotic interpretations*, Dordrecht, Mouton de Gruyter.

Føllesdal, D. (1979) 'Hermeneutics and the hypothetico-deductive method', *Dialectica*, 33:3–4, pp. 319–36.

Foster, P., Gomm, R., and Hammersley, M. (1996) *Constructing Educational Inequality*, London, Falmer Press.

Fox, N. and Alldred, P. (2016) *Sociology and the New Materialism*, London, Sage.

Francis, D. and Hester, S. (2004) *An Invitation to Ethnomethodology*, London, Sage.

Friedrichs, R. (1970) *A Sociology of Sociology*, New York, Free Press.

Frisby, D. (1981) *Sociological Impressionism: A reassessment of Georg Simmel's social theory*, London, Heinemann.

Frisby, D. (1984) *Georg Simmel*, London, Routledge. (Second edition, London, Routledge, 2002.)

Frisby, D. (1986) *Fragments of Modernity: Theories of modernity in the theories of Simmel, Kracauer and Benjamin*, Cambridge, MA, MIT Press.

Fuchs, S. (1989) 'Second thoughts on emergent interaction orders', *Sociological Theory*, 7:1, pp. 121–3.

Gallant, M. and Kleinman, S. (1983) 'Symbolic interactionism vs. ethnomethodology', *Symbolic Interaction*, 6, pp. 1–18.

Garcez, P. (1997) 'Microethnography', in Hornberger, N. and Corson, D. (eds) *Encyclopedia of Language and Education*, Vol. 8, Dordrecht, Kluwer, pp. 187–96.

Garfinkel, H. (1940) 'Color trouble', *Opportunity*, 18, pp. 144–51.

Garfinkel, H (1948/2005) *Seeing Sociologically: the routine grounds of social action*, Boulder, CO, Paradigm.

Garfinkel, H. (1952) *The Perception of the Other: A Study in Social Order*, PhD thesis, Harvard University.

Garfinkel, H. (1952/2008), *Toward a Sociological Theory of Information*, Boulder, CO, Paradigm.

Garfinkel, H. (1956a) 'Some sociological concepts and methods for psychiatrists', *Psychiatric Research Reports of the American Psychiatric Association*, 6, pp. 181–95.

Garfinkel, H. (1956b) 'Conditions for successful degradation ceremonies', *American Journal of Sociology*, 61:5, pp. 420–4.

References

Garfinkel, H. (1960/1972) 'A comparison of decisions made on four 'pre-theoretical' problems by Talcott Parsons and Alfred Schuetz', unpublished paper, Department of Sociology, University of California, Los Angeles (first circulated in 1960; retyped and redistributed in 1972).

Garfinkel, H. (1962) 'The rational properties of scientific and common sense activities', *Behavioral Science*, 5, pp. 72–83. (Republished in Garfinkel, H. (1967a) *Studies in Ethnomethodology*, Englewood Cliffs, NJ, Prentice-Hall.)

Garfinkel, H. (1963) 'A conception of, and experiments with, "trust" as a condition of stable concerted actions', in Harvey, O. J. (ed.) *Motivation and Social Interaction: Cognitive determinants*, New York, Ronald Press.

Garfinkel, H. (1967a) *Studies in Ethnomethodology*, Englewood Cliffs, NJ, Prentice-Hall.

Garfinkel, H. (1967b) 'Practical sociological reasoning: some features in the work of the Los Angeles Suicide Prevention Center', in Shneidman, E. (ed.) *Essays in Self-Destruction*, New York, Science House.

Garfinkel, H. (1968) 'The origin of the term "ethnomethodology"', excerpt from Hill, R. and Crittenden, K. (eds) *Proceedings of the Purdue Symposium on Ethnomethodology*, Institute Monograph Series No. 1, Institute for the Study of Social Change, Purdue University, pp. 5–11. (Reprinted in Turner, R. (ed.) (1974) *Ethnomethodology*, Harmondsworth, Penguin.)

Garfinkel, H. (ed.) (1986) *Ethnomethodological Studies of Work*, London, Routledge.

Garfinkel, H. (1990) 'The curious seriousness of professional sociology', Réseaux, Hors Série 8, n°1, 1990. Les formes de la conversation vol. 1, pp. 69–78. Available at: http://www.persee.fr/docAsPDF/reso_0984–5372_1990_hos_8_1_3531.pdf (accessed 4 Jan. 2018).

Garfinkel, H. (2002) *Ethnomethodology's Program: Working out Durkheim's aphorism*, Lanham, MD, Rowman and Littlefield.

Garfinkel, H. and Livingston, E. (2003) 'Phenomenal field properties of order in formatted queues and their neglected standing in the current situation of inquiry', *Visual Studies*, 18:1, pp. 21–8.

Garfinkel, H., Lynch, M., and Livingston, E. (1981) 'The work of a discovering science construed with materials from the optically discovered pulsar', *Philosophy of the Social Sciences*, 11, pp. 131–58.

Garfinkel, H. and Sacks, H. (1970) 'On formal structures of practical action', in J. C. McKinney and E. A. Tiryakian (eds) *Theoretical Sociology*, New York, Appleton-Century-Crofts, pp. 338–66. (Reprinted in Garfinkel, H. (ed.) (1986) *Ethnomethodological Studies of Work*, London, Routledge, pp. 160–93.)

Garfinkel, H. and Wieder, D. L. (1992) 'Two incommensurable, asymmetrically alternate technologies of social analysis', in Watson, G. and Seiler, R. (eds) *Text in Context: Studies in ethnomethodology*, Newbury Park, Sage, pp. 175–206.

Gellner, E. (1975) 'Ethnomethodology: the re-enchantment industry or the Californian way of subjectivity', *Philosophy of the Social Sciences*, 5, pp. 431–50.

Gerhardt, U. (2003) 'Of kindred spirit: Erving Goffman's oeuvre and its relationship to Georg Simmel', in Treviño, A. J. (ed.) *Goffman's Legacy*, Lanham, MD, Rowman and Littlefield.

References

Gerhardt, U. (2011) *Talcott Parsons: An intellectual biography*, Cambridge, Cambridge University Press.

Giacomoni, P. (2002) 'Georg Simmel between Goethe and Kant on "life" and "force"', in Tymieniecka, A-T. (ed.) *Life Energies, Forces and the Shaping of Life*, Book 1, *Analecta Husserliana*, 74, pp. 51–68.

Giddens, A. (1984) *The Constitution of Society*, Cambridge, Polity Press.

Girton, G. (1986) 'Kung Fu: towards a praxiological hermeneutic of the martial arts', in Garfinkel, H. (ed.) *Ethnomethodological Studies of Work*, London, Routledge.

Goffman, E. (1953) 'Communication Conduct in an Island Community', PhD thesis, University of Chicago. Available at: http://cdclv.unlv.edu/ega/documents/eg_phd.pdf (accessed 4 Jan. 2018).

Goffman, E. (1956a) 'The nature of deference and demeanor', *American Anthropologist*, 58, pp. 478–502.

Goffman, E. (1956b) *The Presentation of Self in Everyday Life*, New York, Doubleday Anchor.

Goffman, E. (1961) *Asylums*, Harmondsworth, Penguin.

Goffman, E. (1964) 'The neglected situation', *American Anthropologist*, 66:6, part II, pp. 133–6.

Goffman, E. (1967) *Interaction Ritual: Essays in face to face behavior*, Garden City, NY, Doubleday.

Goffman, E. (1968) *Stigma*, Harmondsworth, Penguin.

Goffman, E. (1969) *Strategic Interaction*, Oxford, Blackwell.

Goffman, E. (1974) *Frame Analysis*, Harmondsworth, Penguin.

Goffman, E. (1981a) *Forms of Talk*, Philadelphia, University of Pennsylvania Press.

Goffman, E. (1981b) 'Reply to Denzin and Keller', *Contemporary Sociology*, 10:1, pp. 60–8.

Goffman, E. (1983a) 'The interaction order', *American Sociological Review*, 48, pp. 1–17.

Goffman, E. (1983b) 'Felicity's condition', *American Journal of Sociology*, 89:1, pp. 1–53.

Goffman, E. (1989) 'On fieldwork', *Journal of Contemporary Ethnography*, 18:2, pp. 123–32.

Goldthorpe, J. (1973) 'A revolution in sociology?', *Sociology*, 7:3, pp. 449–62.

Goldthorpe, J. (1974) 'A rejoinder to Benson', *Sociology*, 8:1, pp. 131–3.

Goldthorpe, J. (2016) *Sociology as a Population Science*, Cambridge, Cambridge University Press.

Goodenough, W. (1956) 'Componential analysis and the study of meaning', *Language*, 32:2, pp. 195–216.

Goodwin, C. (2000) 'Practices of seeing, visual analysis: an ethnomethodological approach', in van Leeuwen, T. and Jewitt, C. (eds) *Handbook of Visual Analysis*, London, Sage, pp. 157–82.

Gorard, S. (2010) 'Measuring is more than assigning numbers', in Walford, G., Tucker, E., and Viswanathan, M. (eds) *The Sage Handbook of Measurement*, London, Sage.

Gordon, P. (2010) *Continental Divide: Heidegger, Cassirer, Davos*, Cambridge, MA, Harvard University Press.

Gouldner, A. (1970) *The Coming Crisis of Western Sociology*, New York, Basic Books.

Grabiner, G. (1975) 'The situational sociologies', *Insurgent Sociologist*, 5:4, pp. 80–1.

References

Grathoff, R. (ed.) (1978) *The Theory of Social Action: The correspondence of Alfred Schutz and Talcott Parsons*, Bloomington, Indiana University Press.

Greiffenhagen, C., Mair, M., and Sharrock, W. (2011) 'From methodology to methodography: a study of qualitative and quantitative reasoning in practice', *Methodological Innovations Online*, 6:3, pp. 93–107.

Greiffenhagen, C., Mair, M., and Sharrock, W. (2015) 'Methodological troubles as problems and phenomena: ethnomethodology and the question of "method" in the social sciences', *British Journal of Sociology*, 66:3, pp. 460–85.

Grice, H. P. (1975) 'Logic and conversation', in P. Cole and J. Morgan (eds) *Studies in Syntax and Semantics III: Speech Acts*, New York: Academic Press, pp. 183–98.

Gubrium, J. and Holstein, J. (1997) *The New Language of Qualitative Method*, New York, Oxford University Press.

Gumperz, J. and Hymes, D. (eds) (1972) *Directions in Sociolinguistics: The ethnography of communication*, New York, Holt, Rinehart and Winston.

Gurwitsch, A. (1964) *The Field of Consciousness*, Pittsburgh, PA, Dequesne University Press.

Gurwitsch, A. (1974) 'Edmund Husserl's conception of phenomenological psychology', in Gurwitsch, A., *Phenomenology and the Theory of Science*, Evanston, IL, Northwestern University Press.

Haack, S. (2007) *Defending Science, Within Reason: Between scientism and cynicism*, Amherst, NY, Prometheus Books.

Haack, S. (2009) *Evidence and Inquiry*, 2nd edn, Amherst, NY, Prometheus Books.

Hama, H. (2009) 'The primal scene of ethnomethodology: Garfinkel's short story "Color Trouble" and the Schutz-Parsons controversy', in Nasu, H., Embree, L., Psathas, G., and Srubar, I. (eds) *Alfred Schutz and his Intellectual Partners*, Konstanz, UVK Verlagsgesellschaft mbH.

Hamilton, P. (1983) *Talcott Parsons*, London, Routledge.

Hammersley, M. (1981) 'Putting competence into action', in French, P. and MacLure, M. (eds) *Adult–Child Conversation*, London, Croom Helm.

Hammersley, M. (1989a) *The Dilemma of Qualitative Method*, London, Routledge.

Hammersley, M. (1989b) 'The Problem of the concept: Herbert Blumer on the relationship between concepts and data', *Journal of Contemporary Ethnography*, 18:2, pp. 133–59.

Hammersley, M. (2003) '"Analytics" are no substitute for methodology: a response to Speer and Hutchby', *Sociology*, 37:2, pp. 339–51.

Hammersley, M. (2008) *Questioning Qualitative Inquiry*, London, Sage.

Hammersley, M. (2010a) 'Reproducing or constructing? Some questions about transcription in social research', *Qualitative Research*, 10:5, pp. 553–69.

Hammersley. M. (2010b) 'The case of the disappearing dilemma: Herbert Blumer on sociological method', *History of the Human Sciences*, 23:5, pp. 70–90.

Hammersley, M. (2011) *Methodology: Who Needs It?*, London, Sage.

Hammersley, M. (2012) 'Troubling theory in case study research', *Higher Education Research and Development*, 31:3, pp. 393–405.

Hammersley, M. (2014) *The Limits of Social Science*, London, Sage.

References

Hammersley, M. (2015a) 'Reflections on Paul Atkinson's For Ethnography', unpublished paper. Available at: https://martynhammersley.wordpress.com/documents (accessed 4 Jan. 2018).

Hammersley, M. (2015b) 'The mis-selling of academic social science', unpublished paper. Available at: https://martynhammersley.wordpress.com/documents (accessed 4 Jan. 2018).

Hammersley, M. (2017a) 'Is there any such thing as social science evidence? On a Winchian critique', *Ethnographic Studies*, 14. Available at: https://zenodo.org/record/823047#.Wk55O99I-Uk (accessed 4 Jan. 2018).

Hammersley, M. (2017b) 'Interview data: a qualified defence against the radical critique', *Qualitative Research*, 17:2, pp. 173–86.

Hammersley, M. (2018a) 'Is phronesis necessarily virtuous?', in Emmerich, N. (ed.) *Virtue Ethics in the Conduct and Governance of Social Science Research*, Bingley, Emerald.

Hammersley, M. (2018b) 'Was Blumer a cognitivist? Assessing an ethnomethodological critique', *Journal for the Theory of Social Behaviour*, 48 (3)273–287, 2018.

Hammersley, M. (2019a) 'On a dispute about ethnomethodology: Watson and Sharrock's response to Atkinson's "critical review"', 'Understanding a Dispute About Ethnomethodology: Watson and Sharrock's Response to Atkinson's "Critical Review", *Forum Qualitative Research* 20, 1, article no. 1, 2019. Available at: http://www.qualitative-research.net/index.php/fqs/article/view/3048/4319

Hammersley, M. (2019b) 'On ethnomethodology and suicide', .Understanding a Dispute About Ethnomethodology: Watson and Sharrock's Response to Atkinson's "Critical Review", *Forum Qualitative Research* 20, 1, article no. 1, 2019. Available at: http://www.qualitative-research.net/index.php/fqs/article/view/3048/4319

Hammersley, M. (2019c) 'Ethnomethodological criticism of ethnography', unpublished paper. 'Ethnomethodological criticism of ethnography', Qualitative Research, 2019, 19(5) 578–593.

Hammersley, M. and Gomm, R. (2008) 'Assessing the radical critique of interviews', in Hammersley, M., *Questioning Qualitative Inquiry*, London, Sage.

Harman, G. (2009) *The Prince of Networks: Bruno Latour and metaphysics*, Melbourne, Re.Press.

ten Have, P. (2002a) 'Ontology or methodology? Comments on Speer's "Natural" and "contrived" data: a sustainable distinction?' *Discourse Studies*, 4:4, pp. 527–30.

ten Have, P. (2002b) 'The notion of member is the heart of the matter: on the role of membership knowledge in ethnomethodological inquiry', *Sozialforschung/Forum: Qualitative Social Research*, 3:3, Art. 21. Available at: http://www.qualitative-research.net/index.php/fqs/article/view/834 (accessed 4 Jan. 2018).

ten Have, P. (2004) *Understanding Qualitative Research and Ethnomethodology*, London, Sage.

ten Have, P. (2008) *Doing Conversation Analysis: A practical guide*, 2nd edn, London, Sage.

Hayek, F. (1952) *The Counter-Revolution of Science*, Glencoe, IL, Free Press.

Hayek, F. (1967) *Studies in Philosophy, Politics and Economics*, London, Routledge and Kegan Paul.

Heap, J. (1975) 'Non-indexical action', *Philosophy of the Social Sciences*, 5:4, pp. 393–409.

Heap, J. (1976) 'What are sense-making practices?', *Sociological Inquiry*, 46:2, pp. 107–15.

References

Heap, J. (1980) 'Description in ethnomethodology', *Human Studies*, 3:1, pp. 87–106.

Heath, C. and Luff, P. (1992) 'Collaboration and control: crisis management and multimedia technology in London Underground Line control rooms', *Computer Supported Cooperative Work*, 1, pp. 69–94.

Heath, C. and Luff, P. (2000) *Technology in Action*, Cambridge, Cambridge University Press.

Heidegger, M. (1962) *Being and Time*, New York, Harper and Row. (First published in German in 1927.)

Helling, I. (1984) 'A. Schutz and F. Kaufmann: sociology between science and interpretation', *Human Studies*, 7, pp. 141–61.

Helling, I. (1988) 'Alfred Schutz, Felix Kaufmann, and the economists of the von Mises Circle: Personal and methodological continuities', in List, E. and Srubar, I. (eds) *Alfred Schütz: Neue Beiträge zur Rezeption seines Werkes*, Amsterdam, Rodopi, pp. 43–68.

Helm, D. (1982) 'Talk's form: comments on Goffman's *Forms of Talk*', *Human Studies*, 5:2, pp. 147–57.

Hennis, W. (1987) 'A science of man: Max Weber and the political economy of the German Historical School', in Mommsen, W. and Osterhammel, J. (eds) *Max Weber and his Contemporaries*, London, Allen and Unwin.

Hennis, W. (1988) *Max Weber: Essays in Reconstruction*, London, Allen and Unwin.

Hennis, W. (2000a) *Max Weber's Central Question*, Newbury, Threshold Press.

Hennis, W. (2000b) *Max Weber's Science of Man*, Newbury, Threshold Press.

Heritage, J. (1978) 'Aspects of the flexibilities of natural language use', *Sociology*, 12:1, pp. 79–103.

Heritage, J. (1984) *Garfinkel and Ethnomethodology*, Cambridge, Polity Press.

Heritage, J. (2003) 'Presenting Emanuel Schegloff', in Prevignano, C. and Thibault, P. (eds) *Discussing Conversation Analysis: Emanuel Schegloff*, Amsterdam, John Benjamins, pp. 1–10. Available at: http://www.sscnet.ucla.edu/soc/faculty/heritage/Site/Publications_files/Presenting_Schegloff.pdf.

Heritage, J. (2016) 'Epistemics, conversation analysis, and 'post-analytic' ethnomethodology: A rebuttal'. This was a draft of Heritage 2018.

Heritage, J. (2018) 'The ubiquity of epistemics: A rebuttal to the "epistemics of epistemics" group', *Discourse Studies*, 20:1, pp. 14–56.

Heritage, J., Robinson, J., Elliott, M., Beckett, M., and Wilkes, M. (2007) 'Reducing patients' unmet concerns in primary care: The difference one word can make', *Journal of General Internal Medicine*, 22:10, pp. 1429–33.

Hester, S. and Eglin, P. (1992) *A Sociology of Crime*, London, Routledge.

Hester, S. and Eglin, P. (eds) (1997) *Culture in Action: Studies in membership categorization analysis*, Washington, DC, University Press of America.

Hester, S. and Francis, D. (2000) 'Ethnomethodology, conversation analysis, and "institutional talk"', *Text*, 20:3, pp. 391–413.

Hester, S. and Francis, D. (2001) 'Is institutional thought a phenomenon? Reflections on ethnomethodology and applied conversation analysis', in McHoul, A. and Rapley, M. (eds) *How to Analyse Talk in Institutional Settings*, London, Continuum.

Hilbert, R. (1992) *The Classical Roots of Ethnomethodology*, Chapel Hill, University of North Carolina Press.

References

Hill, R. and Crittenden, K. (eds) (1968) *Proceedings of the Purdue Symposium on Eth-nomethodology*, Institute for the Study of Social Change, Department of Sociology, Purdue University. Available at: https://aiemcanet.files.wordpress.com/2010/07/purdue.pdf (accessed 4 Jan. 2018).

Hindess, B. (1973) *The Use of Official Statistics in Sociology: A critique of positivism and ethnomethodology*, London, Macmillan.

Holstein, J. (2009) 'Defining deviance: John Kitsuse's modest agenda', *American Sociologist*, 40, pp. 51–60.

Holstein, J. and Gubrium, J. (eds) (2008) *Handbook of Constructionist Research*, New York, Guilford.

Holstein, J. and Miller, G. (eds) (1993) *Reconsidering Social Constructionism*, Hawthorne, NY, Aldine de Gruyter.

Hopper, R. (1990/91) 'Ethnography and conversation analysis after *Talking Culture*', *Research on Language and Social Interaction*, 24, pp. 161–387.

Houtkoop-Steenstra, H. (2000) *Interaction and the Standardized Survey Interview*, Cambridge, Cambridge University Press.

Huber, J. (1995) 'Institutional perspectives on sociology', *American Journal of Sociology*, 101, pp. 194–216.

Huemer, W. (2003) 'Logical empiricism and phenomenology: Felix Kaufmann', in F. Stadler (ed.) *The Vienna Circle and Logical Empiricism: Re-evaluation and future perspectives*, Dordrecht, Kluwer, pp. 151–61.

Hughes, E. C. (1955) 'Foreword', in Simmel, G., *Conflict and the Web of Group-Affiliations*, New York, Free Press.

Hughes, E. C. (1958) 'Review of *Brücke und Tür: Essays des Philosophen zur Geschichte, Religion,Kunst, und Gesellschaft (Bridge and Door: Essays of the Philosopher on History, Religion, Art, and Society)*, by Georg Simmel', *American Journal of Sociology*, 63:6, pp. 670–2.

Hughes, E. (1965) 'A note on Georg Simmel', *Social Problems*, 13:2, pp. 117–18.

Hughes, J. (2001) 'Of ethnography, ethnomethodology and workplace studies', *Ethnographic Studies*, 6, pp. 7–16.

Husserl, E. (1965) 'Philosophy as a rigorous science', in Lauer, Q. (ed.) *Phenomenology and the Crisis of Philosophy*, New York, Harper and Row.

Husserl, E. (1970) *The Crisis of European Sciences and Transcendental Phenomenology*, Evanston, IL, Northwestern University Press.

Husserl, E. (1983) *Ideas Pertaining to a Pure Phenomenology and to a Phenomenological Philosophy*, Book 1 *General Introduction to a Pure Phenomenology* (trans. F. Kersten), The Hague, Martinus Nijhoff.

Husserl, E. (1989) *Ideas Pertaining to a Pure Phenomenology and to a Phenomenological Philosophy, Book 2: Studies in the phenomenology of constitution*, Dordrecht, Kluwer. (First published in German in 1952.)

Hutchby, I. and Wooffitt, R. (2008) *Conversation Analysis*, 2nd edn, Cambridge, Polity Press.

Hutchinson, P., Read, R., and Sharrock, W. (2008) *There is No Such Thing as a Social Science: In defence of Peter Winch*, Aldershot, Ashgate.

Hutchison, T. (2000) *On the Methodology of Economics and the Formalist Revolution*, Cheltenham, Edward Elgar.

References

Hutchison, T. (ed. R. Backhouse) (2009) 'A formative decade: methodological controversy in the 1930s', *Journal of Economic Methodology*, 16:3, pp. 297–314.

Hymes, D. (1984) 'On Erving Goffman', *Theory and Society*, 13:5, pp. 621–31.

Ingarden, R. (2005) 'About the motives which led Husserl to transcendental idealism', in Bernet, R., Welton, D., and Zavota, G. (eds) *Edmund Husserl: Critical assessments of leading philosophers*, Vol. 1, London, Routledge, pp. 72–89.

Jacobsen, M. (ed.) (2009) *Encountering the Everyday: An introduction to the sociologies of the unnoticed*, Basingstoke, Palgrave Macmillan.

Jaworski, G. (1990) 'Simmel's contribution to Parsons' action theory and its fate', in Kaern, M., Phillips, B. and Cohen, R. (eds) *Georg Simmel and Contemporary Sociology*, Dordrecht, Kluwer.

Jaworski, G. (1997) *Georg Simmel and the American Prospect*, Albany, NY, State University of New York Press.

Jefferson, G. (1989) 'Letter to the Editor Re: Anita Pomerantz' Epilogue to the Special Issue on Sequential Organization of Conversational Activities, Spring 1989', *Western Journal of Speech Communication*, 53, pp. 427–9.

Jenkings, K. N. (2009) 'Studies in *and* as ethnomethodology: Garfinkel and his ethnomethodological "bastards" Part Two', *Sociology*, 43:4, pp. 775–81.

Johnstone, B. (2008) *Discourse Analysis*, Oxford, Blackwell.

Kalekin-Fishman, D. (2013) 'Review article: sociology of everyday life', *Current Sociology*, 61:5–6, pp. 714–32.

Kaplan A. (1964) *The Conduct of Inquiry: Methodology for behavioral science*, San Francisco, Chandler.

Käsler, D. (1983) 'In search of respectability: the controversy over the destination of sociology during the conventions of the German Sociological Society, 1910–1930', in Jones, A. and Kuklick, H. (eds) *Knowledge and Society: Studies in the sociology of culture past and present*, Vol. 4, Greenwich, CT, JAI Press, pp. 227–72.

Kaufmann, F. (1936a) *Methodenlehre Der Sozialwissenschaften*, Vienna, Julius Springer. (English translation: Cohen, R. S. and Helling, I. K. (eds) (2014) *Felix Kaufmann's Theory and Method in the Social Sciences*, Boston Studies in the Philosophy and History of Science, Cham, Springer.)

Kaufmann, F. (1936b) 'Remarks on methodology of the social sciences', *Sociological Review*, 28, pp. 64–84.

Kaufmann, F. (1944) *Methodology of the Social Sciences*, New York, Oxford University Press.

Kaufmann, F. (1950) 'Basic issues in logical positivism', in Farber, M. (ed.) *Philosophic Thought in France and the United States*, Buffalo, NY, University of Buffalo Publications in Philosophy.

Kawano, K. (2009) 'On methodology of the social sciences: Schutz and Kaufmann', in Nasu, H., Embree, L., Psathas, G., and Srubar, I. (eds) *Alfred Schutz and his Intellectual Partners*, Konstanz, UVK Verlagsgesellschaft.

Kelly, G. A. (1955) *The Psychology of Personal Constructs*: Vols 1 and 2, New York, W. W. Norton.

Kendrick, K. (2017) 'Using conversation analysis in the lab', *Research on Language and Social Interaction*, 50:1, pp. 1–1.

References

Kettler, D. (2012) 'Introduction to *Soul and Culture*', *Theory, Culture and Society*, 29:7–8, pp. 279–85.

Kitsuse, J. (1962) 'Societal reaction to deviant behavior: problems of theory and method', *Social Problems*, 9, pp. 247–56.

Kitsuse, J. and Cicourel, A.V. (1963) 'A note on the uses of official statistics', *Social Problems*, 11, pp. 131–9.

Knorr-Cetina, K. (1981) 'Introduction: the micro-sociological challenge of macro-social theory', in Knorr-Cetina, K. and Cicourel, A. (eds) *Advances in Social Theory and Methodology*, London, Routledge and Kegan Paul.

Kockelmans, J. (1983) 'Phenomenology and the critique of the scientific tradition, in Embree, L. (ed.) *Essays in Memory of Aron Gurwitsch*, Washington, DC, University Press of America.

Krausser, P. (1968) 'Dilthey's revolution in the theory of the structure of scientific inquiry and rational behavior', *Review of Metaphysics*, 22, pp. 262–80.

Kuhn, T. (1970) *The Structure of Scientific Revolutions*, 2nd edn, Chicago, University of Chicago Press.

Kusch, M. (1995) *Psychologism: A case study in the sociology of philosophical knowledge*, London, Routledge.

Latour, B. (2005) *Reassembling the Social*, Oxford, Oxford University Press.

Latour, B., Harman, G., and Erdélyi, P. (2011) *The Prince and the Wolf: Latour and Harman at the LSE*, Alresford, Zero Books.

Lee, S. (2016) 'Occasionalism', *The Stanford Encyclopedia of Philosophy*, https://plato.stanford.edu/archives/win2016/entries/occasionalism.

vom Lehn, D. (2014) *Harold Garfinkel: The creation and development of ethnomethodology*, Walnut Creek, CA, Left Coast Press.

Leiter, K. (1980) *A Primer on Ethnomethodology*, New York, Oxford University Press.

Lerner, B. (2002) *Rules, Magic and Instrumental Reason: A critical interpretation of Peter Winch's philosophy of the social sciences*, London, Routledge.

Leudar, I. and Costall, A. (eds) (2009) *Against Theory of Mind*, Basingstoke, Palgrave Macmillan.

Levine, D. (1989) 'Parsons' structure (and Simmel) revisited', *Sociological Theory*, 7:1, pp. 110–17.

Levine, D. (1991) 'Simmel and Parsons reconsidered', *American Journal of Sociology*, 96:5, pp. 1097–116.

Levinson, S. (1983) *Pragmatics*, Cambridge, Cambridge University Press.

Levinson, S. (2006) 'On the human "interaction engine"', in Enfield, N. J. and Levinson, S. C. (eds) *Roots of Human Sociality*, Oxford, Berg, pp. 39–69.

Liberman, K. (2007) *Husserl's Criticism of Reason: With ethnomethodological specifications*, Lanham, MD, Lexington Books.

Liberman, K. (2008) 'Larry Wieder's radical ethno-inquiries', *Human Studies*, 31:3, pp. 251–7.

Liberman, K. (2013) *More Studies in Ethnomethodology*, Albany, NY, State University of New York Press.

Liberman, K. (2017) 'What can the human sciences contribute to phenomenology?', *Human Studies*, 40, pp. 7–24.

References

Lichtblau, K. (1991) 'Causality or interaction? Simmel, Weber and interpretive sociology', *Theory, Culture and Society*, 8, pp. 33–62. (Reprinted in Frisby, D. (ed.) *Georg Simmel: Critical assessments* (1994), London, Routledge, Vol. 2.)

Lipset, S. M., Trow, M. and Coleman, J. S. (1956) *Union Democracy: The internal politics of the International Typographical Union*, New York, Free Press.

Livingston, E. (1986) *The Ethnomethodological Foundations of Mathematics*, London, Routledge and Kegan Paul.

Livingston, E. (1987) *Making Sense of Ethnomethodology*, London, Routledge and Kegan Paul.

Llewellyn, N. and Hindmarsh, J. (eds) (2010) *Organisation, Interaction and Practice*, Cambridge, Cambridge University Press.

Louch, A. R. (1966) *Explanation and Human Action*, Berkeley, University of. California Press.

Lübbe, H. (1978) 'Positivism and phenomenology: Mach and Husserl', in Luckmann, T. (ed.) *Phenomenology and Sociology*, Harmondsworth, Penguin.

Luff, P. (1992) 'Collaboration and control: crisis management and multimedia technology in London underground line control rooms', *Journal of Computer Supported Cooperative Work*, 1:1, pp. 24–48.

Luff, P., Hindmarsh, J. and Heath, C. (eds) (2000) *Workplace Studies: Recovering work practice and informing system design*, Cambridge, Cambridge University Press.

Lynch, M. (1985) *Art and Artifact in Laboratory Science*, London, Routledge and Kegan Paul.

Lynch, M. (1988), 'Alfred Schutz and the sociology of science', in Embree, L. (ed.) *Worldly Phenomenology: The influence of Alfred Schutz on human science*, Washington, DC, University Press of America, pp. 71–100.

Lynch, M. (1993) *Scientific Practice and Ordinary Action: Ethnomethodology and social studies of science*, Cambridge, Cambridge University Press.

Lynch, M. (1999) 'Silence in context: Ethnomethodology and social theory', *Human Studies*, 22, pp. 211–33.

Lynch, M. (2000a) 'Against reflexivity as an academic virtue and source of privileged knowledge', *Theory, Culture & Society*, 17:3, pp. 26–54.

Lynch, M. (2000b) 'A new disease of the intellect? Some reflections on the therapeutic value of Peter Winch's philosophy for social and cultural studies of science', *History of the Human Sciences*, 13:1, pp. 140–56.

Lynch, M. (2000c) 'The ethnomethodological foundations of conversation analysis', *Text*, 20:4, pp. 517–32.

Lynch, M. (2002) 'From naturally occurring data to naturally organized ordinary activities: comment on Speer', *Discourse Studies*, 4:4, pp. 531–7.

Lynch, M. (2004) 'Misreading Schutz: a response to Dennis on "Lynch on Schutz on Science"', *Theory and Science*, 5:1, pp. 1–9. Available at: http://theoryandscience.icaap.org/content/vol5.1/lynch.html (accessed 4 Jan. 2018).

Lynch, M. (2013) 'Ontography: investigating the production of things, deflating ontology', *Social Studies of Science*, 43:3, pp. 444–62.

Lynch, M. (2016a) 'Radical ethnomethodology', paper given at a conference on Radical Ethnomethodology, June. Available at: https://radicalethno.org/documents/lynchposition.pdf (accessed 4 Jan. 2018).

References

Lynch, M. (2016b) 'Notes on a display of epistemic authority: a post-closure rejoinder to John Heritage's rebuttal to "The epistemics of Epistemics"'. Available at: https://radicalethno.org/documents/lynchrejoinder.pdf (accessed 4 Jan. 2018).

Lynch, M. (2017) 'Garfinkel, Sacks and formal structures: collaborative origins, divergences and the vexed unity of ethnomethodology and conversation analysis', A Half-Century of Studies, International Institute for Ethnomethodology and Conversation Analysis (IIEMCA), Otterbein College, Westerville, OH. Available at: https://radicalethno.org/documents/lynchbanquet.pdf (accessed 4 Jan. 2018).

Lynch, M. (2018) 'Garfinkel's Studies of Work', 2015 draft prepared for Maynard, D. and Heritage, J. (eds) *Harold Garfinkel: Praxis, Social Order, and the Ethnomethodology Movement*, Oxford, Oxford University Press.

Lynch, M. and Bogen, D. (1994) 'Harvey Sacks' primitive natural science', *Theory, Culture and Society*, 11, pp. 65–104.

Lynch, M. and Jordan, K. (1995) 'Instructed actions in, as, and of molecular biology', *Human Studies*, 18:2–3, pp. 227–44.

Lynch, M. and Macbeth, D. (2016) 'The epistemics of epistemics', *Discourse Studies*, 18:5, pp. 493–9.

Lynch, M. and Sharrock, W. (eds) (2003) *Harold Garfinkel*, 4 volumes, London, Sage.

Macfarlane, B. (2009) *Researching with Integrity: The ethics of academic inquiry*, London, Routledge.

MacIntyre, A. (1999) *Dependent Rational Animals*, Chicago, Open Court.

Mannheim, K. (1952) *Essays in the Sociology of Knowledge*, London, Routledge and Kegan Paul.

Manning, P. (1992) *Erving Goffman and Modern Sociology*, Stanford, CA, Stanford University Press.

Maroules, N. and Smelser, N. (2006) 'Review of Garfinkel, *Seeing Sociologically*', *Contemporary Sociology*, 35:5, pp. 526–8.

Martin, B. (1981) *A Sociology of Contemporary Cultural Change*, Oxford, Blackwell.

Martin, P. and Dennis, A. (eds) (2010) *Human Agents and Social Structures*, Manchester, Manchester University Press.

Matza, D. (1969) *Becoming Deviant*, Englewood Cliffs, NJ, Prentice-Hall.

Maynard, D. (1996) 'Introduction of Harold Garfinkel for the Cooley-Mead Award', *Social Psychology Quarterly*, 59:1, pp. 1–4.

Maynard, D. (1998) 'On qualitative methodology and extramodernity', *Contemporary Sociology*, 27:4, pp. 343–5.

Maynard, D. (2006) 'Ethnography and conversation analysis: what is the context of an utterance?', in Hesse-Biber, S. and Leavy, P. L. (eds) *Emergent Methods in Social Research*, Thousand Oaks, CA, Sage.

Maynard, D. (2012) 'An intellectual remembrance of Harold Garfinkel: imagining the unimaginable, and the concept of the "surveyable society"', *Human Studies*, 35:2, pp. 209–21.

Maynard, D. and Clayman, S. (1991) 'The diversity of ethnomethodology', *Annual Review of Sociology*, 17, pp. 385–418.

Maynard, D. and Clayman, S. (2018) 'Mandarin ethnomethodology or mutual interchange?', *Discourse Studies*, 20:1, pp. 120–41.

References

Maynard, D., Houtkoop-Steenstra, H. Schaeffer, N. C. and van der Zouwen, J. (eds) (2002) *Standardization and Tacit Knowledge: Interaction and practice in the survey interview*, New York, Wiley Interscience.

Maynard, D. and Schaeffer, C. (2006) 'Standardization-in-interaction: the survey interview', in Drew, P., Raymond, G. and Weinberg, D. (eds) *Talk and Interaction in Social Research Methods*, London, Sage.

McHoul, A. (1982) *Telling How Texts Talk: Essays on reading and ethnomethodology*, London, Routledge and Kegan Paul.

McHoul, A. (1998) 'How can ethnomethodology be Heideggerian?', *Human Studies*, 21:1, pp. 13–26.

McHoul, A. (2009) 'What are we doing when we analyse conversation?', *Australian Journal of Communication*, 36:3, pp. 15–21.

McHugh, P. (1970) 'On the failure of positivism', in Douglas, J. D. (ed.) *Understanding Everyday Life*, Chicago, Aldine.

McHugh, P., Raffel, S., Foss, D., and Blum, A. (1974) *On the Beginning of Social Inquiry*, London, Routledge and Kegan Paul.

McNall, S. and Johnson, J. (1975) 'The New Conservatives: ethnomethodologists, phenomenologists, and symbolic interactionists', *Insurgent Sociologist*, 5:4, pp. 49–65.

Mehan, H. and Wood, H. (1975) *The Reality of Ethnomethodology*, New York, Wiley.

Mehan, H. and Wood, H. (1976) 'De-secting ethnomethodology', *American Sociologist*, 11, pp. 13–21.

Menger, K. (1985) *Investigations into the Method of the Social Sciences, with Special Reference to Economics*, New York, New York University Press. (First published in German in 1883.)

Merton, R. K. (1956) Comments in Witmer, H. and Kotinsky, R. (eds) *New Perspectives for Research on Juvenile Delinquency*, Washington, DC, US Government Printing Office.

Michell, J. (1999) *Measurement in Psychology: Critical history of a methodological concept*, Cambridge, Cambridge University Press.

Michell, J. (2007) 'Measurement', in Turner, S. P. and Risjord, M. W. (eds) *Philosophy of Anthropology and Sociology*, Amsterdam, Elsevier.

Mills, C. Wright (1959) *The Sociological Imagination*, New York, Oxford University Press.

von Mises, L. (1949) *Human Action: A treatise on economics*, New Haven, CT, Yale University Press.

von Mises, L. (1962) *The Ultimate Foundation of Economic Science: An essay on method*, Princeton, NJ, van Nostrand.

Moerman, M. (1988) *Talking Culture: Ethnography and Conversation Analysis*, Philadelphia, University of Pennsylvania Press.

Moerman, M. (1992) 'Life after C.A.: An ethnographer's autobiography', in Watson, G. and Seiler, R. (eds) *Text in Context: Contributions to ethnomethodology*, Newbury Park, CA, Sage.

Moran, D. (2005) *Edmund Husserl: The founder of phenomenology*, Cambridge, Polity Press.

Moran, D. (2012) *Husserl's Crisis of the European Sciences and Transcendental Phenomenology: An introduction*, Cambridge, Cambridge University Press.

Moran, D. and Cohen, J. (2012) *The Husserl Dictionary*, London, Bloomsbury.

References

Mullins, N. (1972) *Theories and Theory Groups in Contemporary American Sociology*, New York, Harper and Row.

Murphy, E., Dingwall, R., Greatbatch, D. Parker, S., and Watson, P. (1998) 'Qualitative research methods in health technology assessment: a review of the literature', *Health Technology Assessment*, 2:16, pp. 1–260.

Oakes, G. (1990) *Weber and Rickert: Concept formation in the social sciences*, Cambridge, MA, MIT Press.

Odum, H. (1951) *American Sociology: The story of sociology in the United States through 1950*, New York, Greenwood.

O'Neill, J. (1973) 'On Simmel's "sociological apriorities"', in Psathas, G. (ed.) *Phenomenological Sociology: Issues and applications*, New York, Wiley.

Parsons, T. (1937) *The Structure of Social Action*, New York, McGraw Hill.

Parsons, T. (1951) *The Social System*, New York, Free Press.

Parsons, T. (1978) 'Retrospect', in Grathoff, R. (ed.) *The Theory of Social Action: The correspondence of Alfred Schutz and Talcott Parsons*, Bloomington, Indiana University Press.

Parsons, T., Bales, R., and Shils, E. (1953) *Working Papers in the Theory of Action*, Glencoe, IL, Free Press.

Parsons, T. and Barber, B. (1948) 'Sociology, 1941–46', *American Journal of Sociology*, 53:4, pp. 245–57.

Parsons, T. and Shils, E. (eds) (1951) *Toward a General Theory of Action*, Cambridge, MA, Harvard University Press.

Phillips, J. (1978) 'Some problems in locating practices', *Sociology*, 12, pp. 56–77.

Piaget, J. (1971) *Structuralism*, London, Routledge and Kegan Paul. (First published in French in 1968.)

Pickering, A. (ed.) (1992) *Science and Culture and Practice*, Chicago, University of Chicago Press.

Pink, S. (2012) *Situating Everyday Life*, London, Sage.

Polanyi, M. (1962) *Personal Knowledge*, Chicago, University of Chicago Press.

Polanyi, M. (1966) 'The logic of tacit inference', *Journal of the Royal Institute of Philosophy*, 41:155, pp. 1–18.

Pollner, M. (1974) 'Sociological and common-sense models of the labelling process', in Turner, R. (ed.) *Ethnomethodology*, Harmondsworth, Penguin.

Pollner, M. (1975) '"The very coinage of your brain": the anatomy of reality disjunctures', *Philosophy of the Social Sciences*, 5, pp. 411–30.

Pollner, M. (1978) 'Constitutive and mundane versions of labeling theory', *Human Studies*, 1:3, pp. 269–88.

Pollner, M. (1979) 'Explicative transactions: Making and managing meaning in traffic court', in Psathas, G. (ed.) *Everyday Language: Studies in ethnomethodology*, New York, Irvington.

Pollner, M. (1987) *Mundane Reason: Reality in everyday and sociological discourse*, Cambridge, Cambridge University Press.

Pollner, M. (1991) 'Left of ethnomethodology: the rise and decline of radical reflexivity', *American Sociological Review*, 56:3, pp. 370–80.

Pollner, M. (2012a) 'The end(s) of ethnomethodology', *American Sociologist*, 43:1, pp. 7–20.

References

Pollner, M. (2012b) 'Ethnomethodology from/as/to business', *American Sociologist*, 43:1, pp. 21–35.

Pollner, M. and Emerson, R. (2011) 'Ethnomethodology and ethnography', in Atkinson, P., Coffey, A., Delamont, S., Lofland, J., and Lofland, L. (eds) *Handbook of Ethnography*, London, Sage.

Pomerantz, A. (1989) 'Epilogue', *Western Journal of Speech Communication*, 53, pp. 242–6.

Potter, J. (2002) 'Two kinds of natural', *Discourse Studies*, 4:4, pp. 539–42.

Potter, J. and Hepburn, A. (2005) 'Qualitative interviews in psychology: problems and possibilities', *Qualitative Research in Psychology*, 2:4, pp. 281–307.

Potter, J. and Wetherell, M. (1987) *Discourse and Social Psychology: Beyond attitudes and behaviour*. London: Sage.

Prendergast, C. (1986) 'Alfred Schutz and the Austrian School of Economics', *American Journal of Sociology*, 92:1, pp. 1–26.

Prevignano, C. and Thubault, P. (eds) (2003) *Discussing Conversation Analysis*, Amsterdam, John Benjamins.

Psathas, G. (ed.) (1973) *Phenomenological Sociology: Issues and applications*, New York, Wiley.

Psathas, G. (1980) 'Approaches to the study of the world of everyday life', *Human Studies*, 3:1, pp. 3–17.

Psathas, G. (1995) '"Talk and social structure" and "studies of work"', *Human Studies*, 18:2–3, pp. 139–55.

Psathas, G. (1999) 'On the study of human action: Schutz and Garfinkel on social science', in Embree, L. (ed.) *Schutzian Social Science*, Dordrecht, Kluwer, pp. 47–68.

Psathas, G. (2004) 'Alfred Schutz's influence on American sociologists and sociology', *Human Studies*, 27:1, pp. 1–35.

Psathas, G. (2008) 'Reflections on the history of ethnomethodology: The Boston and Manchester "schools"', *American Sociologist*, 39:1, pp. 38–67.

Psathas, G. (2009) 'The correspondence of Alfred Schutz and Harold Garfinkel', in Nasu, H., Embree, L., Psathas, G., and Srubar, I. (eds) *Alfred Schutz and his Intellectual Partners*, Konstanz, UVK Verlagsgesellschaft.

Psathas, G. (2010) 'Ethnomethodology and conversation analysis at Boston University', in Leeds-Hurwitz, W. (ed.) *The Social History of Language and Social Interaction*, Cresskill, NJ, Hampton Press.

Psathas, G. (2012) 'On Garfinkel and Schutz: contacts and influence', *Schutzian Research*, 4, pp. 23–31.

Pyle, A. (2003) *Malebranche*, London, Routledge.

Raffel, S. and Sandywell, B. (eds) (2016) *The Reflexive Initiative: On the grounds and prospects of analytic theorizing*, London, Routledge.

Randall, D. and Sharrock, W. (2011) 'The sociologist as movie-critic', in Rouncefield, M. and Tolmie, P., *Ethnomethodology at Work*, London, Routledge.

Rawls, A. (1985) 'Reply to Gallant and Kleinman on symbolic interactionism vs. ethnomethodology', *Symbolic Interaction*, 8, pp. 121–40.

Rawls, A. (1989) 'Simmel, Parsons and the interaction order', *Sociological Theory*, 7:1, pp. 124–9.

References

Rawls, A. (2002) 'Editor's introduction', in Garfinkel, H., *Ethnomethodology's Program; Working out Durkheim's aphorism*, Lanham, MD, Rowman and Littlefield.

Rawls, A. (2003) 'Orders of interaction and intelligibility: intersections between Goffman and Garfinkel by way of Durkheim', in Treviño, A. J. (ed.) *Goffman's Legacy*, Lanham, MD, Rowman and Littlefield.

Rawls, A. (2004) *Epistemology and Practice: Durkheim's* The Elementary Forms of Religious Life, Cambridge, Cambridge University Press.

Rawls, A. (2006) Introduction, in Garfinkel, H. (1948/2005) *Seeing Sociologically: the routine grounds of social action*, Boulder CO, Paradigm.

Rawls, A. (2008) 'Editor's introduction', in Garfinkel, H. (1952/2008), *Toward a Sociological Theory of Information*, Boulder, CO, Paradigm.

Rawls, A. (2013) 'The early years, 1939–1953: Garfinkel at North Carolina, Harvard, and Princeton', *Journal of Classical Sociology*, 13:2, pp. 303–12.

Reeder. H. (1991) *The Work of Felix Kaufmann*, New York, University Press of America.

Reeder, H. (2009) 'Alfred Schutz and Felix Kaufmann: the methodological brackets', in Nasu, H., Embree, L., Psathas, G., and Srubar, I. (eds) *Alfred Schutz and his Intellectual Partners*, Konstanz, UVK Verlagsgesellschaft.

Rescher, N. (1978) *Peirce's Philosophy of Science*, Notre Dame, IN, University of Notre Dame Press.

Ritzer, G. (2010) *Classical Sociological Theory*, 6th edn, New York, McGraw-Hill.

Ritzer, G. and Stepnisky, J. (2011) *The Wiley-Blackwell Companion to Major Social Theorists*, Vol. 1, Chichester, Wiley.

Robbins, L. (1932) *The Nature and Significance of Economic Science*, 2nd edn, London, Macmillan.

Robillard, A. (1999) *Meaning of a Disability: The lived experience of paralysis*, Philadelphia, PA, Temple University Press.

Robinson, J. (2016) 'Accountability in social interaction', in Robinson, J. (ed.) *Accountability in Social Interaction*, New York, Oxford University Press.

Rock, P. (1979) *The Making of Symbolic Interactionism*, London, Macmillan.

Roger, D. and Bull, P. (eds) (1988) *Conversation*, Clevedon, Multilingual Matters.

Rouncefield, M. and Tolmie, P. (2011) *Ethnomethodology at Work*, London, Routledge.

Rule, J. (1997) *Theory and Progress in Social Science*, Cambridge, Cambridge University Press.

Ryave, L. and Schenkein, J. (1974) 'Notes on the art of walking', in Turner, R. (ed.) *Ethnomethodology*, Harmondsworth, Penguin.

Sacks, H. (1963) 'Sociological Description', *Berkeley Journal of Sociology*, 8, pp. 1–16.

Sacks, H. (1967) 'The search for help: no one to turn to', in Shneidman, E. (ed.) *Essays in Self Destruction*, New York, Science House, pp. 203–23.

Sacks, H. (1972a) 'An initial investigation of the usability of conversational data for doing sociology', in Sudnow, D. (ed.) *Studies in Social Interaction*, New York, Free Press, pp. 31–74.

Sacks, H. (1972b) 'On the analysability of stories by children', in Gumperz, J. and Hymes, D. (eds) *Directions in Sociolinguistics: The ethnography of communication* (pp. 325–45), New York, Rinehart and Winston. (Reprinted in Turner, R. (ed.) (1974) *Ethnomethodology*, Harmondsworth, Penguin.)

References

Sacks, H. (1972c) 'Notes on police assessment of moral character', in Sudnow, D. (ed.) *Studies in Social Interaction*, New York, Free Press.

Sacks, H. (1974) 'On the analysability of stories by children', in Turner, R. (ed.) *Ethnomethodology*, Harmondsworth, Penguin, pp. 216–32.

Sacks, H. (1984) 'Notes on methodology', in Atkinson, M. and Heritage, J. (eds) *Structures of Social Action: Studies in conversation analysis*, Cambridge, Cambridge University Press.

Sacks, H. (1992a) *Lectures on Conversation*, Vol. 1, Oxford, Blackwell.

Sacks, H. (1992b) *Lectures on Conversation*, Vol. 2, Oxford, Blackwell.

Sacks, H., Schegloff, E., and Jefferson, G. (1974) 'A simplest systematics for the organization of turn-taking for conversation', *Language*, 50:4, pp. 696–735.

Scharff, R. (1995) *Comte after Positivism*, Cambridge, Cambridge University Press.

Schegloff, E. A. (1968) 'Sequencing in conversational openings', *American Anthropologist*, 70, pp. 1075–95.

Schegloff, E. (1972) 'Notes on a conversational practice: formulating place', in Sudnow, D. (ed.) *Studies in Social Interaction*, New York, Free Press.

Schegloff, E. (1979), 'Identification and recognition in telephone conversation openings', in Psathas, G. (ed.) *Everyday Language: Studies in Ethnomethodology*, New York, Irvington, pp. 23–78.

Schegloff, E. (1988a) 'Goffman and the analysis of conversation', in Drew, P. and Wootton. T. (eds) *Erving Goffman: Exploring the Interaction Order*, Cambridge, Polity Press.

Schegloff, E. (1988b) 'On an actual virtual servo-mechanism for guessing bad news: a single case conjecture', *Social Problems*, 35:4, pp. 442–57.

Schegloff, E. (1991) 'Reflections on talk and social structure', in Boden, D. and Zimmerman, D. (eds) *Talk and Social Structure*, Cambridge, Polity Press.

Schegloff, E. (1992a) 'On talk and its institutional occasions', in Drew, P. and Heritage, J. (eds) *Talk at Work: Interaction in institutional settings*, Cambridge, Cambridge University Press.

Schegloff, E. (1992b) 'Introduction', in Sacks, H. *Lectures on Conversation*, Vol. 1, Oxford, Blackwell.

Schegloff, E.A. (1997) 'Whose text? Whose context?', *Discourse and Society*, 8, pp. 165–87.

Schegloff, E.A. (1999) 'On Sacks on Weber on ancient Judaism', *Theory, Culture and Society*, 16:1, pp. 1–29.

Schegloff, E. (2005) 'On integrity in inquiry … of the investigated, not the investigator', *Discourse Studies*, 7:4–5, pp. 455–80.

Schegloff, E. (2007) *Sequence Organization in Interaction: A primer in conversation analysis*, Volume 1, Cambridge, Cambridge University Press.

Schmaus, W. (1998) 'Commentary and debate, Rawls, Durkheim, and causality: a critical discussion', *American Journal of Sociology*, 104:3, pp. 872–86.

Schmidt, P. (1978) 'Towards a History of the Department of Social Relations, Harvard University, 1946–72', PhD thesis, Harvard University.

Schutz, A. (1943) 'The problem of rationality in the social world', *Economica*, 10, pp. 130–49. (Reprinted in Schutz, A. *Collected Papers*, Vol. II, pp. 64–88.)

Schutz, A. (1945) 'On multiple realities', *Philosophy and Phenomenological Research*, 5:4, pp. 533–76. (Reprinted in Schutz, A. (1962) *Collected Papers*, Vol. I, pp. 207–59.)

References

Schutz, A. (1962) *Collected Papers*, Vol. I, *The Problem of Social Reality* (ed. Maurice Natanson), The Hague, Martinus Nijhoff.

Schutz, A. (1964) *Collected Papers*, Vol. II: *Studies in Social Theory* (ed. A Brodersen), The Hague, Martinus Nijhoff.

Schutz, A. (1966) *Collected Papers*, Vol. III, *Studies in Phenomenological Philosophy* (ed. Ilse Schutz), The Hague, Martinus Nijhoff.

Schutz, A. (1967) *The Phenomenology of the Social World*, Evanston, IL, Northwestern University Press. (First published in German in 1932.)

Schutz, A. (1996) *Collected Papers*, Vol. IV (ed. H. Wagner, G. Psathas and F. Kersten), Dordrecht, Kluwer.

Schutz, A. and Luckmann, T. (1973) *The Structures of the Life-World*, Evanston, IL, Northwestern University Press.

Schwartz, H. (1971) 'Mental disorder and the study of subjective experience: Some uses of each to elucidate the other', PhD dissertation, UCLA.

Schwartz, H. (1978) 'Data, who needs it?', *Analytic Sociology*, 2:1. (Reprinted in Lynch, M. and Sharrock, W. (eds) *Harold Garfinkel*, Vol. 3, London, Sage.)

Scott, J. (ed.) (2007) *Fifty Key Sociologists*, London, Routledge.

Selznick, P. (1948) 'Foundations of the theory of organization', *American Sociological Review*, 13:1, pp. 25–35.

Sharrock, W. (1974) 'On owning knowledge', in Turner, R. (ed.) *Ethnomethodology*, Harmondsworth, Penguin.

Sharrock, W. (1977) 'The problem of order', in Worsley, P. (ed.) *Introducing Sociology*, Harmondsworth, Penguin.

Sharrock, W. (1999) 'The omnipotence of the actor: Erving Goffman on "the definition of the situation"', in Smith, G. (ed.) *Goffman and Social Organization: Studies in a socio- logical legacy*, London, Routledge.

Sharrock, W. (2000) 'Where the simplest systematics fits: a response to Michael Lynch's "The ethnomethodological foundations of conversation analysis"', *Text*, 20:4, pp. 533–9.

Sharrock, W. (2001) 'Fundamentals of ethnomethodology', in Ritzer, G. and Smart, B. (eds) *Handbook of Social Theory*, London, Sage.

Sharrock, W. (2004) 'What Garfinkel makes of Schutz: The past, present and future of an alternate, asymmetric and incommensurable approach to sociology', *Theory and Science*, 5. Available at: http://theoryandscience.icaap.org/content/vol5.1/sharrock.html (accessed 4 Jan. 2018).

Sharrock, W. and Anderson, R. (1982) 'On the demise of the native: some observations on and a proposal for ethnography', *Human Studies*, 5:2, pp. 119–35.

Sharrock, W. and Anderson, R. (1986) *The Ethnomethodologists*, London, Tavistock.

Sharrock, W. and Anderson, B. (1991) 'Epistemology: professional scepticism', in Button, G. (ed.) *Ethnomethodology and the Human Sciences*, Cambridge, Cambridge University Press.

Sharrock, W. and Button, G. (1991) 'The social actor', in Button, G. (ed.) *Ethnomethodology and the Human Sciences*, Cambridge, Cambridge University Press.

Sharrock, W. and Button, G. (2011) 'Conclusion: ethnomethodology and constructionist studies of technology', in Rouncefield, M. and Tolmie, P. (eds) *Ethnomethodology at Work*, London, Routledge.

References

Sharrock, W. and Coulter, J. (2009) '"Theory of mind": A critical commentary continued', in Leudar, I. and Costall, A. (eds) *Against Theory of Mind*, Basingstoke, Palgrave Macmillan.

Sharrock, W. and Randall, D. (2004) 'Ethnography, ethnomethodology and the problem of generalisation in design', *European Journal of Information Systems*, 13, pp. 186–94.

Sharrock, W. and Read, R. (2002) *Kuhn*, Cambridge, Polity Press.

Sharrock, W. and Watson, D. R. (1984) 'What's the point of "rescuing motives"?', *British Journal of Sociology*, 35:3, pp. 435–51.

Sharrock, W. W. and Watson, D. R. (1988) 'Autonomy among social theories: the incarnation of social structures', in Fielding, N. (ed.) *Actions and Structure: Research methods and social theory*, London, Sage.

Sidnell, J. and Stivers, T. (eds) (2013) *The Handbook of Conversation Analysis*. Malden, MA, Blackwell.

Silverman, D. (1989) 'Six rules of qualitative research: a post-Romantic argument', *Symbolic Interaction*, 12:2, pp. 215–30.

Silverman, D. (1993a) 'The machinery of interaction: remaking social science', *Sociological Review*, 41:4, pp. 731–52.

Silverman, D. (1993b) *Interpreting Qualitative Data*, London, Sage.

Silverman, D. (1998) *Harvey Sacks: Social science and conversation analysis*, Cambridge, Polity Press.

Simmel, G. (1907/2004) *The Philosophy of Money* (trans. T. Bottomore and D. Frisby), London, Routledge and Kegan Paul. (3rd enlarged edn, 2004).

Simmel, G. (1908) *Soziologie*, Leipzig, Duncker and Humblot.

Simmel, G. (1971) *Individuality and Social Forms*, ed. and intro. D. Levine, Chicago, University of Chicago Press.

Simmel, G. (1995) *Philosophie der Mode; Die Religion; Kant und Goethe; Schopenhauer und Nietzsche*, Georg Simmel Gesamtausgabe Band 10, Frankfurt am Main, Suhrkamp.

Sismondi, S. (2010) *An Introduction to Science and Technology Studies*, 2nd edn, Oxford, Wiley-Blackwell.

Smith, D. E. (1978) '"K is Mentally Ill": the anatomy of a factual account', *Sociology*, 12, pp. 23–53.

Smith, D. W. (2010) 'Science, intentionality and historical background', in Hyder, D. and Rheinberger, H-J. (eds) *Science and the Life-World: Essays on Husserl's Crisis of European Sciences*, Stanford CA, Stanford University Press.

Smith, G. (1989) 'A Simmelian Reading of Goffman', PhD thesis, University of Salford.

Smith, G. (2003) 'Ethnomethodological readings of Goffman', in Treviño, A. J. (ed.) *Goffman's Legacy*, Lanham, MD, Rowman and Littlefield.

Smith, G. (2006) *Erving Goffman*, London, Routledge.

Smith, R. and Atkinson, P. (2016) 'Method and measurement, 50 years on', *International Journal of Social Research Methodology*, 19:1, pp. 99–110.

Sormani, P. (2015) *Respecifying Lab Ethnography: Experimental physics in ethnomethodological perspective*, Farnham, Ashgate.

Spector, M. and Kitsuse, J. (1977) *Constructing Social Problems*, Menlo Park, CA, Cummings.

References

Speer, S. A. (2002a) '"Natural" and "contrived" data: a sustainable distinction?', *Discourse Studies*, 4:4, pp. 511–25.

Speer, S. A. (2002b) 'Transcending the 'natural'/'contrived' distinction: a rejoinder to ten Have, Lynch and Potter', *Discourse Studies*, 4:4, pp. 543–8.

Speer, S. A. and Hutchby, I. (2003) 'From ethics to analytics: aspects of participants' orientations to the presence and relevance of recording devices', *Sociology*, 37:2, pp. 315–37.

Speigelberg, H. (1960) *The Phenomenological Movement*, Vol. 1, The Hague, Martinus Nijhoff.

Stivers, T. (2007) *Prescribing Under Pressure*, Oxford, Oxford University Press.

Stivers, T. and Majid, A. (2007) 'Questioning children: interactional evidence of implicit bias in medical interviews', *Social Psychology Quarterly*, 70, pp. 424–41.

Stokoe, E. and Sikveland, R. (2017) 'The conversation analytic role-play method: simulation, endogenous impact and interactional nudges', in Fors, V., O'Dell, T. and Pink, S. (eds) *Theoretical Scholarship and Applied Practice*. Oxford: Berghahn Books.

Stones, R. (2017) *Key Sociological Thinkers*, 3rd edn, London, Palgrave.

Strauss, A. (1996) 'A partial line of descent: Blumer and I', *Studies in Symbolic Interaction*, 20, pp. 3–22.

Strodtbeck, F. and Hare, A. P. (1954) 'Bibliography of small group research: 1900 through 1953', *Sociometry*, 17, pp. 107–78.

Stubbs, M. (1983) *Discourse Analysis*, Oxford, Blackwell.

Sturtevant, W. (1964) 'Studies in ethnoscience', *American Anthropologist*, n.s., 66:3, pp. 99–131.

Suchman, L. (1987) *Plans and Situated Actions: The problem of human–machine communication*, Cambridge, Cambridge University Press.

Sudnow, D. (1965) 'Normal crimes', *Social Problems*, 12, pp. 255–76.

Sudnow, D. (1967) *Passing On: The social organization of dying*, Englewood Cliffs, NJ, Prentice-Hall.

Sudnow, D. (1978) *Ways of the Hand: The organisation of improvised conduct*, Cambridge, MA, MIT Press. (See also *Ways of the Hand: A rewritten account*, Cambridge, MA, MIT Press, 2002.)

Sztompka, P. (2008) 'The focus on everyday life: a new turn in sociology', *European Review*, 16:1, pp. 1–15.

Taylor, C. (1964) *The Explanation of Behaviour*, London, Routledge and Kegan Paul.

Tenbruck, F. (1987) 'Max Weber and Eduard Meyer', in Mommsen, W. and Osterhammel, J. (eds) *Max Weber and his Contemporaries*, London, Allen and Unwin.

Tessier, S. (2012). From field notes, to transcripts, to tape recordings: evolution or combination?, *International Journal of Qualitative Methods*, 11, pp. 446–60.

Tieszen, R. (2005) 'Science as a triumph of the human spirit and science in crisis: Husserl and the fortunes of reason', in Gutting, G. (ed.) *Continental Philosophy of Science*, Oxford, Blackwell.

Tolmie, P. and Rouncefield, M. (eds) (2013) *Ethnomethodology at Play*, London, Routledge.

Torgerson, W. (1958) *Theory and Method of Scaling*, New York, Wiley.

References

Travers, M. (1997) *The Reality of Law: Work and talk in a firm of criminal lawyers*, Aldershot, Ashgate.

Travers, M. (1999) *The British Immigration Courts: A study of law and politics*, Bristol, Policy Press.

Travers, M. (2007) *The New Bureaucracy: Quality assurance and its critics*, Bristol, Policy Press.

Treviño, A. J. (ed.) (2001) *Talcott Parsons Today*, Lanham, MD, Rowman and Littlefield.

Tribe, K. (1995) *Strategies of Economic Order: German economic discourse, 1750–1950*, Cambridge, Cambridge University Press.

Truzzi, M. (ed.) (1968) *Sociology and Everyday Life*, Englewood Cliffs, NJ, Prentice-Hall.

Tucker, K. (1998) *Anthony Giddens and Modern Social Theory*, London, Sage.

Turner, R. (1970) 'Words, utterances and activities', in Douglas, J. D. (ed.) *Understanding Everyday Life*, Chicago, Aldine.

Turner, S. P. (2007) 'A life in the first half-century of sociology: Charles Ellwood and the division of sociology', in Calhoun, C. (ed.) *Sociology in America: A History*, Chicago, University of Chicago Press. p. 122.

Vaihinger, H. (1924) *The Philosophy of 'As if': A system of the theoretical, practical and religious fictions of mankind* (trans. C. K. Ogden), London, Routledge and Kegan Paul.

Vanderstraeten, R. (2002) 'Parsons, Luhmann and the theorem of double contingency', *Journal of Classical Sociology*, 2:1, pp. 77–92.

Wagner, H. (1970) *Alfred Schutz on Phenomenology and Social Reality*, Chicago, University of Chicago Press.

Wagner, H. (1983) *Alfred Schutz: An intellectual biography*, Chicago, University of Chicago Press.

Wagner, H. (1988) 'Alfred Schutz's long-range influence on American Sociology', in Embree, L. (ed.) *Worldly Phenomenology*, Washington D.C., Center for Advanced Research in Phenomenology and University Press of America.

Watson, D. R. (1983) 'Goffman, talk and interaction: some modulated responses', *Theory, Culture and Society*, 2:1, pp. 103–8.

Watson, D. R. (1984) 'Review of Goffman's *Forms of Talk*', *British Journal of Sociology*, 35:1, pp. 155–6.

Watson, D. R. (1992) 'The understanding of language use in everyday life: is there a common ground?', in Watson, G. and Seiler, R. (eds) *Text in Context*, Newbury Park, CA, Sage.

Watson, D. R. (1997) 'Some general reflections on "categorization" and "sequence" in the analysis of conversation', in Hester, S. and Eglin, P. (eds) *Culture in Action: Studies in Membership Categorization Analysis*, Washington, DC, University Press of America.

Watson, D. R. (1998) 'Ethnomethodology, consciousness and self', *Journal of Consciousness Studies*, 5:2, pp. 202–23.

Watson, D. R. (1999) 'Reading Goffman on interaction', in Smith, G. (ed.) *Goffman and Social Organization: Studies in a socio-logical legacy*, London, Routledge.

Watson, D. R. (2008) 'Comparative sociology, laic and analytic: some critical remarks on comparison in Conversation Analysis', *Cahiers de Praxématique*, 50, pp. 197–238. Available at: http://journals.openedition.org/praxematique/967 (accessed 4 Jan. 2018).

Watson, D. R. (2012) *Analyzing Practical and Professional Texts*, Aldershot, Ashgate.

References

Watson, D. R. (2016) 'Harold Garfinkel and pragmatics', in Östman, J-O, and Verschueren, J. (eds) *Handbook of Pragmatics Online*, Vol. 20, Amsterdam: John Benjamins. Available at: https://benjamins.com/online/hop/ (accessed 4 Jan. 2018).

Watson, D. R. (2017) 'Harold Garfinkel', in Östman, J-O. and Verschueren, J. (eds) *Handbook of Pragmatics Online*, Amsterdam, John Benjamins. Available at: https://benjamins.com/online/hop/ (accessed 4 Jan. 2018).

Watson, D. R. and Coulter, J. (2008) 'The debate over cognitivism', *Theory, Culture and Society*, 25:2, pp. 1–17.

Watson, D. R. and Sharrock, W. (1991) 'On the provision of "ethnographic context" in ethnomethodological and conversation-analytic research', paper presented at the International Conference on Current Work in Ethnomethodology and Conversation Analysis, University of Amsterdam, The Netherlands, July.

Webb, H., Heath, C., vom Lehn, D., and Gibson, W. (2013) 'Engendering responses: professional gesture and the assessment of eyesight in optometry consultations', *Symbolic Interaction*, 36:2, pp. 137–58.

Webb, H., vom Lehn, D., Heath, C., Gibson, W., and Evans, D. (2013) 'The problem with "problems": the case of openings in optometry consultations', *Research on Language and Social Interaction*, 46:1, pp. 65–83.

Weber, M. (1927) *General Economic History*, New York, Greenberg. (First published in German in 1923.)

Weber, M. (1968) *Economy and Society: An outline of interpretive sociology*, New York, Bedminster Press. (First published in German in 1922.)

Weinberg, D. (2009) 'On the social construction of social problems and social problems theory: a contribution to the legacy of John Kitsuse', *American Sociologist*, 40, pp. 61–78.

Weinberg, D. (2014) *Contemporary Social Constructionism*, Philadelphia, PA, Temple University Press.

Weller, J. (2000) 'Tests of concepts in Herbert Blumer's method', *Social Thought and Research*, 23:1/2, pp. 65–86.

Wetherell, M., and Edley, N. (1999) 'Negotiating hegemonic masculinity: imaginary positions and psycho-discursive practices', *Feminism & Psychology*, 9, pp. 335–56.

Wetherell, M. and Potter, J. (1992) *Mapping the Language of Racism*, Chichester, Harvester Wheatsheaf.

White, L. (1977) *The Methodology of the Austrian Economists*, New York, Center for Libertarian Studies.

Wieder, D. L. (1970) 'On meaning by rule', in Douglas, J. D. (ed.) *Understanding Everyday Life*, Chicago, Aldine.

Wieder, D. L. (1974) *Language and Social Reality: The case of telling the convict code*, The Hague, Mouton.

Wieder, D. L. (1977) 'Ethnomethodology and ethnosociology', *Mid-American Review of Sociology*, 2:2, pp. 1–18.

Wieder, D. L., and Pratt, S. (1990) 'On being a recognizable Indian among Indians', in D. Carbaugh (ed.) *Cultural Communication and Intercultural Contact*, Hillsdale, NJ, Lawrence Erlbaum, pp. 45–64.

References

Wieder, D. L., Zimmerman, D., and Raymond, G. (2010) 'UCLA: then and now', in Leeds-Hurwitz, W. (ed.) *The Social History of Language and Social Interaction*, Cresskill, NJ, Hampton Press, pp. 127–58.

Wilkins, J. (1968) 'Review of Harold Garfinkel, *Studies in Ethnomethodology*', *American Journal of Sociology*, 73, pp. 642–5.

Willer, D. and Willer, J. (1973) *Systematic Empiricism: Critique of a Pseudoscience*, Englewood Cliffs, NJ, Prentice-Hall.

Williams, M. (2001) *Problems of Knowledge*, Oxford, Oxford University Press.

Williams, R. (1983) 'Sociological tropes: a tribute to Erving Goffman', *Theory, Culture and Society*, 2:1, pp. 99–102.

Williams, R. (1988) 'Understanding Goffman's methods', in Drew, P. and Wootton. T. (eds) *Erving Goffman: Exploring the Interaction Order*, Cambridge, Polity Press.

Wilson, T. P. (1970a) 'Conceptions of interaction and forms of sociological explanation', *American Sociological Review*, 35:4, pp. 697–710.

Wilson, T. P. (1970b) 'Normative and interpretive paradigms in sociology', in Douglas, J. D. (ed.) *Understanding Everyday Life*, London, Routledge and Kegan Paul.

Wilson, T. P. (2003) 'Garfinkel's radical program', *Research on Language and Social Interaction*, 36:4, pp. 487–94.

Wilson, T. P. (2005) 'The problem of subjectivity in Schutz and Parsons', in Endress, M., Psathas, G., and Nasu, H. (eds) (2005) *Explorations of the Life-World*, Dordrecht, Springer.

Wilson, T. P. (2012) 'Classical ethnomethodology, the radical program, and conversation analysis', in Nasu, H. and Waksler, F. C. (eds) *Interaction and Everyday Life: Phenomenological and ethnomethodological essays in honor of George Psathas*, Lanham, MD, Lexington Books.

Winch, P. (1958) *The Idea of a Social Science*, London, Routledge. (2nd edn with new intro., 1990).

Winch, P. (1964) 'Understanding a primitive society', *American Philosophical Quarterly*, 1:4, pp. 307–24.

Winkin, Y. (1991) 'Erving Goffman: Outline of an Intellectual Biography', unpublished manuscript, Department of Landscape Architecture, University of Pennsylvania. (Cited in Chriss, J. (1993) 'Looking back on Goffman: the excavation continues', *Human Studies*, 16:4, pp. 469–83.)

Winkin, Y. and Leeds-Hurwitz, W. (2013) *Erving Goffman: A critical introduction to media and communication theory*, New York, Peter Lang.

Wittgenstein, L. (1972) *Philosophical Investigations*, Oxford, Blackwell. (First published 1958.)

Wolff, K. (ed.) (1950) *The Sociology of Georg Simmel*, New York, Free Press.

Wolff, K. (ed.) (1971) *From Karl Mannheim*, New York, Oxford University Press.

Woolgar, S. (ed.) (1988) *Knowledge and Reflexivity: New frontiers in the sociology of knowledge*, London, Sage.

Woolgar, S. and Lezaun, J. (2013) 'The wrong bin bag: the turn to ontology in science and technology studies', *Social Studies of Science*, 43:3, pp. 321–40.

Wootton, A. (1975) *Dilemmas of Discourse*, London, Allen and Unwin.

References

Wootton, A. (1988) 'The methodology of conversation analysis', in Roger, D. and Bull, P. (eds) *Conversation*, Clevedon, Multilingual Matters.

Zimmerman, D. (1970a) 'Record keeping and the intake process in a public welfare agency', in Wheeler, S. (ed.) *On Record*, New York, Basic Books, pp. 319–54.

Zimmerman, D. (1970b) 'The practicalities of rule use', in Douglas, J. (ed.) *Understanding Everyday Life*, Chicago, Aldine, pp. 221–38.

Zimmerman, D. (1976) 'A reply to Professor Coser', *American Sociologist*, 2, pp. 4–13.

Zimmerman, D. (1978) 'Ethnomethodology', *American Sociologist*, 13, pp. 6–14.

Zimmerman, D. and Pollner, M. (1970) 'The everyday world as a phenomenon', in Douglas, J. (ed.) *Understanding Everyday Life*, Chicago, Aldine.

Zimmerman, D. and Wieder, D. L. (1970) 'Ethnomethodology and the problem of order', in Douglas, J. (ed.) *Understanding Everyday Life*, Chicago, Aldine.

Zollschan, G. and Hirsch, W. (eds) (1964) *Explorations in Social Change*, London, Routledge and Kegan Paul.

Name index

Name index

Sharrock, W. 1, 3, 5, 8, 14, 16, 17, 26, 32, 46, 56, 65, 68, 69, 71, 76, 77, 79, 82, 83, 84, 87, 88, 97, 101, 108, 110, 111, 112, 134, 135, 137, 139, 140, 144, 145, 146, 147, 148, 150, 151, 152, 153, 155, 158, 162
Silverman, D. 9, 17, 127, 130
Simmel, G. 2, 3, 12, 18, 24, 46–57, 59, 61, 62, 65, 86, 91, 150
Smith, D. 112
Smith, G. 46, 47, 49, 50, 51, 52, 57, 60, 61–2, 63, 65, 66
Srubar, I. 41
Sudnow, D. 6, 7, 16, 70, 105, 133, 138, 159

ten Have, P. 11, 16, 111, 130, 145, 159
Tenbruck, F. 42–3
Turner, R. 111, 145
Turner, S. P. 47

Warner, W. Lloyd 7, 47, 49, 62
Watson, D. R. 6, 16, 17, 46, 55, 63, 64, 65, 79, 82, 97, 106, 112, 135, 138, 139, 148, 149, 150, 154, 157, 158

Weber, Marianne 36
Weber, Max 18, 32, 35, 36–7, 38, 39, 40, 41, 42–3, 45, 52, 74, 91, 93, 161, 163
Wetherell, M. 128
Whitehead, A. N. 93, 107
Wieder, D. L. 4, 6, 7, 11, 16, 28, 46, 57, 68, 69, 101, 109, 119, 128, 133, 141, 144, 154, 161
Wieser, F. von 34
Willer, D. and J. 122
Williams, R. 64–5, 112
Wilson, T. 6, 8, 32, 42, 77, 79, 85, 99, 106, 109, 115, 116, 126, 134, 136, 141, 148, 161
Winch, P. 5, 11, 24, 75, 107
Winkin, Y. 47, 49, 60, 61, 64, 66
Wittgenstein, L. 14, 15, 23, 75, 92, 96, 107, 144, 158, 159
Wood, H. 4, 8, 11–12, 65, 110, 115, 133, 155, 158

Zimmerman, D. 6, 7, 8, 12–13, 14, 16, 28, 68, 75, 81, 98, 99, 104, 105, 106, 107–8, 110, 124, 133, 134

Subject index

Subject index

EU authorised representative for GPSR:
Easy Access System Europe, Mustamäe tee 50,
10621 Tallinn, Estonia
gpsr.requests@easproject.com